THE DETERMINANTS OF ENTREPRENEURSHIP: LEADERSHIP, CULTURE, INSTITUTIONS

T0347333

Perspectives in Economic and Social History

Series Editor: *Robert E. Wright*

Titles in this Series

Forthcoming Titles

THE DETERMINANTS OF ENTREPRENEURSHIP: LEADERSHIP, CULTURE, INSTITUTIONS

EDITED BY

José L. García-Ruiz and Pier Angelo Toninelli

Routledge
Taylor & Francis Group

LONDON AND NEW YORK

First published 2010 by Pickering & Chatto (Publishers) Limited

Published 2016 by Routledge
2 Park Square, Milton Park, Abingdon, Oxfordshire OX14 4RN
711 Third Avenue, New York, NY 10017, USA

First issued in paperback 2015

Routledge is an imprint of the Taylor & Francis Group, an informa business

BRITISH LIBRARY CATALOGUING IN PUBLICATION DATA

The determinants of entrepreneurship: leadership, culture, institutions. –
(Perspectives in economic and social history)
1. Entrepreneurship. 2. Leadership. 3. Corporate culture.
I. Series II. Garcia Ruiz, Jose Luis, 1959– III. Toninelli, Pierangelo Maria.
338'.04-dc22

ISBN-13: 978-1-138-66137-0 (pbk)
ISBN-13: 978-1-8489-3071-1 (hbk)

Typeset by Pickering & Chatto (Publishers) Limited

CONTENTS

LIST OF FIGURES AND TABLES

LIST OF CONTRIBUTORS

Franco Amatori is Full Professor of Economic History at the Bocconi University, head of the Istituto di Storia Economica, president of the Fondazione Associazione ASSI di Storia e Studi sull'Impresa, president of the Istituto per la Cultura e la Storia d'Impresa Franco Momigliano and past president of the European Business History Association. He is a member of the boards of *Business History Review*, *Enterprise and Society* and *Business History* and a member of the advisory board of the Business History Conference. He is editor of *Annali di storia dell'impresa* and co-editor of *Comparative Perspectives in Business History*, a series of volumes from Cambridge University Press. His main publications are *Big Business and the Wealth of Nations* (1997, co-edited with A. D. Chandler and T. Hikino), *Comunità di imprese: Sistemi locali in Italia tra Ottocento e Novecento* (2001, co-edited with A. Colli) and *Business History around the World* (2003, co-edited with G. Jones).

Carlos Dávila is Full Professor of Business History, member of the board of trustees and director of the Research Group 'Historia y Empresariado' at the University of the Andes (Colombia). His main publications are *Business History in Latin America* (1999, co-edited with R. Miller), Empresas y empresarios en la historia de Colombia. Siglos XIX y XX (2003, editor), 'La historia empresarial en América Latina', in C. Erro (ed.), *Historia empresarial: Pasado, presente y retos de futuro* (2003), 'Books that Made a Difference: *On the Theory of Social Change: How Economic Growth Begins*, by Everett Hagen', *Business History Review* (2006) and *Una mirada a la historia del mercadeo en Colombia* (2008, with L. F. Molina, G. Pérez and J. M. Ospina).

Paloma Fernández-Pérez is Associate Professor of Economic History at the University of Barcelona and a member of the board of Business History and Investigaciones de Historia Económica. She is also member of the board of the Centre d'Estudis en Economia i Història Econòmica Antoni de Capmany. Her recent publications are 'Small Firms and Networks in Capital Intensive Industries: The Case of Spanish Steel Wire Manufacturing', *Business History* (2007), 'A Silent Revolution: The Internationalization of Large Spanish Family Firms',

Business History (2009, with N. Puig) and *Innovation and Entrepreneurial Networks in Europe* (2010, co-edited with M. B. Rose).

James Foreman-Peck is Director of the Welsh Institute for Research in Economics and Development of the Cardiff Business School. He is a former president of the European Historical Economics Society and economic adviser at HM Treasury concerned with micro-economic policy issues. His main publications are *European Industrial Policy: The Twentieth-Century Experience* (1999, with G. Federico), 'Business and Social Mobility into the British Elite, 1870–1914', *Journal of European Economic History* (2004, with J. Smith) and 'Measuring Historical Entrepreneurship', in Y. Cassis and I. Pepelasis Minoglou (eds), *Entrepreneurship in Theory and History* (2005).

José L. García-Ruiz is Associate Professor at the Complutense University of Madrid and co-director of the Grupo de Investigación Complutense de Historia Empresarial (GICHE). His recent publications are 'Cultural Resistance and the Gradual Emergence of Modern Marketing and Retailing Practices in Spain, 1950–1975', *Business History* (2007), *Educación, instituciones y empresa: Los determinantes del espíritu empresarial* (2008, with G. Tortella, J. M. Ortiz-Villajos and G. Quiroga) and 'AmCham Spain and the Transformation of Spanish Business, 1917–2007', in *American Firms in Europe* (2009, with N. Puig).

Ignacio Moral holds a PhD in Economics from the University of Cantabria (Spain). He is a statistician and researcher at the Instituto de Estudios Fiscales (Ministry of Finance) and a researcher in a project directed by Professor Gabriel Tortella on the determinants of entrepreneurship in the history of Spain. He has provided technical assistance as a statistician in *Educación, instituciones y empresa: Los determinantes del espíritu empresarial* (2008).

Ioanna Sapfo Pepelasis is Assistant Professor of Economic History with a tenure at the Athens University of Economics and Business. She has served as a member of the boards of the European Business History Association, the European Association of Evolutionary Political Economy and the *International Journal of Maritime History*. Her main publications are *Diaspora Entrepreneurial Networks: Four Centuries of History* (2005, edited with I. B. McCabe and G. Harlaftis), *Entrepreneurship in Theory and History* (2005, co-edited with Y. Cassis), *Country Studies in Entrepreneurship: A Historical Perspective* (2006, co-edited with Y. Cassis).

Núria Puig is Associate Professor of Economic History at the Complutense University of Madrid and a member of the boards of *Revista de Historia Industrial* and *Business History Review*. Her recent publications are 'A Silent Revolution:

The Internationalization of Large Spanish Family Firms', *Business History* (2009, with P. Fernández-Pérez), 'Global Lobbies for a Global Economy: The Creation of the Spanish Institute of Family Firms in International Perspective', *Business History* (2009, with P. Fernández-Pérez) and 'Patterns of International Investment in Spain, 1850–2005', *Business History Review* (2009, with R. Castro).

Gloria Quiroga holds a PhD in Economic History from the University of Alcalá. She is a researcher in a project directed by Professor Gabriel Tortella on the determinants of entrepreneurship in the history of Spain. She has recently published *Educación, instituciones y empresa: Los determinantes del espíritu empresarial* (2008, with G. Tortella, J. L. García-Ruiz and J. M. Ortiz-Villajos).

Pier Angelo Toninelli is Full Professor of Business and Contemporary History at the Faculty of Economics of the University of Milano-Bicocca, where he is in charge of the organization of the economic and social studies. He is a member of the board of scientific institutions (Associazione ASSI di Storia e Studi sull'Impresa and Instituto per lo studio della Storia contemporanea) and journals (*Imprese e Storia*, *Annali di storia d'impresa*). His main publications are *The Rise and Fall of State-Owned Enterprise in the Western World* (2000, editor) and *Storia d'Impresa* (2006).

Gabriel Tortella is Emeritus Professor of Economic History at the University of Alcalá (Spain), founder of the *Revista de Historia Económica* and co-founder of the *Asociación Española de Historia Económica*. He is a former president of the International Economic History Association (1994–8). His main publications are *The Development of Modern Spain* (2000), *Educación, instituciones y empresa: Los determinantes del espíritu empresarial* (2008, with J. L. García-Ruiz, J. M. Ortiz-Villajos and G. Quiroga) and *The Origins of the Twenty-First Century* (2009).

Michelangelo Vasta is Associate Professor of Economic History at the Università di Siena, co-director of *Imprese e Storia* and co-founder of the Centro di Ricerca Interuniversitario per gli studi economici applicati (CERISE). His main publications are *Storia dell'impresa industriale italiana* (2005, with R. Giannetti), *Evolution of Italian Enterprises in the Twentieth Century* (2006, co-edited with R. Giannetti) and *Forms of Enterprise in Twentieth-Century Italy* (forthcoming, co-edited with A. Colli).

Peng Zhou is a PhD student at the Julian Hodge Institute of Applied Macroeconomics (JHIAM) of the Cardiff Business School. The subject of his thesis is 'Inequality and Economic Growth under Heterogeneous Agent Model'.

INTRODUCTION

José L. García-Ruiz and Pier Angelo Toninelli

Even though recent troubles have disrupted the world's economic scenario, they do not seem to have affected the renewed interest towards entrepreneurship and/or the entrepreneurial function which has emerged in the last decades. This sentiment has been stimulated primarily by the Information and Communication Technologies (ICT) revolution and the emergence of a 'new entrepreneurial economy'.[1] This cluster of innovations assumed the character of a General Purpose Technology (GPT) and as such its effects were felt first in the activities directly connected with its production and implementation, giving rise to the dot.com entrepreneurial boom; later the wave of innovations progressively spread over the global economy, stimulating productivity and the creation of new firms. But when the undertow backwash came, it left behind a lot of victims, its effects made dramatically worse by the incumbent recession.[2]

Therefore once more innovation seems to have played a fundamental role in determining entrepreneurship. But if this relationship actually exists, how strong is it? And, conversely, is there a link between the expansion and/or the renewal of the entrepreneurial class and economic growth? Is it possible to figure out some generalization about the reciprocal behaviour?

Recent investigations by specialized institutions have shown how difficult it is to grasp these associations, particularly with regard to the complex and manifold impact exerted by the social, cultural and political context on the implementation of entrepreneurial capacities and entrepreneurial opportunities.[3] Certainly the task has not been facilitated by the contributions coming from theory. If the entrepreneur constitutes 'one of the most intriguing' characters acting in the economic game, economics has so far failed to offer a sound and convincing analysis of its basic features as well as of its role in economic development.[4] Reasons may be at least twofold: one pertains to its conceptually most elusive character and analytical vagueness[5] – made up of virtues and capabilities changing over time, therefore extremely dynamic and volatile – which can hardly be portrayed through the traditional (analytical and quantitative) tools of the 'dismal science', or forced into a general model which can prove valid beyond time and space. The other is that in an ideal type market economy, without uncertainty, asymmetric information, factor-market imperfections and externalities, such as the one considered by mainstream economics, entrepreneurial initiatives are not only unnecessary but not even hypothesized.

However, to be more precise, if we regard the evolution of the concept of entrepreneur, as well as the allocation of the entrepreneurial function, what seems to emerge is quite a dichotomy in the history of economic thought between the British (and later the American) approach – which can be modelled along the line of what in epistemology is usually called the analytical school – and the Continental one. Such a dichotomy would emphasize, on the one side, the Anglo-Saxon, the centrality of the firm and, on the other, the Old Continental, the role of the entrepreneur. Different epistemological backgrounds are likely to explain the diverging conceptualizations that lie behind the two traditions of research.[6] In classical economics – from Smith to Marx – the entrepreneur is hardly mentioned if mentioned at all. Production and the investment of capital were regarded as types of automatic process, which involved no critical decision-making, no risky judgement or imagination of any kind. In this tradition 'capitalist' was the only term which seemed to appeal to the student. On the Continent, instead, a long-standing tradition going back to late medieval and early Renaissance Italy, as well as to Minorite economics and late Scolastic thought, singled out risk and uncertainty (*periculum*) as the fundamental element which legitimated merchant (business) profits.[7] Besides, it was a French contemporary of Smith, Richard Cantillon, who introduced the term entrepreneur for one who could take advantage of the unrealized profit opportunities created by discrepancies between demand and supply, which means those who 'are willing to buy at a certain price and sell to an uncertain price'.[8] If later on John Stuart Mill popularized the term entrepreneur among British economists (1848), he failed to break the Smith-Ricardo tradition of the entrepreneur as simply a 'multifaceted capitalist'.[9] Yet towards the end of the century some interesting openings came from Alfred Marshall who hypothesized that 'it seems best sometimes to reckon Organization a part as a distinct agent of production'. It was that factor which allowed the business undertaker successfully to face risks and to win competition.[10] However Marshall's concern was addressed primarily towards small and medium firms, in particular the ones acting in the wholesale and retail trade. These activities have been labelled by Mark Casson as the 'low level of entrepreneurship' which although equally important should not be confused with the 'high level' which would become the main concern of the theorists of the twentieth century.[11]

In any case, theoretical attitude would not change much, but for a few major exceptions, in the next century. First of all, on the Continental side social scientists/economists like Max Weber and Werner Sombart produced major efforts to offer typologies and/or taxonomies of all the characters acting in the economy, including entrepreneurs. Nor should the contribution of the American institutionalism be dismissed, particularly of Thorstein Veblen. Both the German and the American schools had quite an influence on theories elaborated later on by Frank Knight and Joseph Schumpeter. In Knight's *Risk, Uncertainty and Profit* (1921), where echoes coming from the Renaissance tradition as well as from the nineteenth-century German tradition surface, the distinction between risk and uncertainty is fully analysed. Risks are those uncertainties of economic life whose objective probability can be evaluated and calculated; therefore they can be shifted via insurance to the shoulders of others. Such risks become part of the production cost. But there are uncertainties which cannot be evaluated and measured because they involve totally new and unknown situations. In this perspective the role of the entrepreneur becomes crucial and cannot be ignored as it usually is in the mainstream. However it is the contribution of Schumpeter (1934, 1939) which is still regarded as the classic statement of entrepreneurship.[12] As the entrepreneur is the one who innovates in the economy by carrying out new combinations – new products, new processes of production, new forms of organization, the discovery of new export markets as well as of new sources of raw materials – he is the prime mover in economic development: therefore a dynamic actor and a disequilibrating force which precipitates structural changes in the economy.

For quite a long time Knight's and Schumpeter's influence remained limited. But the presence of them both can be felt in an outstanding representative of the (Keynesian) orthodoxy, Nicholas Kaldor. In the concluding remarks of his 1954 fundamental contribution he pays an explicit tribute to the Schumpeterian concept of entrepreneur and implicitly to Knight, as he singles out the attitudes to speculation and risk together with the innovative spirit as the basic, disequilibrating factor which brings economic growth.[13] But, generally speaking, within neo-classic modelling entrepreneurship was long deemed a useless false glitter. Here the entrepreneurial factor could be considered at most as a residual. In such an elusive element the growth accounting theory confined all that could not be explained through its classic analytical tool, however important it could be. It is in such a way that theory reckons with productivity. For instance in his analysis of the sources of economic growth of the United States, Edward Denison is eager to recognize the contribution given by technical progress, human capital formation, resources reallocation, institutional change and so on. Nevertheless he explicitly dismisses the role of entrepreneurship because automatically counted in the inputs growth.[14]

Conversely all through the century institutionalism kept on exerting its influence on a minor but nevertheless not negligible stream of thought. As a consequence growing attention to the firm as an organized institution began to be paid:[15] whereas 'the concept of entrepreneurship played a formative role in the emergence of business history as a distinct academic field',[16] the dynamics of that institution was to become a major field of research within business history, which, in its 'organizational synthesis' variant (as Lou Galambos in 1970 happily labelled Chandler's approach),[17] was bound to have a profound impact on the theory of the firm itself. This in turn revitalized the question who is the ultimate repository of the entrepreneurial function, already raised by Schumpeter's late works:[18] the individual entrepreneur, the firm, the dynasties, the managers, either private or public (for instance Alfred Sloan or Enrico Mattei). Hence the relevant questions are: do we have to distinguish between a capitalist entrepreneurship and a non-capitalist one?[19] Or, between innovative and replicative entrepreneurs or, further, between productive and unproductive ones? How different institutions and/or cultural influences impact on determining entrepreneurship? Some of the essays in this collection will try to answer these questions.

On the other hand the emergence of a new entrepreneurial economy and the suggestions coming from history and sociology – together with the current economic turmoil – have recently cast serious doubts on the perfect functioning of the invisible hand in large sectors of the economic orthodoxy. As nowadays former generalization and rigid assumptions are getting progressively weaker, entrepreneurship is likely to become more and more part of economics. Think, for instance, of what has been recently suggested by Paul Romer:

> Economic growth occurs whenever people take resources and rearrange them in ways that are more valuable. A useful metaphor for production in an economy comes from the kitchen ... Human history teaches us ... that economic growth springs from better recipes, not just from more cooking.[20]

Or, again, think of the title which headed one of the contributions presented in the special supplement devoted to entrepreneurship by the *Economist* on 12 March 2009: 'Is Entrepreneurship becoming Mainstream?'

If heterogeneity of cases and behaviours has so far prevented us from having a convincing statistical model as well as a formal theory of entrepreneurship, history can provide 'the most fertile field for the germination and gathering of ideas for policy'.[21] The contributions gathered in this book try to improve our knowledge on entrepreneurship in that way.

The book is organized in three parts: I: Entrepreneurial Typologies; II: The Business Leaders; III: Culture or Institutions? Thirty years ago the *Business History Review* published an essay by Franco Amatori under the title 'Entrepreneurial Typologies in the History of Industrial Italy'.[22] That paper underlined the differences between state-oriented entrepreneurship identified with the city of Genoa and the contrasting market-oriented entrepreneurship more commonly associated with the city of Milan. Actually three typologies were outlined: the 'private' entrepreneur, the 'supported' entrepreneur and the 'public' entrepreneur. The work by Professor Amatori that opens this book ('Determinants and Typologies of Entrepreneurship in the History of Industrial Italy') focuses on the macro-determinants of Italian entrepreneurship which the author singles out in three elements: how Italy's economic environment evolved (with its weaknesses as well as its strengths) from the moment of the nation's political unification; the actions and the role played by the state; and stimulants from the international economy which reflected on the dynamism of Italy's domestic market. Able to call upon the wealth of data to be found in the unpublished *Biographical Dictionary of Italian Entrepreneurs* (with its 600 entries of entrepreneurs who operated in Italy from Unification in the middle of the nineteenth century up to the beginning of the twenty-first century) together with a number of more recent secondary sources, this time the typologies are articulated in more detail and cover a longer time span. Amatori incorporates some new aspects, giving a more comprehensive snapshot of the conquests – as well as the limits – of Italian capitalism.

The other work in the first part is presented by Ioanna Sapfo Pepelasis ('Entrepreneurial Typologies in a Young Nation State: Evidence from the Founding Charters of Greek Société Anonymes, 1830–1909'). This paper examines entrepreneurs(hip) in Greece between National Independence in 1830 and 1909, the year of the 'peaceful revolution' of the bourgeoisie. The formation of new companies is perceived as an outcome of entrepreneurial initiatives. The analysis here is based on an exciting new database constructed from the 251 founding charters of the total group of 303 joint-stock company type Société Anonyme start-ups established in this period. This database offers information on the identities and actions of company founders. It also gives a unique opportunity to conceptualize the general contours of entrepreneurs(hip) in the macroscopic context of Greece, a latecomer economy/young nation state. This essay argues that the mercantile diaspora, modern nation-building and the legacies of the past were the most important determinants of entrepreneurship in the nascent 'corporate sector'. It also proposes that entrepreneurship was multifaceted; it did not fit within one single theoretical typology. Moreover, the analysis here makes the case that incorporation unleashed new entrepreneurial forces that fostered new economic activities and spaces while also developing synergies with the sphere of tradition in business. Finally, this paper unveils the rich mosaic of founders of Société Anonymes. In examining the body of company founders we could perhaps speculate the following: had Westerners been the (sole) direct physical carriers of foreign technologies and capital the synergies between tradition and modernity would have been less pronounced.

The second part of this book is devoted to leadership. It opens with a contribution by Pier Angelo Toninelli and Michelangelo Vasta ('Italian Entrepreneurship: Conjectures and Evidence from a Historical Perspective'). This paper is the first product of an ongoing research into the determinants and the role of entrepreneurship in Italian economic development. Its primary aim is the creation of a data-set of Italian entrepreneurs for the period encompassed between Unification and the end of the twentieth century. The main source of the research is a collection of 390 entrepreneurial biographies, prepared for the ongoing *Biographical Dictionary of Italian Entrepreneurs*. The first part of the paper presents a descriptive analysis of the main peculiarities of the country's entrepreneurship on the basis of a few standard variables traditionally used in economic analysis. The second one refines the descriptive approach through a methodology – Multiple Correspondence Analysis and Cluster Analysis – usual by now in standard statistics, yet not very familiar to scholars in economic and/or business history. This has allowed the authors to single out a few entrepreneurial typologies from the history of Italian capitalism which partly confirm the 'traditional' features already emphasized by historiography; such as the prominence of northern entrepreneurs, the strong relations both with entrepreneurs' own and their partners' families, the almost total absence of female entrepreneurs and an essentially middle-class rooted entrepreneurship. However a few novel interesting aspects emerge, the most surprising being the high level of formal education of the sample: a majority (60 per cent) has a medium/high degree and almost one-third a university degree.

In the second part there are two contributions about the Spanish case that are also based on biographical dictionaries: 'Entrepreneurship: A Comparative Approach', by Gabriel Tortella, Gloria Quiroga and Ignacio Moral, and 'Dynasties and Associations in Entrepreneurship: An Approach through the Catalan Case', by Paloma Fernández-Pérez and Núria Puig. According to Tortella et al., entrepreneurial studies are proliferating and a question which is cropping up often is: what moves entrepreneurs? Is it just a matter of genes or are there more general factors (social, psychological) which move people to become entrepreneurs; and not only this: what makes entrepreneurs successful? What makes some behave in a certain way and others differently? Using a sample of English and Spanish entrepreneurs, the paper of Tortella et al. tests the role of education in the formation of the entrepreneurial spirit to conclude that education is a key variable.[23] In their turn, Fernández-Pérez and Puig try to shed light on the role played by dynasties in the creation of social capital and the accumulation and transfer of entrepreneurship in Catalonia, the region that led the Spanish industrialization process. In their paper, Fernández-Pérez and Puig present advanced results of a research in progress about large family firms in Catalonia.

The third part of this book debates the role played by culture and institutions in the promotion of entrepreneurship. In 'Entrepreneurial Culture or Institutions? A Twentieth-Century Resolution', James Foreman-Peck and Peng Zhou test the strength and persistence of cultural influences on entrepreneurship over the best part of a century. Comparison of self-employment propensities of United States immigrant groups in 1910 and 2000 suggests a number of stable customary stimuli, deduced from national origins. In accordance with the 'cultural critique', the English were less prone to entrepreneurship than other United States immigrant groups, once controls for other influences are included. The Dutch consistently exhibited about average levels of entrepreneurial activity, not as precocious as might be expected if the predominant Protestant religion encouraged entrepreneurship. Conversely Weber's identification of nineteenth-century Catholic culture as inimical to economic development is not borne out in the twentieth century by the sustained entrepreneurship of Cubans and Italians in the United States. The strongest entrepreneurial cultures were exhibited by those originating from the Middle East, Greece and Turkey, though some historical interpretation is necessary to establish who these people were. The inference from these patterns is that entrepreneurial culture must be of minor significance for economic development compared with institutional influences.

Following this is 'Entrepreneurship and Cultural Values in Latin America, 1850–2000: From Modernization, National Values and Dependency Theories towards a Business History Perspective', written by Carlos Dávila. Focusing on the historical determinants of entrepreneurship in Latin America, and in particular the influence of cultural factors, this paper analyses the eventful path of the literature dealing with the role of values (from 'traditional' to 'modern') and its relationships to entrepreneurship in Latin America between 1850 and 2000, and examines the potential that the growing business historiography on this region of the world offers to advance its understanding. For this purpose, the papers draws selectively on surveys of the field and explores the challenges and opportunities confronting future research into the historical explanation of entrepreneurship in this area; in particular, the potential for conducting studies of entrepreneurial typologies is delineated. With this in mind, key features and patterns of Latin American entrepreneurship based upon business history research output are also identified. Within Latin America's broad scope and diversity (the region consists of 21 countries), this paper encompasses Mexico and seven South American nations (Argentina, Brazil, Chile, Colombia, Peru, Venezuela and Uruguay), with particular emphasis on Colombia. The contents of this paper could prove useful to policymakers fostering entrepreneurship in Latin America, as well as to business schools engaged in valuable discussion about the extent to which culture – and in particular values – is a key issue in today's concerns to foster entrepreneurship.

The last contribution to this book is 'Education and Entrepreneurship in Twentieth-Century Spain: An Overview', where José L. García-Ruiz offers statistical information on the evolution of the level of education among Spanish entrepreneurs between 1964 and 2004 through the data provided by the official survey on the working population (the Encuesta de Población Activa, EPA). The EPA data show an important improvement in the education of the Spanish entrepreneurs, in a trend that resembles that for the whole Spanish population. The structural transformation of the Spanish economy was accompanied by a clear improvement in the education levels. But, contrary to some popular beliefs, García-Ruiz has found that the more ambitious entrepreneurs, those that create jobs and are not merely self-employed, have always enjoyed an educational level well above the average for the whole working population. If the training of Spanish entrepreneurs as a whole has been deficient it is due to the late implementation of business studies. The conclusion is clear: education improves the quality of entrepreneurship rather than entrepreneurship itself.

1 DETERMINANTS AND TYPOLOGIES OF ENTREPRENEURSHIP IN THE HISTORY OF INDUSTRIAL ITALY

Franco Amatori

Introduction: Entrepreneurship and its Environment

Entrepreneurship is a difficult subject to grasp. Notwithstanding its much acknowledged centrality for the wealth and the competitiveness of a nation, it is an elusive phenomenon, a concept very difficult to define clearly, a concept so protean that it is impossible to categorize in a mathematically formalized discourse.

Entrepreneurship appears in different sizes: it can be found in large corporations as well as in the small workshops of artisans. It can present itself under various forms. There is, of course, the Schumpeterian hero capable of constructing an empire but it can also be found in a manager in an entrepreneurial position who has the capacity not only to maintain a strong grip on the organization but also to make it even bigger. It is possible for an entrepreneur to be self-employed or even someone with a couple employees who is capable of being highly reactive in responding to customized demands and fitting his actions into a limited niche. Innovation is a good litmus test to verify the degree of entrepreneurship in an economic national system, but it is not enough to explain everything. Entrepreneurship can be a long, day-by-day accumulation or it might just present itself in a dramatic leap ahead. But, again, not all the people we tend to identify as entrepreneurs are actually exceptional innovators.[1]

In any case, having studied the phenomenon of entrepreneurship under various angles and in different realities over the course of time, I have become profoundly convinced that *de facto* it is impossible to separate the entrepreneur from his environment. Especially pertinent are the simple but profound observations of Carlo Cipolla in his wonderful book *Before the Industrial Revolution*. Looking at the crucial issue of productivity, Cipolla declared that the correlation with the increase of material inputs was not sufficient to explain it. At the same time, he was not convinced that the 'surplus' could be identified with the Schumpeterian creative reaction of history. In Cipolla's mind, the Austrian economist made the error of reducing the whole to one part (in this case entrepreneurial activity).[2] If Cipolla had a positive way of persuading me of the existence of this tight connection between the entrepreneur and his environment, I was left with the opposite effect by *Entrepreneurship: A Comparative and Historical Study*. In order to explain the impact of entrepreneurship on economic development of different nations, Paul Wilken, an American sociologist, singled out four variables: 'O' (opportunities), 'Y' (economic growth), 'X' (non-economic factors) and 'E' (entrepreneurship). He examined the cases of Great Britain, France, Germany, Japan, the United States and Russia in the nineteenth century, reaching results that were, to say the least, disconcerting. For instance, Wilken affirmed that both Great Britain and the United States were among the countries where entrepreneurship played a minor role.[3] The entrepreneur and the environment cannot be separated. If we reconsider each on its own, it might become easier to analyse both.

Sketching Italian History and the Macro-Determinants of Entrepreneurship[4]

Given these premises it is necessary to sketch an evolution of the Italian economic environment since Unification in 1861. From this, we can draw some determinants of entrepreneurship together with some entrepreneurial typologies. For this task my main source has been the *Biographical Dictionary of Italian Entrepreneurs* (*BDIE*; see the appendix to this chapter).

Italian economic history since Unification can be broken down into six phases:

1. 1861–6: Italy was primarily an agricultural society which, at least up to 1880, exported agricultural products and raw materials to the countries at the heart of international capitalism. Starting in the 1880s, given the huge crisis of agriculture (due to a remarkable increase of imports because of steam navigation from United States and railways from Russia), a first layer of industry in the northern part of the country started to be visible, together with better-designed policies that supported industry and that materialized in protectionist measures in favour of basic products such as steel. *De facto*, in 1884 the state promoted a steel company in central Italy – Terni – for military reasons and three years later, when the firm was on the brink of bankruptcy, proceeded to rescue it by ordering the Bank of Italy to print new currency. This was a limited – but expensive – episode which represents just the beginning of state involvement in industry.

2. 1896–1918: This is the era of the first industrialization, a blend of the First and Second Industrial Revolutions, and was based on the evolution of international technology. Up until 1914 the international context played a strong role; for Italy this meant new technologies, new demands, new entrepreneurial and managerial capacities as well as new and original sources of financing (in particular, the remittances of emigrants). In this phase the main characters were northern Italy's entrepreneurs, but the state still played an important role with protectionism, orders, subsidies to industry and also, once again, with a huge rescue – this time an entire sector (steel) in 1911. During the First World War, the state was the main engine of industry. Its actions strengthened heavy industries and conferred the phenomenon of a high industrial concentration in the so-called 'industrial triangle' in the north-west between the cities of Milan, Turin and Genoa. In the end, the war constituted the point of 'no return' for Italian industrialization.

3. 1918–45: In this period, too, we have wars and industrial rescues. Of the latter, especially important was the one of 1933, when – via the creation of IRI (Istituto Ricostruzione Industriale) – the industrial shares of Italy's universal banks (Banca Commerciale Italiana, Credito Italiano and Banco di Roma) were bailed out. Even if these years were very turbulent in Italy from an economic point of view, important sectors of the Second Industrial Revolution were developed and consolidated (chemicals, electricity and automobiles are good examples). By the end of the Second World War, Italy was the only industrialized country in Southern Europe.

4. 1945–70: Often referred to as the glorious years, this era represents the definitive modernization of the country, when industry took over the role as leader of the nation's economy. In the 1950s and 1960s Gross National Product (GNP) grew at an annual rate of almost 6 per cent. Italy became a part of the Western economic community. It received help from the Marshall Plan and was among the founding members of the European Common Market. Private big business flourished, especially in the automobile sector thanks to Fiat, but the area of state-owned enterprises also grew stronger. IRI was joined by ENI (Ente Nazionale Idrocarburi) and in both state ownership was matched with an entrepreneurial and managerial style more typical of private enterprise. New sectors such as household appliances emerged and in this period it was possible to see the passage from craftsmanship to industrial dimensions in various sectors.

5. 1970–90: These decades are often described as the period of Italy's 'failed landing' and limited recovery. At the peak of the 'economic miracle' in 1961, Italian GNP reached a record rate of growth of 8.6 per cent; it seemed feasible for Italy to become a first-rate economic power. Some scholars have outlined its similarities with Japan: both as regarded the timing of the industrialization process as well as the crucial role played by the state. The major difference, how-

ever, is that Italy did not reach the world economic frontier; its main weakness was linked to the political and institutional boundaries. Unlike Japan, in Italy the state did not withdraw from direct economic activity but, instead, actually increased its sphere according to social and political criteria. In addition, the political side failed to come up with a proper legal and institutional framework to favour the development and consolidation of big business.

Italy in this period had no anti-trust legislation, offered little protection for investors in the stock exchange, failed to promote mutual and pension funds, and suffered from ineffective banking legislation following the end the Universal Bank model in 1936. Furthermore, the government was not capable of controlling and channelling the enormous social change that came about as a consequence of the great economic transformation (primarily illustrated by the massive migration of workers from the south to the northern regions of the country). This kind of situation put big business in serious difficulty. The lack of rules made recovery in the 1980s ephemeral.

Still, Italy in the 1970s was the Western country with the highest rate of growth after Japan. How was this possible? It happened thanks to small businesses which in several areas of the country were organized into industrial districts, those homogeneous territories that concentrated on the manufacture of a specific product. In order to reach this goal, the firms of an industrial district created a sophisticated division of labour: horizontal for separating and specializing production in different phases, and vertical since industrial equipment and intermediate products used for the manufacture of goods were also produced. Italy's industrial districts were the humus for the rise of a 'Fourth Capitalism', meaning firms that are neither small nor big private or state-owned businesses. At the end of the twentieth century in Italy there were 1,500 companies with revenues between 150 million euro and 1.5 billion euro. They focused on a niche, which was often global in extent. These firms were defined as 'pocket multinationals'.

6. 1990–2010: The past twenty years have been characterized by stagnation and relative decline. In Italy, globalization has created some problems for industrial districts and Fourth Capitalism because of much harsher competition brought about primarily by the Asiatic giants, especially China. Still, these firms continue to be the backbone of the Italian economy. At the other end, state-owned companies, submerged by debts and liabilities, have been in large part privatized. Overall, big business has definitely shrunk. Major companies like chemical manufacturers Montedison and SNIA or Olivetti in electronics no longer exist. Fourth Capitalism has many advantages but its weak points are also evident. We see this when examining family businesses and the sectors where these firms usually operate – consumer goods (products for persons and households) are not exactly frontier productions.

Reflecting on Italian history, one feels the need to outline some macro-determinants of entrepreneurship, including: 1. the evolution of the economic environment at the moment of the nation's political unification with its weaknesses as well as its strengths; 2. the actions of the state; and 3. stimulants of the international economy which reflect on the dynamism of the domestic market.

As regards the first point, without a doubt Italy is a nation that – starting in the seventeenth century up to the present day – has lost its economic world primacy. It is also a country in which it is evident that there is a territorial dualism between north and south that is very difficult to overcome. At the same time, Italy is also a country generously endowed with technical skills, scientific and cultural institutions, a cosmopolitan attitude towards trade, refined consumption given its numerous small capitals and an agricultural system that over the course of centuries has been able to accumulate resources and in which there is room for initiative together with a hard-work ethic.[5]

Regarding the second point, the state's actions, we must remember that since Unification (let us remember Franco Bonelli, who defined it as 'precocious State capitalism'),[6] and especially since the 1880s, the state has been a very active player, with its goal that Italy should catch up with the most advanced nations. For this purpose, the state chose to pursue this strategy via the use of subsidies, orders, protectionism and – a truly original element – four industrial 'rescues' over the course of fifty years (until the birth of the state-entrepreneur in 1933).

Shifting to the last aspect, I do not think that it is correct to define this as globalization. Rather, I believe that we should take a Braudelian view of the world economy with its concentric circles. In this vision, Italy is situated at the periphery of the first circle (or, it can also be said, at the extreme limit of the semi-periphery) but it is enough to reflect on what happened in the years that Giorgio Mori defines as the 'true Italian miracle' (1896–1914), when entrepreneurs, technologies, capital in various forms, managerial know-how and strong demand came to Italy from the outside world.[7]

Heritage

Scientific Knowledge, Technological Capacities, Workers' Skills

In the first decades of the twentieth century, Giovanni Agnelli created the nation's largest industrial concern, Fiat (Fabbrica Italiana Automobili Torino). Agnelli was one of a small group of noblemen, financiers, professionals and landholders in Turin who founded the firm. Unlike the others, however, Agnelli was the first to understand that automobiles were not just a toy for the affluent but represented a means of transportation that could be distributed on large scale and eventually change our way of life. His intuition regarding mass production led Fiat to build up a vertically integrated firm – from foundries to the garages where the automobiles would be sold.

In 1923, using hefty profits procured during the First World War, Agnelli inaugurated Lingotto, Europe's most modern automobile factory. All this was possible thanks to the favourable conditions that surrounded Fiat at the time. In fact in the last part of the nineteenth century we see the first signs of the various elements that would favour the birth as well as the growth of the most important automotive centre in Italy. The Piedmont region had a long tradition in body shops, going back to the sixteenth century when Italian manufactured carriages were considered to be among the finest in all of Europe. Over time these shops were able to adapt to new market demands, like those of the railways. Even a difficult economic period (like that which occurred between 1888 and 1895) did not destroy the solidity of a metal machinery sector that was based not only on military and civilian orders from the state (for example, the arsenal and the railway plants) but also offered a breeding ground for an important nucleus of specially skilled workers who could be found in the plants of companies such as Ansaldi, Dubosc, Officine di Savigliano and Ferriere Piemontesi. With experienced workforces, these companies were able to supply some rather sophisticated products: from high precision machine tools to motors, electrical equipment and special casts in iron. Also of note is the fact that the financial downturn of the early 1890s did not destroy the significant financial resources that were available for investment in secondary sectors. The strong future prospects of the automobile industry did much to make sure that adequate funding was set aside. It is equally important to understand the premises for the significant advances made by Turin's industries in the first fifteen years of the twentieth century. The intellectual climate of the time was dominated by *positivism*, which considered a cognizance of the surrounding world to be a tool for realizing socio-economic progress. In Turin a number of educational and cultural institutions played an important role in this scenario as they were oriented towards favouring industrial development: institutions like a laboratory for economic policy, professional schools and, most of all, a polytechnic university. An equally important role was played by Turin's political leadership which from the outset of the twentieth century vigorously focused on offering those elements which were most important for industrial growth: low-priced sources of electric energy, an extensive rail network, low-cost housing for workers and technical training. Turin's first steps in the automotive industry go back to 1895 when David Federmann started up an activity as commercial representative of Daimler while Michele Lanza, a chemical industrialist, ordered a vehicle from Fratelli Martina, a local firm which up to then had supplied machinery for Lanza's plant. These early attempts, while ephemeral, grew in number until the end of the century. Almost always using foreign manufactured motors, attempts to break into the auto industry were made by firms like Bender & Marty, bicycle manufacturer Luigi Storero, Carlo Racca (a lawyer) and engineers such as Caramagna and Emanuel Rosselli. Even then, observers of the time could not help but ask why Turin, rather than Milan, had transformed itself into the nation's most important centre for automobiles. Of course it was in this fertile terrain that Giovanni Agnelli based his undertaking.[8]

If Turin's polytechnic was a hive of technicians and managers for Fiat (and this became especially visible following the inauguration of the Lingotto plant when the company undertook an extensive hiring campaign), in the same way Milan's polytechnic showed itself to be an invaluable source for Lombardian entrepreneurs in the electric industry.[9]

Although the race to secure guaranteed profit centres over the course of time shows the entrepreneurial limitations of a society not accustomed to competition, it is equally important to highlight Italy's ability to put together important technical and scientific resources that were capable of realizing complex engineering projects such as the mountain plants that took advantage of artificial lakes to provide a sure and constant source of energy. It was in this sense that Milan Politecnico played a key role. The only independent institution in Italy's university system, the Politecnico took advantage of the support of local associations both private and public. The school was able to react quickly to the needs of the new electric industry. Already in 1883 students were taught some of the new applications made possible by electricity; the 1887–8 academic year produced the nation's first graduates of electrical engineering. Among these new engineers were Aldo Foscarini, who would eventually serve as technical director at Edison, Angelo Sonda (future managing director of Società Anglo-Romana per l'illuminazione) and Carlo Paolo Colti, who would go on to be appointed the president of Società Elettrica Bergamasca. A few years earlier the Politecnico had also produced engineers who eventually played an important role in the Italian economy. These were people such as Ettore Conti, a key actor in Edison's expansion, and Giacinto Motta, who served as head of the same in the interwar years.[10] In 1886 a generous donation from pharmaceutical industrialist Carlo Erba made possible the creation of Istituzione Elettrotecnica (Electro-Technical Institute) Carlo Erba inside the school of engineering. Over time the institute would actively advise businesses, developing services for testing, refining and verifying new technological inventions for industrial use. In 1902, Cesare Saldini, who was an instructor at the Politecnico after receiving his degree from there, worked together with the Società Umanitaria, a local cultural initiative, to create an electro-technical laboratory. During the day the laboratory was full of engineering students while in the evening the same classrooms filled up with workers who had already studied electricity at the secondary level in the school of Società di Incoraggiamento di Arti e Mestieri (Association for the Encouragement of Arts and Trades): the latter then went on to become some of the most sought-after workers in the industry's principal firms. Finally, no history of the technical schools and engineering universities of northern Italy would be complete without mentioning one of its most important actors, Giuseppe Colombo, who, together with Francesco Brioschi, established Milan Politecnico in 1863. Colombo was renowned as a scholar, an entrepreneur and a resourceful politician, as well as the force behind numerous cultural and scientific initiatives.

In fact, many of the characters who played an important role in the Italian industrial scenario were engineers by training. This was the background of Giovanni Battista Pirelli,[11] one of Milan Politecnico's most brilliant graduates. After completing his studies, in 1870 Pirelli received a grant to travel to various areas of industrialized Europe in search of a new sector that could be transplanted in Italy. Ernesto Breda[12] was also an engineer, who succeeded in transforming an old machinery producer, Elvetica, into a firm that specialized in manufacturing locomotives; as was Oscar Sinigaglia,[13] the big reformer of the Italian steel industry who (for most of the first half of the twentieth century) fought for a rationalization plan that would transform the industry into a major player. Other engineers who would go on to play a key role in industrial Italy included Guido Donegani,[14] creator of Montecatini, the largest Italian chemical manufacturer, and Agostino Rocca,[15] a follower of Oscar Sinagaglia. At the conclusion of the Second World War, Rocca emigrated to Argentina where he created an important multinational for the construction of big industrial plants. Adriano Olivetti,[16] too, was an engineer by training. He did not limit his attentions to the technical and organizational aspects of work, however. More than the others, Olivetti understood that the factory was both a place of production and of socialization and human achievement. For these reasons, Olivetti believed that an entrepreneur's viewpoint had to take into account the surrounding territory and its problems as well.

Skills that Came from Afar

In 1824 the mayor of Recanati, a small town in the central Italian region of Le Marche, replied to a questionnaire sent by the pontificial government asking for information regarding the situation of the territory for which he was responsible. The answers he provided were recorded by historians because the mayor in question was Monaldo Leopardi, father of one of Italy's most revered poets, Giacomo Leopardi. In his reply, Monaldo Leopardi mentioned above all the role played by agriculture in the area, then referred to some commercial activities and finally, almost as an afterthought, mentioned the minor activity of some artisans who used ox horn to produce women's decorative haircombs. Leopardi was of the opinion that this was doubtless a transitional activity because it had as its basis neither agriculture nor support from the state. But the mayor was wrong as a similar activity exists even today. The ox horn used by the artisans was replaced with plexiglas in the 1930s thanks to the Guzzini family. The family had its origins as sharecroppers and, starting in the early 1900s, would make small objects with ox horn in the winter and in those moments when the demands of agriculture were few. Over time the Guzzinis started producing not only hair ornaments but also various household objects. Today the company employs more than 3,000 people and its products are sold around the world.[17]

Le Marche had always offered a combination of sharecropping and village industries scattered across many of the 220 towns and cities of the region which today has a total of 1.4 million inhabitants, making the entire area less populated than the city of Milan. The combination of these industries can be found in sectors deemed important for the region such as shoes and musical instruments, or in other activities such as agricultural machinery produced by Pieralisi[18] in the town of Jesi or white goods produced by Merloni,[19] an international player which has its headquarters in Fabriano. Le Marche is a region rich in social capital, as can be seen by the Istituto Tecnico (Technical Institute) in Fermo that was created during Napoleonic times as a secondary school for technical training and which, over time, has become an incubator of entrepreneurs such as the Benelli brothers[20] (manufacturers of motorbikes), Adriano Cecchetti[21] (active in numerous sectors from heavy machinery to agricultural machinery as well as shipbuilding and railcars) and the previously mentioned Aristide Merloni, who created a true dynasty in the household appliances industry. Just as Fermo was important for the technical training offered to young people, the school of pharmaceutical studies in Camerino also produced a number of entrepreneurs including Francesco Angelini, who in the 1950s created a pharmaceutical group bearing his name which continues to be among the most important in the industry.

A tradition of refined consumers and widespread technical abilities are the key elements to the success of 'Made in Italy' fashion. It was Giovanni Battista Giorgini,[22] a headstrong gentleman from Tuscany who, starting in 1951 with the fashion shows of Florence, brought Italian couture to the United States and then across Europe. He is often seen as the inventor of 'Made in Italy'. Giorgini's first attempts were met with mistrust but then consumers became enthusiastic for the tasteful fashion items being produced in Italy. Via fashionable clothing, Giorgini felt that Italian intuition would be rewarded by the international markets. Giorgini started his career as a buyer of tailor-made products that showed creativity, fantasy, good taste and ties with both the Italian sense of tradition as well as the artistic sensibilities for which the country is so well known. The first ambassadors of Italian high fashion included important tailors such as Zoe Fontana[23] and Elvira Leonardi.[24] Soon, however, new designers appeared on the scene; people such as Giorgio Armani, Walter Albini[25] or Enrico Coveri[26] knew how to blend creativity with their expertise in fabrics and ability to establish long-term relationships with producers. But 'Made in Italy' is not limited to clothing. The concept spread to other sectors such as machinery and arms manufacturing. Beretta,[27] for example, is a dynasty which has been producing shotguns since the sixteenth century; in the seventeenth century a large forge was built in the region of Brescia. Over time, the forge helped to insulate the firm from the periods of crisis that affected the manufacturers of weapons for war; Beretta shifted its focus to hunting rifles. In the post-Second World War period, Beretta expanded its product line; today its pistols are used by many police departments in the United States.

This enlargement of the concept of 'Made in Italy' helps explain the success of Agusta,[28] a machinery firm that has its origins in an area in north-western Lombardy known around the world for its tradition of producing goods ranging from motorbikes to helicopters. Enzo Ferrari,[29] too, was an eloquent international ambassador of Italian products; the company which bears his name was born in a district of Italy which seems to be based on speed. In fact one of Ferrari's historical rivals, Maserati, also has its plants in the Modena area. Other firms with a well-established international presence include food and beverage manufacturers like Barilla,[30] Buitoni,[31] Ferrero[32] and Lavazza.[33] In these firms we find an ability to transform artisan-made items into goods for mass consumption as well as a special talent for marketing, as can be seen by the advertising campaigns which turned these companies into household names in Italy and around the world.

The Challenge of Realizing Complex Projects[34]

In a somewhat forced move, in 1861 Italy became a unified nation. Therefore the country does not really have a long tradition similar to what we find in the United Kingdom or in France. Nor, as can be found in Germany, was there a strong compact culture or a sense of national identity based on important states. A long-standing institutional continuity and a strong bureaucracy are important components for system that wants to embark on the realization of technologically complex projects. This gap can be seen in the failures of the electro-technical sector in early nineteenth-century Italy, in the experiences of Bartolomeo Cabella and in the fact that a speciality chemicals industry never really established a hold in Italy. To be successful, it would have been necessary to have a national system of innovation with strong coordination between the state, businesses and secondary schools of specialization. This dilemma is even more pronounced in the period following the Second World War. A good example is the field of electronics which Adriano Olivetti had slowly and carefully built up in his Ivrea firm with its specialization on office machinery. This time the state, which many times in the past had intervened to rescue productions considered strategic, did not lift a finger for the development of the electronics sector. Instead, coming to the rescue of Olivetti in 1964 (which found itself in a moment of difficulty because of the unexpected death of its founder) were four of the country's most important industrial firms and financial institutions: Fiat, Pirelli, Mediobanca and IMI. As none of these firms had experience in the sector, they were convinced that the electronics segment was holding back the company, so their first decision was to sell it off to the American General Electric. Even more clamorous was Italy's experience in the field of nuclear energy. Euroatom – the United Nations agency which promoted peace-time uses for nuclear power – had envisioned Italy as the possible leader in Europe. But Italian policies for the sector showed how uncoordinated things really were in the nation. In the 1950s three power plants were constructed but each was built by a different firm (ENI, Edison and Finelettrica) and each used a different form of technology. By the time the decision to implement a unified policy for the nuclear sector was made and Felice Ippolito, a well-respected scientist from Naples, was appointed as the person responsible for this, a battle (brought on by the lobbyists of the oil industry) broke out. The oil companies feared that a unified policy would cut down on the amount that they were supplying to thermo-electric plants as oil producers would not be needed once nuclear power took off. They blocked the project by launching an attack on Ippolito; though the accusations were quickly determined to be false, it was enough to put an end to the project.

The Burden of the South

Without a doubt, over the past century there has been no lack of talented entrepreneurs in the southern regions of Italy. For example, in the food industry we find firms such as Divella[35] (Apulia) and De Cecco[36] (Abruzzo), two pasta manufacturers whose brands have been appreciated around the world since the beginning of the 1900s. There are other sectors as well with important tales of entrepreneurship – for example, Giuseppe Calabrese, based in Apulia and active in the field of transportation, or Salvatore D'Amato,[37] an entrepreneur from Campania who has established a reputation as one of the most modern as well as technologically innovative firms in the packaging industry. Still, neither these examples nor others to be found among small and medium-sized companies have been able to pull all firms together into developing the south of Italy. Some of the companies which made the attempt failed. A good example is Florio[38] which, in the second half of the nineteenth century, assembled an extensive group based in Sicily that spread out into many sectors. This Italian 'Zaibatsu' reached its peak in 1881 with the creation of Società di Navigazione Generale (Society for General Navigation) as a result of the merger with the Genoese shipping line Rubattino. The Italian colossus was, however, essentially based on a concession in the postal services monopoly; much criticized, by the end of the century the whole firm was declared a failure. In addition to its activities in this area, Florio also produced an outstanding wine (Marsala), supported tuna fishing, owned a sulphur mine and had begun activities in the steel sector. But the privileges attained from the monopoly in maritime activities were actually an obstacle to a modern and attentive form of management: while the profits reliably arrived on a regular basis, the process of investing in the modernization of a quickly antiquated system was much slower. In 1893 only 34 of the 103 streamers owned by Florio were less than 20 years old while another 32 vessels were more than 30 years old. In the course of a few years, the company entered into a downward spiral that could not be stopped.

The attempts of other southern Italian enterprises to grow in the period between Unification and the Second World War also had a bitter ending. One example is Bruno Canto Canzio's firm, Manifatture Cotoniere Meridionali.[39] At the eve of the Second World War, the biggest economic power in the south was SME (which operated in the electricity sector), but most of the merit can be attributed to the fact that the company had an extensive international network and could count on the involvement of a group of foreign investors who supported this initiative of Maurizio Capuano[40] and Giuseppe Cenzato,[41] two business leaders who were also somewhat 'distant' from the industrial fabric of southern Italy. In reality, the industrial firm of southern Italy which benefited from important state support was Ilva, which as a result of the 1904 'Naples legislation' was able to construct the Bagnoli steel plant. Ilva's Bagnoli stayed on this path but the firm never really took off and simply survived by special financing and orders received from the state. This was a policy that revealed itself to be a failure and which pushed southern Italy ever further from being connected with the rest of Europe, eventually even putting into question the idea of a truly unified nation.

The Role of the State

Patriotism and Business

The actions of the state are the second macro-determinant of Italian entrepreneurship. From Unification up to the First World War, examples of entrepreneurs who have state actions as their reference point emerge; there is an evident confusion between patriotism and business. Let us take, for instance, the case of Pietro Bastogi, a revolutionary patriot when he was young (he was very close to Giuseppe Mazzini, one of the leaders of the Unification movement) but who became increasingly moderate in later life, leading a family firm that was active in trading and banking. He was an authoritative member of the right wing and was appointed minister of finance in the first government of a unified Italy led by Camillo Cavour. In 1862 Bastogi foresaw the great opportunity of his life: constructing the railways between the cities of Ancona and Brindisi on the Adriatic coast and another line between Naples and Foggia (effectively linking the east coast with the west coast), thereby forming a skeleton for the railways in southern Italy. The government had assigned the operation to the Rothschilds but Bastogi, taking advantage of the ardent patriotism of those days (this was a period when Garibaldi wanted to conquer Rome and take it back from papal domination at any price), succeeded in convincing Parliament to reverse its decision. He declared that he had assembled what today we would define as a network of Italian capitalists, raising a sum considered enormous at the time – 100 million lire. In reality, it was later discovered that the majority of the capital was French, that one of the major shareholders of the new company was also the president of the parliamentary commission which made the decision and that Bastogi himself – by acquiring the rights to subcontract work – would earn the considerable sum of 14 per cent of that allocation. The episode was the first economic-financial scandal in the history of a united Italy. Bastogi left the political scene for a short while but quickly returned without any problems and as a main actor, maintaining the management of his company Le Strade Ferrate Meridionali.[42]

In a certain sense the story of Vincenzo Stefano Breda is similar. He, too, was a patriot and politician as well as a leader of one of the most important Italian companies: Società Veneta di Costruzioni, the major national operator in the field of big public works. The government entrusted Breda with building the first important Italian industrial initiative, the steelworks in Terni, for which subsidies and protection were granted. Terni was assigned the production of the steel needed for constructing battleships. Breda grabbed the opportunity and tried to go beyond state support with a project that was difficult (but brilliant) and that would make Terni the most important Italian steel producer. Nevertheless by 1887 the company was on the verge of bankruptcy for lack of technical sophistication, for the difficult economic situation and also for clear administrative irregularities. Breda had entrusted Terni with a foundry that he owned, assigning it a higher value that its actual worth. He probably utilized state funds to solve the precarious situation of Società Veneta, trapped in the economic crisis of the late 1880s. Breda went on trial but, before a decision could be taken, he was appointed senator and this meant that he could only be judged by a special court. For that occasion the Senate transformed itself into a high court of justice and absolved Breda (probably because a great part of the ruling class identified itself with a project that wanted to give the country the raw materials, the steel, indispensable for any initiative of foreign policy).[43] Terni was then bailed out by the National Bank which, in order to raise the funds, resorted to printing money.

Equally close to the state were Ferdinando Maria Perrone and his sons, Mario and Pio. The family owned and managed Ansaldo, a large corporation in Genoa with a production line that went from locomotives to battleships. The Perrones could not help but be attentive observers of the system: in the early part of the twentieth century, the state would often advance a manufacturer up to 144 per cent of the cost of its supplies. It is evident that pressure on public powers was a decisive part of their entrepreneurial action, so much that they purchased news-papers and specialist magazines, hired high-ranking officers of the navy, tried to put faithful functionaries in the diplomatic posts and paid political figures for alleged consulting projects.[44]

These ambiguous situations should not hide the fact that significant results were obtained. Even if Bastogi's behaviour was hardly orthodox, three years after the founding of Strade Ferrate Meridionali, the railway segment Ancona–Brindisi had been completed. Notwithstanding various tribulations of Breda at the beginning of the 1890s, Terni had gained the status of a modern steel fac-tory that was able to offer a wide scope of production lines. Similarly Ansaldo was able to initiate a courageous programme of vertical integration to deliver a ship ready for combat. The British partners, Armstrong, thought that Perrone's project was crazy but, in 1913, the German military attaché expressed his admi-ration for the Genovese naval shipyards at Ansaldo.[45]

The Negotiators

It is possible to single out another segment close to the typology outlined: those who pursued big dimensions or diversified production so as to place themselves in a position of major bargaining force with the political power. Probably the person who best represents this type of character is Arturo Bocciardo. Leader of Terni after the First World War, a difficult time for the steel industry, he moved the company into electric and electrochemical productions. Still, Bocciardo did not dismiss the original core sector so that he was able to make an agreement with the government, exchanging a 'patriotic sacrifice' for preferential tariffs in electric supplies and a solid position in the chemical cartels that were regulated by the government.[46] Bocciardo is not an isolated case. It is enough to remember the leaders of the steel trust[47] at the beginning of the century or the leaders of the most important chemical companies in the 1970s.[48]

Another entrepreneur experienced in negotiating with the state was Guido Donegani, the leader of Montecatini.[49] He chose to invest the fabulous prof-its Montecatini accumulated during the First World War in the mining sector (pyrites and sulfites – essential components of explosives – and copper that was used for bullets) into an operation of forward integration in the chemical sec-tor. In 1920 he was able to realize his objective, taking over Unione Concimi and Colla e Concimi, the two most important Italian producers of fertilizers. In any case, his most important accomplishment in the chemical field of the 1920s was the production of synthetic nitrogen via the innovative Fauser method that functioned by utilizing only the 'autarchic' ingredients of water, air and electricity. Montecatini invested an enormous amount in constructing hydroelectric power plants for the production of synthetic nitrogen and needed to hinder the Italian farmers' consumption of nitrogen fertilizers imported from Germany in order to control the vital domestic market. Inevitably Donegani 'signed a pact with the devil' (Mussolini), when he asked for the creation of fierce protectionist measures. In exchange, Donegani was compelled by Mussolini to make a series of rescues (dyestuff producer Acna, mining company Montevecchio and companies involved in Carrara marble) and to keep obsolete productions alive for the Duce's autarkic objectives.

Italian Samurai

Nevertheless, at the beginning of the twentieth century figures of entrepreneurs who appear to be disinterested also emerge. These were entrepreneurs who, in a certain sense, even if they were external to public administration, could be qualified as real state servants.

Let us take the case of Oscar Sinigaglia who, while very young (he was seventeen at the time), effected an incredible turnaround of the almost bankrupt family company that traded steel products. Immediately after, Sinigaglia drafted a brilliant project of rationalization of the Italian steel sector. His project was an alternative to the rescue outlined by the Bank of Italy for the industry in 1911, a project that had envisioned the formation of trusts and cartels, crystallizing a productive apparatus that had been inefficient and irrational. Sinigaglia, who enrolled himself as a volunteer at the onset of the First World War, donated his company to the state. He was engaged in industrial mobilization, an agency that supported the Italian military effort during the war. In the post-war period he flanked the poet and nationalistic leader Gabriele D'Annunzio in the military enterprise of bringing the Istrian town of Fiume (now Rijeka) inside the borders of Italy. Sinagaglia would spend the rest of his life in various states of fortune but was finally successful in solving what he saw as the central question of Italy's economy – the steel problem.[50]

Alberto Beneduce, the creator of the state-owned holding IRI, represented – in an even more apparent way – the figure of the civil servant entrepreneur. Beneduce, born in 1877 in Caserta near Naples, collaborated with and followed Francesco Saverio Nitti, a politician born in the deep south of Italy who envisioned the industrialization process as the only way to solve the problems of his native area. After the First World War, Beneduce worked to make Nitti's ideas a reality, founding two financial institutions (Crediop and ICIPU). Thanks to a system of bonds guaranteed by the state, these institutions were able to fund the big projects necessary for the electrification of the south. It was the same system that Beneduce used to finance IRI, born after the very serious crises of the Italian universal banks in the early 1930s. Beneduce, accused by some historians of short-term vision and substantial support to big private capital, in reality oriented his actions on the basis of some precise ideas. First of all, the state was expected to assume its responsibilities as an owner, not underselling the shareholders acquired to private business leaders. It was a strong position that shows up in various episodes of IRI's history but the subsequent step did not bring him to pursue the nationalization of the economy. Together with state ownership, Beneduce expected that there should be an entrepreneurial and managerial style able to compete in the marketplace. In those sectors and companies where private capitalism had failed, Beneduce entrusted IRI's properties to the 'right hands' of manager-state entrepreneurs such as Rocca, Cenzato and Reiss Romoli.[51]

A third example of Italian 'samurai', seen as entrepreneurs who were sincerely patriotic and provided disinterested and essential services to the state, was Enrico Mattei, a man new to the scene. Mattei quickly became an important protagonist in the years of the Italian 'economic miracle'. Immediately after the Second World War he transformed a state-owned company, AGIP, which had been created by the Fascist government in 1926 in order to guarantee a supply of oil for the country. Head of the Catholic partisans, Mattei came to AGIP as *Commissaire* in 1945 and, instead of shutting it down as had been requested, chose to keep it alive and made it even more powerful, in 1953 founding ENI (Ente Nazionale Idrocarburi), the second public holding after IRI.[52] Mattei gave new focus to oil drilling in the Padana area and launched the construction of a network of natural gas pipelines to take advantage of methane gas in the area; ENI also financed research in the area of nuclear power. Under his guidance, ENI negotiated important drilling concessions in the Middle East as well as an important commercial agreement with the Soviet Union. These were initiatives which contributed to breaking up the Seven Sisters oligopoly which dominated world oil production at the time.

The Crisis of the State as Entrepreneur

After 1960, the state as entrepreneur underwent boundless expansion with few limits on the actions of IRI and ENI as well as two other state-owned holdings, EFIM (engineering and glass industries) and EGAM (mining). The growth of the state as entrepreneur was not based on economic criteria but, rather, on objectives for increasing employment, gaining consensus and procuring votes for the parties of the governmental coalition. In this way the state not only opted *not* to privatize companies that could very well have been put back on the market but it also chose to *increase* its area of intervention.

The consequence was the crisis and defeat of the state entrepreneur and of the heirs of people like Beneduce and Sinagaglia. A major turning point was in 1956 with the creation of the Ministry of State Shareholdings through which a real chain of command was created. At the top was the minister and, below, the superholdings IRI and ENI, the sectorial financial holding and finally the companies themselves. In reality, when the Ministry was created it was a puppet in the hands of Enrico Mattei and the other most important state entrepreneurs. But property rights have their own weight; when the economic situation became more difficult in the second part of the 1960s the chain of command showed all its effects and limitations. Now politicians were in command and they looked for consensus while imposing their choices on the heads of the various holdings.

In this respect, it is interesting to examine the case of Alberto Capanna,[53] a state entrepreneur who in some ways embodies the opposite of Sinagaglia's heritage. Capanna, too, came from a long experience in the steel sector but he was much more in tune with the desires of the political powers. First as CEO, then as chairman of Finsider (the holding that controlled IRI's steel companies), he fought for the continuous enlargement of the operations in Taranto (by the late 1960s Italy's largest steel plant), putting the focus on mass production with very low added value. In this market, the Italian integral cycle plant stood little chance of competing with Japan and other emerging countries. Capanna fiercely opposed plans for restructuring Finsider and succeeded in preserving it both in its role of financial holding as well as headquarters for operative companies. He defined himself as being a navigator of the short distance between the rocks of the political and union powers. His years as leader marked the beginning of the end of IRI in the steel sector. In 1988 – with 25,000 billion lire of debts – Finsider found itself bankrupt.

Influences from Abroad

From Unification to the First World War

At the beginning of industrialization in Italy, between the end of the nineteenth century and the beginning of the twentieth, one of the most decisive elements was the country's openness to stimulants that came from the international scene. In concrete terms, this meant being able to reach rich markets, acquire new technologies and import cutting-edge business concepts. The latter appeared in new organizational and entrepreneurial factors as well as the appearance of new actors such as the Universal Banks based on the German example, together with enormous flows of new financial resources thanks to the remittances of Italy's numerous emigrants scattered around the world. In the period between Unification and the First World War, we find three entrepreneurs who are especially representative of the ability to follow up quickly on stimuli from abroad and their application to internal markets: Alessandro Rossi, Giovanni Battista Pirelli and Giorgio Enrico Falck.

Rossi, a wool producer from Schio in the Venetian region, was the most important Italian industrialist in the first post-Unification years. He was one of the great advocates of the protectionist tariffs of the 1880s. In fact, he affirmed that the ideology of free trade was nothing more than protectionism of the strong nations. But, notwithstanding all this, Rossi's rise was due to his travels abroad, to his capacity to grasp technological innovations as they were at the frontier and integrate them into his long-term view in building a modern factory with the right size by utilizing the most advanced legal corporate set-ups (joint-stock corporations, for example).[54]

As mentioned earlier, after finishing his studies at Milan Politecnico, Pirelli received a grant to make a grand tour in Europe with the aim of searching out new industries to be brought back to Italy; he identified rubber. The company he founded in 1872 which bears his name certainly did not disdain state orders like those for submarine cables or for telegraph wires that came from the navy and Ministry of Military Infrastructures. But Pirelli quickly jumped into international competition and rapidly created a multinational enterprise with factories in Spain, in South America and even in the heart of world capitalism – the United Kingdom.[55]

Finally, I want to mention Giorgio Enrico Falck, a third-generation member of a steel dynasty with Alsatian origins. In 1906, he set up Acciaierie e Ferriere Lombarde in Milan. Falck did not produce only those big products associated with steel that the state wanted. Instead, he looked carefully at the needs of the local market and urban infrastructures, at a civil and industrial housing in strong expansion, at a flourishing engineering industry. Falck did not build the very expensive integral cycle steel plants; production was based on scrap iron so that it was possible to utilize more and more the electric oven, a technique that guaranteed an increased flexibility.[56]

After the Second World War

After the Second World War, Italy actually got into the Western market economy thanks to some good decisions by political figures such as Alcide De Gasperi (prime minister between 1945 and 1953) as well as Cesare Merzagora and Ugo LaMalfa (both ministers for foreign trade in the early 1950s). Their choices advanced both the nation's position as well as the entrepreneurs themselves who were frightened by international competition and in many cases preferred the protection they had enjoyed during the years of Fascism. Probably the best example of these important choices of Italy's political forces was the fundamental decision to join as a founding member of the European Common Market. In 1953 the other nation members of the Common Market – Western Germany, France, the Netherlands, Belgium and Luxembourg – accounted for a 20.7 per cent share of Italian exports. By the end of that decade they represented more than 35 per cent, eventually reaching 40 per cent in 1966. Above all, Italy exported finished industrial products whose total incidence was more than 60 per cent in 1961. The country enjoyed an especially favourable position in industries such as automotives, metallurgy and new sectors like that of household appliances.

Furthermore the assistance received from the United States via the Marshall Plan permitted the technological renewal of large enterprises. Finsider implemented a plan designed by Oscar Sinigaglia; it envisioned the building of a very modern steel plant near Genoa that was endowed with continuous rolling mills – an American technology bought with Marshall Plan funds – for the indispensable production of durable consumer goods, the specialization of the other two integral cycle centres (Piombino for rails and Bagnoli for large sheets of steel) and the closing of obsolete factories. Thanks to Sinigaglia's plan the Italian steel industry moved from ninth to sixth position in the world.[57]

Vittorio Valletta, the manager who assumed the leadership of Fiat after the death of Giovanni Agnelli, was equally able to grasp some of the opportunities brought about by the Marshall Plan. Valletta envisioned the Americanization process of the Marshall Plan as something more than a means to oppose the advancement of Communism. For Valletta, this was a chance to create a new world of mass production and mass consumption, to elevate living conditions in order to eliminate the harsher aspects of class struggle. Indeed, he reached this goal thanks to the aid obtained via the Marshall Plan. Fiat was able to increase production tenfold over the course of fifteen years (from 100,000 in 1950 to one million in 1965).[58]

Similarly internationally oriented was Adriano Olivetti. At the end of the 1950s he led a multinational company with 50,000 employees and branches around the world. Olivetti pursued a very audacious move – taking over Underwood, a major American producer of office equipment and assuring Olivetti's front-row seat in the global marketplace.[59]

Enrico Mattei, too, understood the necessity of internationalization – at least in the field of oil sources since Italy was very poor in this component so essential for an industrial country. This was why he chose to pursue a very risky international policy favouring oil-producing countries. Mattei was paid for his choices with strong hostility from the major oil companies as well as some Western governments. In the end, his own life was put at stake. It is believed that his death in an air crash in October 1962 was probably caused by sabotage.[60]

In the 1950s other new characters of Italian industry come forth including some white goods producers. In Italy, the household appliances industry did not exist before the war. Craftsmen like Giovanni Borghi,[61] Eden Fumagalli[62] and Lino Zanussi[63] were ready to exploit the domestic as well as the international markets where they directed an important segment of their production.

From Districts to 'Pocket Multinationals'

A third phase of internationalization for the nation was apparent in the 1970s, when the conditions of the Italian domestic market were unstable given economic and social turmoil. In this phase the importance of industrial districts emerged. Each was dedicated to a specific production structured according to a very sophisticated division of work. Not only were they involved in various phases but they also manufactured the equipment and the intermediate products necessary for producing the goods manufactured in the industrial district.[64] Several dominant enterprises emerged. They cannot be defined as big business, either public or private, but neither can they be classed as small business when we realize that around the end of the century there were 1,500 companies with revenues of between 150 million and 1.5 billion euros active in Italy.

These firms have been defined as a 'Fourth Capitalism'. Their competitive advantage was the ability to put together exceptional crafts skills and equally careful attention to the market with a capacity to create international networks. This is the story of the Benetton family (clothing) and Leonardo Del Vecchio (eyewear) and, more recently, of Diego Della Valle (shoes). This so-called Fourth Capitalism did not emerge from industrial districts, but remains a part of them, such as in the case of Ratti, with its origins in the silk district of Como, or Zegna and Loro Piana which their ties to the wool manufacturing district of Biella. A number of these protagonists began their activity after the Second World War, such as Catelli (Chicco products for children), Fossati (Star, food manufacturers) and Ferrero (chocolate).

The ties with the world market are evident in various cases such as the producers of ceramic tiles in the Sassuolo area or chemical companies like Mapei. They also can be seen with other companies, such as suppliers for the automobile sector like Giorgio Bombassei, the owner of Brembo, originally a small mechanical workshop which, by supplying clients such as Alfa Romeo, has become one of the most important producers of disk brakes.[65]

A Community of Entrepreneurs

In the end, it is possible to say that not only today but also over the entire course of Italy's history from Unification onwards, when we think of entrepreneurs we observe a great liveliness and variety. There are entrepreneurs oriented towards the technical side and others who are pioneers. There are those who look at the social context and political engagement. There is a rich tradition of state entrepreneurs and others who have turned bargaining with the government into a formidable tool. We have manager-entrepreneurs but we have also entrepreneurs who are owners and we have both managers and owners who have Schumpeterian dimensions and vigour. We have entrepreneurs of mid-size firms, those whose companies we have defined as Fourth Capitalism whose origins – even if today they are well-known names – can be traced over the entire historical period examined in this paper.

A few years ago, as we prepared the *Biographical Dictionary of Italian Entrepreneurs*, we observed that, while greater numbers of entrepreneurs can be found in the northern part of Italy, the south was not dormant. In this region we can find entrepreneurs such as Giuseppe Calabrese in Apulia, who operated in the transportation sector, Liborio Vincenzo Callia, who made furniture in Basilicata, and Salvatore D'Amato, a leader in the packaging industry who was based in Campania.

In addition, the history of Italy is full of examples of simple people who wake up early in the morning and start working with great earnestness; these are the entrepreneurs that I collocate in the category of 'alertness'. We also should not forget those who seized occasions like Angelo Luigi Colombo who, in post-First World War Milan, manufactured pipes for various uses, Antonino Giuffre, a Sicilian student at Bocconi University in the 1920s whose career in publishing had its origins in selling class notes to other students, or Franco Angeli, who did something similar in the 1950s. Another example is Giuseppe Battista from the southern region of Molise who, starting in the 1860s, moved from flour mills to manufacturing macaroni and from there to a tannery and to a mechanical plant thanks to the help and involvement of his eighteen children. If we venture north, we also find Domenico Dalle Case in the Trentino region, who was active around 1900 in different sectors and finally consolidated in manufacturing construction bricks. But more examples come to mind if we think also of fashion, of high technology, of the gigantic plants of protagonists such as Giovanni Agnelli and Enrico Mattei.

Drawing to a close, I want to modify slightly the Fascist slogan which portrayed Italians as being a population of 'heroes, saints and navigators' by adding 'entrepreneurs'. In my opinion, enterprising attitude is a raw material that is abundant in this nation. It must be promoted and allowed to develop. At the same time, it needs to be disciplined and channelled into a system of rules and institutions so that it can be of benefit to all.

Appendix

The *Biographical Dictionary of Italian Entrepreneurs* (*BDIE*) was started in 2001 under the sponsorship of Enciclopedia Italiana Treccani. At the time, a related series, the *Biographical Dictionary of the Italians*, had already published 200 entries about entrepreneurs but that series had only arrived at the letter 'G'. When *BDIE* started, it was decided that one-third of the entries from the old dictionary were completely obsolete, one-third needed significant revisions, and one-third could be published with minor updates.

An editorial board was set up for *BDIE*, chaired by Franco Amatori (Bocconi University) and Mario Caravale (University of Rome), who was also editor of the larger dictionary. Other members of the editorial board were Giuseppe Berta and Andrea Colli (Bocconi), Augusto De Benedetti (University of Bologna), Giuseppe Pignatelli (Enciclopedia Italiana) and Luciano Segreto (University of Florence).

For *BDIE*, entrepreneurs were defined as 'those who allocated resources at a maximum level of a company regardless of ownership'. For inclusion in *BDIE*, those chosen were to be considered relevant for national or local history. It was decided to include successes as well as failures (and honest as well as dishonest actors). Fundamental was the availability of wide and critical sources; facts mentioned in the entries had to be documented. The entire work was designed to be representative of all of Italian entrepreneurial history – by geographical areas, by sectors and by typologies. All of Italy's regions were considered and it was also decided to single out special categories such as bankers, traders, technicians, women, fashion and movie industries, and managers of state-owned enterprises.

BDIE's organization was structured on a network of decentralized trustees responsible for regions or categories. Each region or category was assigned a certain number of entries. The intention was to arrive at a total of 1,000–1,100 entries. Each trustee was asked to propose twice the number of possible entries for the region or category so that a selection could be made of the 50 per cent considered to be the most representative of that group. Within the selected groups, entrepreneurs were divided into three categories: for the first, entries were to be no more than 8,000 words; for the second, no more than 5,000 words; and entries for the final group were much shorter (no more than 2,000 words). It was decided to include only entrepreneurs who were no longer alive and who had operated in the period between Italy's unification and the beginning of the twenty-first century. The decision to represent all the regions of Italy meant sacrificing thorough coverage of the most industrially advanced regions. For instance, Lombardy as an average represents 25 per cent of Italian GNP but only 170 entries for entrepreneurs from the region were accepted. Manufacturing or industry took the lion's share with almost 70 per cent of the entries. A little less than 5 per cent were from agriculture and slightly less than 4 per cent from commerce. Bankers and financiers represented slightly more than 10 per cent.

Of the entrepreneurs chosen, 351 were basically active between the years of Unification and the First World War, another 377 in the period between the two wars, while 299 came forth in the final half of the twentieth century. The remaining 94 could not be classified according to these criteria. The authors were supplied with a checklist of items for consideration:

1. Family origins and education.

2. Significant incidents that brought the individual to entrepreneurial activity.

3. Strategy and structure (but with relevance to the specific context).

4. The entrepreneur's specific and detailed position in a wider framework (without placing more emphasis on the framework than the individual himself).

5. Quantitative benchmarks.

6. Political vision or action as well as the entrepreneur's relationship with the social context.

It was suggested that some living entrepreneurs be included but they were not because of the conviction that it is impossible to evaluate an individual still in the position of making strategic choices. However, since the editorial board was aware of the latest wave of entrepreneurship in Italy in the past 30 years, plans were made for an eventual fourth volume made up of 300 brief entries dedicated to new enterprises which had emerged more or less in the last three decades of the twentieth century.

The *BDIE* initiative was suspended in 2004 for budgetary reasons even though the project – with close to 600 entries completed – had arrived up to the letter N. Today business historians can consult the pre-print versions which are available in the library of Bocconi's economic history institute. It is the hope of Italian scholars that some day the project will resume once funding has been secured to complete the work.

2 ENTREPRENEURIAL TYPOLOGIES IN A YOUNG NATION STATE: EVIDENCE FROM THE FOUNDING CHARTERS OF GREEK SOCIÉTÉ ANONYMES, 1830–1909

Ioanna Sapfo Pepelasis

Introduction

This essay examines entrepreneurial typologies in Greece, a latecomer economy, between national independence in 1830 and 1909, a landmark year regarding state formation and the empowerment of the bourgeoisie.[1] The analysis is based on the collective body of Société Anonymes founding charters[2] and, following Foreman-Peck, the formation of new companies is perceived as an outcome of entrepreneurial initiatives.[3] This methodological approach offers a unique opportunity to conceptualize the general contours of entrepreneurship in Greece[4] because until now no equivalent database has existed for other types of business start-ups.

The core questions addressed in this essay are: who were the protagonists, the builders of the Société Anonymes? Are theoretical typologies appropriate for 'classifying' entrepreneurial action? Was there economic agency in the nascent 'corporate' sector?[5] Was incorporation cut off from traditional forms of business organization? The analysis opens with a very brief survey of Greek economy and enterprise during the period under review. Emphasis is laid on the coexistence, during this time of deep transition, of imported institutions and the legacies of the pre-independence past. Awareness of this duality is a necessary starting point for the historical exploration of entrepreneurial typologies.

Economy and Enterprise

When Greece won independence from the Ottoman Empire in 1830, it was an economically devastated land striving to catch up with the West. Although it was the cradle of Western civilization, for over a millennium it diverged culturally as a result of the impact/legacy of Byzantium and Ottoman subjugation.[6] Hence, in contrast to the West, private property rights were initially weak in the newborn Greek state. The latter was also in the peculiar position of being small in size while the majority of Hellenes continued to live outside its borders.[7] By 1909 progress had been achieved on many fronts. The territory was much larger and Greece had made the transition from a backward and peripheral agrarian province of the Ottoman Empire to a modern nation state with a parliamentary monarchy. It had a steadily rising bourgeoisie, the elite of which was dominated by Westernized Greeks of diaspora origin. Its legal system provided a clearer framework for property rights and on the economic front it had a higher real per capita income,[8] an industrial core and a more open economy.[9]

Within this milieu of macro-changes and the rise of a 'mercantile' type of capitalism, there were important continuities in the political economy of Greece.[10] As in the past, the majority of enterprise was in commerce and shipping. Οικογενειοκρατία (familiocracy) was widespread and most firms were small, if not tiny single proprietorships or (in)formal partnerships.[11] Entrepreneurs managed risk and capital scarcity through short-termism, a limited degree of specialization and multiple ventures with diverse partners from family- and community-based networks. A successful business person would, at any point in time, be involved in numerous short-term commercial partnerships, some of which were set up only for one specific transaction.[12] Moreover, although each large entrepreneur would be practically in full charge of a 'personal' firm, he deliberately avoided having exclusive ownership in his hands. For example, even in shipping where there was large capital accumulation, wealthy shipowners did not have 100 per cent ownership in any one of their vessels. This was a result of prudent diversification and strategic economizing of capital for other opportunities.[13]

Finally, the divide between the spheres of business and state administration was not clear as, from the early years following the War of Independence, public officials did not rely on their salaries alone for a living. For example, one prominent military officer, Vassos Mavrovouniotis, was also involved in some commercial activities.[14]

It was within this mixed environment that the Société Anonyme was transplanted in Greece. The innovation of this joint-stock type company (henceforth SA) was introduced to post-independence Greece in 1835, through the formal adoption of the 1807 Napoleonic Commercial Code. In terms of capital accumulation the SA was a significant force in the economy during the period under study, as the registered capital of SAs was at least equivalent to 16.6 per cent of non-agricultural Gross Domestic Product.[15] In brief, the SA was a technology transplanted into a society in transition, in which the traditional and the modern coexisted and developed multiple 'synergies' between them.

The Protagonists: Company Founders

The known founding shareholders of the 303 SAs established during the period under review comprised a mosaic of around 7,000 natural personae, 200 business firms, 15 banks and less than 10 public bodies.[16]

The first category, natural personae, consisted basically of male members of the elite, the majority of whom were already well-established business persons prior to their undertaking of entrepreneurial initiatives in the nascent corporate sector. Many founders would declare in the company charter that they were merchants, merchant-entrepreneurs (involved simultaneously in shipping, money-lending or tax-farming) or merchant-landowners. Although founding shareholders often put next to their name the occupation 'landowner', a good number of them were truly merchant entrepreneurs whose landed estates were a spin-off from their other business activities but who described themselves as landowners for reasons of prestige.

Despite the strong presence of the mercantile classes, the body of founding shareholders also included various categories of craftsmen and petty traders. Over time, however, the composition of company founders evolved and, from 1870 onwards, there was a growing core of enterprising professionals such as bankers, engineers and chemists. Usually Western-educated, these technocrats were often scions of first-generation merchants.

Throughout the period under study, members of the non-business elite could also be found among company founders: the occasional lawyer, notary, pharmacist, headmaster, university professor, mayor or other high-ranking civil servant, as well as descendants of ex-Ottoman local officers and dignitaries. There were also some politicians, for example Theodoros Deligiannis, who as minister of foreign affairs was a cofounder of the marine insurance SA I Agyra (est. 1869). There is also the example of the War of Independence hero General (Yiannis) Makriyiannis, who was among the first shareholders of the National Bank of Greece (est. 1841). The involvement of such public figures in incorporations may have been a career choice or a form of valuable political protection needed by business.[17] The opposite facet can also be seen, whereby leading company founders – or their close relatives – involved themselves in politics, often as a way of consolidating links and lobbying power that could protect them from political interference or threats. Through this strategy, business in the emerging corporate sector may have compensated in part for the absence of institutional protection of property rights.

The banker entrepreneurs Andreas Syngros and Stephanos Skouloudes were only two of the elite members of the mercantile diaspora who were SA company founders. Other prominent figures were Theodoros Vlastos, Grigoris Kouppas, Stephanos Franghiadis and the banker Ioannis Pezmazoglou. In contrast to the diaspora, which claimed many names among company founders, there were very few Western European businessmen. In the early years, the latter would usually be merchant entrepreneurs domiciled in Greece, for example the German Theodore Hamburger who lived in Patras. Later, foreign businessmen who participated in SA start-ups were basically bankers or railway tycoons who resided outside Greece. One such businessman was Baron G. de Reuter, who was a cofounder in the railway company Etaireia Ellinikon Sidirodromon (est. 1902).[18]

Finally, a discussion of natural personae would be incomplete without a few words on female SA company founders. These mostly involved ladies of the elite who were acting in the interest of their families. Almost always, they operated in consort with male relations and with the exception of widows they did not display much individual agency.[19]

The second largest category of company founders, business firms, consisted of some two 200 businesses – almost exclusively merchant houses – organized as general or limited partnerships. The involvement of merchant houses in incorporation was more pronounced prior to 1870 and it was partly a vehicle to expand the control of a few powerful SA company shareholders without analogous capital commitment.[20] Indeed, it was often the case that in a particular SA start-up, individuals who were owners of a specific merchant house – as well as the merchant house as an independent entity itself – would be founding shareholders.

The third category, banks (seven Greek, one diaspora and seven foreign), acted as substitutes for pure entrepreneurship and flourished from 1882 onwards. Though far smaller in number, banks were particularly successful at mobilizing local and foreign capitalists and setting up the largest of all SA companies. Banks largely coalesced with the technocratic segment of natural personae company founders and were important in fostering the rise of a managerial/technocratic class.

The fourth and smallest category of company founders, public entities, consisted of the central state and a small number of municipalities.[21] However, in spite of the small number of SAs in which public entities participated, the influence of the central state was large as it played an important indirect role in shaping the wider parameters within which entrepreneurial initiatives materialized.[22]

To sum up, incorporation involved a rich mosaic of players from many segments of society, the composition of which shifted over time. This intermingling of a large variety of entrepreneurial players was part of the wider story of evolution in a young nation state striving to break away from economic backwardness and in which there were no clear divisions either among the diverse social groups of the elite or between the world of politics and business. This complexity and the multiple interactions between the traditional (continuity) and the modern (change) were simultaneously mirrored in the entrepreneurial typologies that emerged in the nascent corporate sector of this latecomer country.

Relevance of Theoretical Typologies

There is a long international discourse on the subject of national typologies of entrepreneurs(hip) in which theory and empirical observations interlock.[23] In the case of Greece, entrepreneurial history and the related dialogue on the relevance of theory are still in an early stage. Two recent attempts at classifying Greek entrepreneurship have interpreted it as an example of Kirznerian alertness to profit opportunities.[24] This classification is basically grounded in the observation that the bulk of entrepreneurship was in commerce/mercantile intermediation and that Greece did not experience an industrial revolution in the nineteenth century. Although this classification is not without basis, it lacks comprehensivity as it applies only to the traditional segment of Greek entrepreneurship, namely that involving commerce. It overlooks the fact, delineated in this paper, that there were elements of economic change in Greece at the time.[25]

Importantly, the body of SA founding charters provides evidence that in the young nation state, the sectoral breakdown of start-ups did not mirror the composition of Gross Domestic Product. Agriculture, the largest sector of the economy, was absent. Sailshipping was also not directly present and trade, the main activity of Greek businessmen, had only a small presence.[26] Therefore, Kirznerian commercial intermediation (which can be identified with a scalar expansion in economic activities) was present only to a small extent. The great majority of entrepreneurial initiatives in the emerging corporate sector was of a higher level order and entailed multifaceted economic agency: the undertaking of new economic activities; the adaptation of imported technologies to local conditions, the opening of new markets as well as of new economic spaces (see section below). These Schumpeterian elements of innovation bring into the picture the Baumolian concept of productive entrepreneurship. Namely, the type of entrepreneurial action that did not entail 'simply a scalar expansion of the economy',[27] but which brought change and had a positive impact on the economy at large.[28] Further theoretical insights that enhance our understanding of the wider productive impact of entrepreneurial initiatives in the Greek corporate sector can be drawn from the work of Nathaniel Leff and Stavros Thomadakis.[29] These two scholars have demonstrated that in the context of latecomer economies, early entrepreneurs had to create from nil the prerequisite institutions and infrastructure which already existed in advanced countries and that were necessary for the expansion of entrepreneurship and economic development. The most blatant examples of the latter in Greece during the period under review were the large transport schemes.

Before proceeding onto an analysis of the diverse facets of agency it should be underlined that the inclination towards productive entrepreneurship should not be exaggerated as the success or failure of many grand modernistic initiatives of incorporation naturally depended on general economic conditions and the foresight (also perhaps morality) of company promoters.[30]

Agency of Company Founders and the Building of New Greece

Entrepreneurial agency in the corporate sector entailed entry into the following new activities: The introduction of marine insurance companies that operated as informal financial institutions, a mechanism *par excellence* for the allocation and management of risk which had social repercussions that went beyond any private benefits, as it produced reserves for the absorption of shocks. In addition, although incorporation was not widespread in shipping as a whole, it was of significance in the birth of the technologically advanced area of 'steam'. Moreover, it had a strong presence within the emerging capital/knowledge-intensive enclaves of Greek industry – i.e. mining, metallurgy, mechanical engineering, electricity production and chemical fertilizers.

In addition to the introduction of new economic activities, incorporation also opened up new economic spaces. First, it enhanced monetization, the spread of the use of symbolic money and the formation of a national market economy.[31] When Greece became a nation-state it had a quasi-subsistence economy: the market was highly underdeveloped, there were no banks and no national currency. The vital importance to the formation of a state of a national currency and a printing bank are well documented.[32] SA company founders brought about what can perhaps be labelled a 'financial revolution', at the centre of which stood the National Bank of Greece and a complex web of formal and informal banking institutions.[33]

Second, the collective entrepreneurial initiatives of SA banks opened new channels for the mobilization of scarce capital and technical know-how for the construction of public utilities/infrastructure. At the centre of these efforts stood the 1,548-km national railway system.[34] This project, together with the opening of the Corinth canal, was seminal for the creation of an integrated national economy and administrative centralization, both of which were centre-pieces of nation-state building. In addition, SA banking groups gave birth to the new economic space of public benefit organizations. The first such entity was the State Monopolies Company, Etaireia Diaheirisis ton Monopolion tis Ellados (est. 1887). It was set up by five banks (two diaspora banks, the National Bank of Greece and two foreign banks)[35] and it unified the collection of taxes on state monopoly goods whose revenues were assigned as security for the 4 per cent 135 million gold franc loan raised by the state in London and Paris in 1887.

Finally, incorporation opened new channels for the mobilization of national technical know-how. Engineer entrepreneurs of Greek or diaspora origin assisted – and in some instances, eventually replaced – the foreign engineers who spearheaded the construction and operation of large infrastructure projects. For example, in 1890 a Greek-based Corinth canal SA took over the work of the French company that had been set up in Paris in 1882. Continuation of construction was assigned to the Greek engineer Antonios Matsas.

Entrepreneurial agency, although present from the early days, became more pronounced within the emerging corporate sector from *c.* 1874/9 onwards. This shift was a result of a Baumolian change in the 'rules of the game' which created a more favourable environment for the undertaking of innovative entrepreneurial initiatives. This change was brought about by several factors, including the land distribution of 1871, which strengthened the institution of private property, and the 1881 abolition of tithes, which curtailed the institution of tax-farming and its rent-seeking advantages. An additional influence was the changing ability of the state to build infrastructures. This was in large part related to the government's renewed access to the international capital market following the lifting in 1879 of a thirty-six-year embargo. Also, of significance was the increasing interest of the international mercantile diaspora in doing business in the homeland.[36] This elite group operated as a key intermediary in the negotiations of the state with foreign bondholders for the lifting of the long financial embargo. Moreover, it acted as a facilitator for the massive transfer of capital and know-how from the West which materialized after 1879.[37] It is, in fact, possible to argue that the rise in agency in the emerging corporate sector would not have been possible had a growing segment of SA company founders not consisted of professionals, basically engineers, bankers and institutions of diaspora origin. The latter were more willing and capable than other Greek entrepreneurial agents of pushing certain activities beyond the familiar spheres of traditional rent-seeking and intermediation.

Company Founders: Shaping the Société Anonyme as a Form of Business Organization

Entrepreneurial initiatives in the emerging corporate sector also had agency over the shape of the SA as a form of business organization. On the one hand, although the legal framework for incorporation remained unchanged, founding shareholders through their own initiative began to introduce new rules and stipulations in the founding charters of companies which brought the Greek SA closer to the Western archetype and provided for better governance, more sophisticated accounting practices and a clearer separation between owner-ship and management.[38] On the other hand, company founders adapted the imported organizational form of the SA to local conditions and embraced cer-tain past legacies. More specifically, they assimilated and elevated to a higher level the customary Greek business practices of relations of trust and defensive diversification. Through this process they maintained tight relations with – and embedded their start-ups in – the traditional world of non-corporate business.

With respect to relations of trust: as mentioned above, the great majority of Greek businesses were family firms during the period under review. The number of SAs that took the shape of pure family firms may have been insignificant but nevertheless most SAs were network-based. In those SA companies that were established by a large number of founders, the latter would be a mixture of interlinked subgroups each one consisting of trusted collaborators and/or individuals related through blood ties or ritual kinship. The spatial dimensions of entrepreneurial networks among SA company founders give evidence of the intermingling of local with wider – national and even international diaspora – portal networks. This was particularly obvious in the case of the networks of SA bankers, which were highly cosmopolitan and had strong ties with the cen-tral state.[39]

Regarding adoption of defensive diversification, initially it prevailed in tradi-tional business as an organizational device to manage uncertainty. In the young corporate sector it adopted two forms: internal and external to a particular SA company. With respect to internal diversification, over a quarter of SAs declared more than one activity in their charters. Multi-diversification within a single enterprise was not a means to expand scale and internalize transaction costs, as was the case with vertical integration in multidivisional firms of the advanced nations. Instead, it was an organizational mechanism used by company found-ers for the management of risk and for dealing with two paramount structural problems of nineteenth-century Greece: capital shortage and the threat of idle capacity as a result of the small size of the market. Low specialization of organi-zations, capital goods and human resources lent themselves to multiple use and allowed entrepreneurs within firms to retain the flexibility to shift activity if a crisis occurred in one sector. Most multipurpose firms were marine insurance companies, or commercial or shipping companies that also provided some type(s) of financial services. A few manufacturing SA firms also pursued com-mercial activities and vice versa.

Turning to external diversification, company charters attest to the fact that founders would often use incorporation as a tool to expand their business operations without deserting their preceding private proprietorships or part-nership-based firm(s). One basic reason behind this organizational strategy was that the new SA would offer some type of service to the pre-existing non-corporate firm(s). Within this context of building dynamic connections with traditional business, diversification may have appeared as 'external' to an indi-vidual SA enterprise, but it was 'internal' at the level of the total affairs of a given entrepreneur.

External diversification also had one more facet. Multidimensional entrepre-neurs would give a corporate form to those business ventures which involved new economic activities (capital-intensive projects of a Schumpeterian or, by extension, Baumolian high-agency bent). Whereas activities with which they were more familiar, were less capital-intensive and/or did not require coordi-nated action among diverse groups of entrepreneurs would be allocated to the non corporate sphere of business.

Especially towards the end of the period, a few select SA company founders made the full transition to the corporate form in organizing their business activi-ties. Two such notable examples were the diaspora-origin Nikolaos Vlangalis in industry and Ioannis Pesmazoglou in banking. Nevertheless, even in these cases it is most likely that some network ties were maintained with individuals and organizations of the non-corporate sector, as the majority of Greek businesses belonged to the latter realm.

To conclude, company founders spontaneously introduced modern organi-zational features from the West while also creatively embracing selected business practices of the past.

Micro-Examples of Entrepreneurial Action in the Nascent Corporate Sector

The analysis of the general trends in entrepreneurial norms is at this point sup-plemented by a micro-level snapshot of major company founders who were individuals (natural personae) and banks. A closer look at both groups of actors is helpful in comprehending the motivation, logic and typologies that defined entrepreneurs(hip).

This section presents nine individuals who invested large amounts of capital in SAs and for whom rather detailed biographical information exists on their overall activities. Three bankers figure in our list of nine leading company found-ers. This is not coincidental. The involvement of banking in incorporation was diverse and extensive. It was usual in the largest SAs for both banks (as insti-tutions) and bankers (as individuals) to participate simultaneously in the same company as founding shareholders. For these reasons bankers drew substantial public attention and hence there exists more biographical information for them compared to other categories of company founders.

Table 2.1 at the end of this chapter presents in a condensed form the following information on these nine individual company founders: social origins and education; non-corporate business activities; entrepreneurial initiatives in the corporate sector; non-business interests such as involvement in politics and social affairs; and any other relevant information. Chronological order is followed in the sequence of the names so as to emphasize evolution over time. Each of these micro-cases has unique characteristics, but as a whole they do confirm, on the one hand, the existence of general behavioural patterns and, on the other hand, evolution over time. In summary, this micro-material demonstrates the following:

1. That the most important company founders were well educated, belonged to the country's elite, were of diaspora origin (or had close contact with it) and often sought out a parallel involvement in politics.

2. The post-1873/4 generational twin evolution whereby more and more company founders (often the sons of merchants) were professionals and in parallel an increasing number of entrepreneurial initiatives in the nascent corporate sector were outside the realm of the familiar.

3. How the entrepreneurial initiatives of many individual company founders were a combination of non-corporate entrepreneurialism (of a Kirznerian bent) and incorporation (of a Schumpeterian/innovative bent). This duality occurred either concurrently or over time, as a transition would be made from the first to the second type of entrepreneurial action.

Information is far richer for banks that were company founders than for the far more numerous category of natural personae. As happened in other backward countries with a low supply of entrepreneurship and market imperfections, banks assumed entrepreneurial leadership.[40] Specifically in the young corporate sector of Greece seven local SA banks – which had strong connections to the diaspora – developed a significant entrepreneurial presence. In order of importance, in terms of the number of SAs they participated in, these financial institutions were: the National Bank of Greece, the General Credit Bank of Greece, the Bank of Industrial Credit, the Bank of Epiro Thessaly, the Bank of Athens, the Currant Bank and the Anatolian Bank. All in all the seven aforementioned local banks set up more than twenty large SAs in collaboration with two types of financial institutions: diaspora owned banks based outside Greece such as the Bank of Constantinople[41] and Western banks (as for example, the Banque d'Escompte de Paris, the Banque de l'Union Parisienne, E. Erlanger & Bros and Hambros & Sons).

As a further point of interest, the registered capital of all Greek SA banks and banking affiliated SA companies amounted to 70 per cent of the total registered capital of corporates during this period.[42] Thus it is no exaggeration to claim that finance-related institutions drove incorporation.

The involvement of banks evolved over time. Prior to the lifting, in 1879, of the thirty-six-year financial embargo and the accession of the region of Thessaly in 1881, the only banks to create SA companies were the National Bank of Greece and the Bank of Constantinople. Thereafter, we have the genesis of the phenomenon of SAs founded also by some other bank or more usually by banking groups.

The entrepreneurial actions of banks involved the creation of three types of SA companies: 1. other joint-stock banks; 2. public utilities and public benefit organizations; and 3. companies providing private (consumption) services and goods. The latter involved steam shipping, marine insurance, general insurance and heavy industry. Often banks would participate in the creation of an SA company not only through share capital but also through the provision of bond loans.[43] It would appear that in many cases SA companies affiliated to financial institutions would be the main customers of the banks which founded them. As for the entrepreneurial initiatives of foreign banks in the incipient Greek corporate sector, their scope was slightly narrower as it did not involve insurance or industry.

To sum up, as in other latecomer countries, collective entrepreneurial action on the part of banks and banking groups was pronounced. However, the Greek case is unique in that financial institutions were able to exhibit superior capabilities in mobilizing scarce resources (capital and skilled/knowledge-intensive labour) because of their connections to the internationally-based cosmopolitan Greek mercantile diaspora networks.[44]

Conclusion

This essay has shown that entrepreneurial action in the corporate sector displayed multifaceted economic agency, thereby enhancing the process of economic change and constituting a rich, dynamic and cumulative 'catch-up' force for the young Greek state. Furthermore, entrepreneurship as incorporation was not divorced from or independent of society. Three historical determinants played a seminal role in shaping it: the mercantile diaspora, modern nation-building and the legacies of the past. The mercantile diaspora acted as a key facilitator for the involvement of foreign capital and know how in incorporation. The building of a modern state system established over time 'new rules of the game' which, on the one hand, curtailed traditional rent-seeking activities and, on the other, provided an institutional environment conducive to the expansion of a Schumpeterian/ Baumolian-type entrepreneurship. The legacies of the past were two-fold. There existed the backward elements in the wider socio-economic environment which blocked productive entrepreneurship and were inherited from pre-revolutionary Greece. In contrast but parallel to these were the long-tested traditional business practices and organizational devices that were creatively assimilated by company founders.

In addition, this paper has illustrated how, during this period of deep transformation, a mosaic of SA company founders existed and there was no uniform entrepreneurial typology. It has been argued that within the emerging corporate sector the presence of Kirznerian-type entrepreneurship was far less pronounced than in traditional business. By contrast, Schumpeterian-type entrepreneurial initiatives prevailed which ventured beyond the 'scalar expansion' of the economy and the narrow horizons of blood ties.

Finally, in the debate about the modernization/Westernization of nineteenth-century Greece, this study brings to the fore the existence of interaction, complementarity and even collaboration between tradition and the new and it supports the argument that there was continuity within change.[45] More specifically, with respect to the issue of Westernization of society I would like as a closing comment to propose that entrepreneurial agency in the nascent corporate sector was a precursor to the wider social changes that followed the 1909 revolution. SA company founders forged links among themselves and with banks, the state and the new professional classes. This was tantamount to the emergence of a transformed elite that underpinned the political change of 1909. It was this incorporation mechanism that bridged the initial conditions of the newly independent state of 1830 to the 'revolutionary' conditions of Greece in 1909. Clearly, there were other confluent processes at work too, and I do not wish to overplay the significance of the incorporation process as a component of change. It should not be ignored, however.

Many questions remain open to further exploration. For example, why did some of the most innovative captains of industry not choose the corporate form of business organization during the period under review? How did the personal dreams/aspirations of leading company founders interact with the grander national vision of the building of the new Greece? Perhaps the most interesting is the following counterfactual question: how would foreign entrepreneurial initiatives and technology transfer have differed in the corporate sector had there been no diaspora involvement? I would like to suggest that if Westerners had been the (sole) direct physical carriers of foreign technologies and capital, the osmosis between modernity and tradition would have been much less pronounced. However, a lot of further research is necessary in order to check the validity of this claim.

Table 2.1: Key Information on Seminal Entrepreneurs SA Company Founders, 1830–1909.[46]

1. Elpidoforos Ladopoulos[47]

Social Origin, Education	Son of a merchant. He studied in Athens (law) and Paris.
Non-Corporate Business Activities	Merchant house Ladopoulos Athanasios and Sons (est. 1860?) in Syros.
Corporate Activity	Cofounder of the SA steam shipping firm Etaireia Ellinikis Atmoploias (est. 1856) and member of its board of directors. He was a powerful presence and acted as a proxy for other shareholders.
Civil and Political Posts	He was on the city council of Syros, served as a commercial judge and was president of the local chamber of commerce.
Other Comments	–

2. Sotiris Gerousis[48]

Social Origin, Education	Son of a merchant.
Non-Corporate Business Activities	He started his commercial career in Smyrna in early 1820s. In 1827 he moved to Trieste. In 1835 he moved to Patras and became active in commerce/money-lending, acquiring substantial real-estate property through these activities.
Corporate Activity	Founder member of SA marine insurance firm I Anatoli (est. 1856) and 'Elliniki Naftiki Trapeza' (est. 1860).
Civil and Political Posts	–
Other Comments	Appears to have made a full transition to the SA form of business organization by the end of his life.

3. Panayotis Halikiopoulos[49]

Social Origin, Education	Ranked among the highest members of the local intelligentsia.
Non-Corporate Business Activities	Lawyer and professor of commerce at the high school of Patras. He specialized in the study of the currant economy and wrote an important treatise in the 1880s on how to improve the country's agriculture. He owned substantial tracts of land and declared his occupation as entrepreneur/landowner.
Corporate Activity	Founder member and director of the SA wine-producing firm Elliniki Oinopoiitiki Etaireia (est. 1858). Founder member and director of the SA transport insurance company Sotir (est. 1858). Cofounder of an SA company dealing in currants, Korinthiaki Stafis (est. 1859). Also founding shareholder and director in the insurance company I Pronoia (est. 1859) which provided insurance for financial assistance to young boys and dowries to girls. This company also accepted deposits.
Civil and Political Posts	–
Other Comments	He was a close friend of the mayor of Patras, Benizelos Roufos.

4. Elias Kehagias[50]

Social Origin, Education	Son of a local dignitary in Amfissa who after the revolution became a politician. He studied in Trieste.

Non-Corporate Business Activities	Started his career in Syros as a money-lender. He also acquired two ships and became well known as a merchant entrepreneur.
Corporate Activity	Director of SA steam shipping company Etaireia Ellinikis Atmoploias (est. 1856). Also founding shareholder in National Bank of Greece (est. 1841).
Civil and Political Posts	–
Other Comments	Cousin of the vice governor of the National Bank of Greece.

5. Georgios Skouzes[51]

Social Origin, Education	Son of a wealthy diaspora merchant.
Non-Corporate Business Activities	Started his career in Trieste where he worked as a trainee in a merchant house. There he developed commercial ties with Charles Hambro and Joseph Erlanger. Over time he evolved into a well-known merchant, entrepreneur, landowner and banker. In 1847 he set up the limited liability partnership bank Trapeza of Georgios P. Skouzes which operated until 1912 and which participated in the financing of railway building, an otherwise corporate activity.
Corporate Activity	Founding Shareholder of the National Bank of Greece (est. 1841). He was also a consultant of this bank. He was a cofounder of the SA Athens Piraeus Railways (a free-standing company set up in London in 1869?) and a founding shareholder in the Athens-based SA bank Trapeza Viomihanikis Pisteos (est. 1873). He was also a shareholder in the London-based Ionian Bank.
Civil and Political Posts	–
Other Comments	He built the most advanced storage houses at the time in Greece in the port of Piraeus. He also maintained his non-corporate interests throughout his lifetime.

6. Alexandros Vlangalis[52]

Social Origin, Education	Of diaspora origin from Constantinople; nephew of the prominent engineer entrepreneur Nicholas Vlangalis from Odessa. He was an electrical engineer with a degree from the Zurich Polytechnic, from which he graduated in 1896.
Non-Corporate Business Activities	Began his career as an engineer at the notorious Vassiliades shipyards.
Corporate Activity	Cofounder and director of the railway company Etaireia Ellinikon Sidirodromon (est. 1902).
Civil and Political Posts	–
Other Comments	Consultant to the SA electric tram railways of Athens.

7. Antonios Z. Matsas[53]

Social Origin, Education	Engineer with a degree from Paris.
Non-Corporate Business Activities	–
Corporate Activity	Cofounder of the construction SA company Geniki Etaireia Ergolipsion (est. 1889). Consultant to the SA Bank of Athens, 1896–1904.
Civil and Political Posts	–
Other Comments	Supervised construction of Athens Piraeus Railways in 1869. He was involved in the last phase of the construction of the Corinth Canal (*c.* 1893).

8. Ioannis Pezmazoglou[54]

Social Origin, Education	Son of a prominent Greek merchant in Smyrna. He studied economics in Paris.
Non-Corporate Business Activities	Started his career at the Credit Lyonnais branch in Alexandria, Egypt. In 1876 he founded a non-corporate bank, Trapeza Ioannis G. Pezmazoglou.
Corporate Activity	In 1896 he merged his bank with the Bank of Athens, of which he became a director. He was personally involved in the creation of the currant board Pronomiouhos Etaireia Pros tin Prostasian tis Paragogis kai tis Emporias tis Stafidos (est. 1905) and the wine/alcohol distillery company Etaireia Oinon kai Oinopnevmaton (est. 1906).
Civil and Political Posts	From 1900 onwards he was elected MP for Athens and to the prefecture of Elia and Kalamon in the Peloponese.
Other Comments	One of the most important modernizers/businessmen in Athens at the turn of the century.

9. Epameinondas Harilaos[55]

Social Origin, Education	His father was a very prominent merchant of Smyrna and Galatsi (Romania). He studied law in Athens and chemistry in France, Belgium and Germany.
Non-Corporate Business Activities	He established three partnership firms of which the first was a soap/oil refinery firm by the name of Epameinondas Harilaos and Nikolaos Kanellopoulos (est. 1892).
Corporate Activity	He was a founder and director of the wine/alcohol distillery company Etaireia Oinon kai Oinopnevmaton (est. 1906).
Civil and Political Posts	He served as president of the Industrial and Commercial Chamber of Athens.
Other Comments	After 1909 he became involved in the foundation of numerous other SA companies.

3 ITALIAN ENTREPRENEURSHIP: CONJECTURES AND EVIDENCE FROM A HISTORICAL PERSPECTIVE

Pier Angelo Toninelli and Michelangelo Vasta

Introduction

The last two decades have seen a renewed interest towards entrepreneurship and/or the individual entrepreneur, which in turn has stimulated research both in the theory and the history of entrepreneurship. This chapter fits this new climate: it is part of an ongoing research project on the determinants and the role of entrepreneurship in Italian economic development. Its primary aims are the creation and a preliminary evaluation of a data set of Italian entrepreneurs for the period encompassed between the Unification of the Kingdom (1861) and the end of the twentieth century.

Several fresh suggestions coming from both economics and history prove useful in our survey. First we would like to mention the broad partition in two main categories – innovative versus replicative entrepreneurs – proposed by William Baumol et al. A further interesting suggestion comes from the taxonomy of capitalism they propose (on the basis of their different rate of innovation and entrepreneurship). They hypothesize in fact the existence of four different categories of capitalism: 1. state guided capitalism; 2. oligarchic capitalism; 3. big firm capitalism; and 4. entrepreneurial capitalism. While each of these shows virtues and pitfalls, according to them, 'the *best* form of "good capitalism" is a blend of "entrepreneurial" and "big-firm" capitalism, although the precise mix will vary from country to country'.[1] Further insights come from the four models of entrepreneurship development, often overlapping, most recently advanced by the Monitor Group.[2] Despite this increasing attention to the issue at the theoretical level, all these suggestions still have as their main reference the Schumpeterian theory (as it is, by the way, in the field of the applied sciences – be they sociology, management and business or entrepreneurial history).

As for history, notwithstanding a number of recent innovative contributions,[3] we are still far from having a set of empirical evidence large enough to support a convincing explanation of the historical determinants of entrepreneurship. Joel Mokyr suggests that the issue of entrepreneurship should be studied looking at various determinants, among which cultural (industrial Enlightenment) and institutional (right incentives) factors play a decisive role: only these could help in understanding, for example, 'Why Britain led'.[4]

Probably the best way to tackle this fundamental question is starting from the bottom: that is assembling the empirical evidence from which to induce possible generalizations. Naturally this can be fruitfully performed only through a clever use of the few suggestions coming from the theory.[5] This endeavor might allow the construction of national typologies empirically supported, in order to make further steps towards the discovery of stylized facts, such as encompassing the national experiences into a more general model.

Our work is organized in the following way. The first section focuses on the historical debate on entrepreneurship in Italy, followed by a description of the sources used, and illustrates the main features of a significant sample of Italian entrepreneurs by means of a descriptive statistical approach. The next part of the chapter refines the descriptive approach through a methodology – Multiple Correspondence Analysis and Cluster Analysis – usual by now in standard statistics, yet not very familiar to scholars in economic and/or business history: first explaining the methodology used and then illustrating the main results obtained by the cluster analysis. In the final section, some conclusive considerations will be suggested.

Entrepreneurship in Italian Historiography: The Issues

But for few exceptions, in Italy until the end of the 1970s contemporary economic history was characterized mostly by a macroeconomic approach dealing with issues such as economic growth and development, structural change, backwardness, dualism and so on. The very few business-oriented historical studies were addressed towards big companies, either private or public. Later on the trend changed and a microeconomic approach emphasizing single behaviours and individual strategies emerged.[6] This was the result of converging factors: on the one side the slow-down of the economic process induced by the energy emergency of the 1970s, the decline of the Keynesian recipes and of the dominant paradigm of growth centred on industrialization and big business; on the other, the growing influence of economic sociology and business history of American origin brought about both by American consulting agencies and Italian scholars visiting the US academic world. Yet at least for a decade – that is before the districts and networks of enterprises were fully considered by the economic and social culture of the country – the primary interest concentrated on the evolution, strategy and organization of single big business, either private or public. Scarce effort was devoted to entrepreneurs and even less to any attempt to figure out some sort of taxonomy or classification.

There were, however, a few major exceptions: the first was the 1980 path-breaking contribution by Franco Amatori, whose title explicitly referred to 'entrepreneurial typologies' of Italian industrial history. Amatori suggested a simple but still substantially unchallenged typology that outlines the enduring threefold structural character of the country's entrepreneurship: 'private', 'supported' and 'public'.[7] In his fundamental bibliographical essay on Italian business history in 1990, Duccio Bigazzi sustained that the remarkable backwardness and poverty of Italian entrepreneurial history did not allow at the time the construction of an Italian repertory of entrepreneurs.[8] Later contributions largely built upon Amatori's, often dwelling on sectoral individual or cluster initiatives.[9] Only recently have new insights into the category of family entrepreneurs and/or outward-looking entrepreneurs been added.[10]

Another reason helps to explain the backwardness and indolence of Italian entrepreneurial history: the ambiguous attitude towards the figure and the role of the entrepreneur which runs throughout the country's economic and social history. In large sections of socio-political as well as cultural circles entrepreneurship has long been scarcely legitimized, its function not being considered as important in the change and modernization of the country as in the other first comers.[11] Alas some entrepreneurial reluctance to compete on the market freely accepting both risks and benefits cannot be certainly ruled out. In this respect it seems highly instructive to contrast two cultural attitudes towards entrepreneurship, the British and the Italian ones, as they emerge from two recent contributions. In the first case, Joel Mokyr points at the climate of dignity and trust surrounding the eighteenth-century British entrepreneurial class as the fundamental informal institution forging the cultural climate propitious to the Industrial Revolution. As for Italy, Roberta Garruccio gives us insights into the socio-cultural approach towards entrepreneurship still dominating in the upper classes of Milan (the economic centre of the country) in the interwar period as she quotes the memories of the nephew of an outstanding textile entrepreneur reporting: 'the entrepreneur didn't have even a quarter of the dignity we nowadays recognize in him'.[12]

In the business history perspective these issues are central to our analysis: is Italy's prolonged backwardness to be explained mostly by the structural absence of those Schumpeterian virtues – innovative capacity and risk-taking – which were at the basis of the Anglo-American success? Did such a frailty ask for substitutive factors such as state intervention and banks support? Or, *au contraire*, has that supposed prolonged process of entrepreneurial accumulation been hampered by the state's political and economic interference and banks' excessive power? Finally and more generally, is the Italian institutional setting on the whole ill-suited to offer opportunities to the most valid entrepreneurial projects?

It is clear to us that to answer these fundamental questions we have to start almost from the beginning, that is we have to construct the basic empirical support on which to build any analytical explanation. Therefore the primary aim of our research programme is the creation of a data set of Italian entrepreneurs for the period between the Unification of the Kingdom (1861) and the end of the twentieth century. Of course the foregoing historical debate as well as insights from theory have guided us in the setting out of the framework of the database.

Descriptive Analysis of the Database

The main source of our research is a collection of entrepreneurial biographies prepared for the ongoing *Biographical Dictionary of Italian Entrepreneurs* (*BDIE*),[13] which has so far processed about 600 'gross' entries: these in fact are comprehensive of figures which might stand out more for political than entrepreneurial reasons or that acted primarily as managers. From a practical point of view this means that such a rough estimate has to be depurated from unsuitable entries, but at the same time increased by the variable number of characters that have been taken into consideration in the dynastic biographies referring not to a single entrepreneur but to an entrepreneurial family. These biographies were classified on the basis of the scheme presented in Table 3.1: of course there is no complete information for all the variables in the table, which enumerates all those for which at least one entry has been found.

Table 3.1: Legend of the Database: Table of Variables.

Who is Who (entrepreneur, manager/entrepreneur …)
Sex
Periodization
Social Class
Education
Graduate degree
Undergraduate degree
High school degree
Training abroad
Type and geographical location of training abroad
First job
Apprenticeship

Family Background
Father's educational degree
Mother's educational degree
Father's prevailing activity
Mother's prevailing activity
Job relationship with other members of the family
Conjugal partner's social class
Job relationship with conjugal partner's family
Information about the Firm
Juridical form of the start-up firm
Start-up sector
Main sector of activity
Multisectoral activity
Maximum number of sectors at the same time
Number of sector changes
Finance: internal or external
Relationship with the banking system
Membership of banks' boards of directors
State financial support
ERP financial aid
Form of governance
Modality of acquisition of the firm
Innovating Entrepreneur?
Product
Process
Sector
New geographical markets
New production markets
New raw materials
New organizational model
New governance
Strategies
Bankruptcies
Social Context
Noble birth
Religion
University teacher
Trade or industrial association
Knight of labour
Freemansory
Lobbies
Direct political commitment
Indirect political commitment
Acknowledgements and awards

So far we have collected data concerning 390 entrepreneurs, i.e. the entries of the first volume of the *BDIE*, which gathers individuals with A–D surnames. To be more precise, such a figure corresponds to the original number of the records of the volume *plus* the entries resulting from all the entrepreneurial characters taken into consideration in a single item (that is a business family), *minus* the characters recorded in the *BDIE* but who acted essentially as politicians, such as for instance Orso Maria Corbino – physician and Italian minister of education – *minus* the Italian entrepreneurs who moved abroad, such as Antonio Devoto – who emigrated to Argentina – *minus* those for whom we have too little information.

To make the journey through the description of the database easier for the reader, we have partitioned the results of the survey in two broad categories: the first concerning the individuals – their background, their formation etc. – the other collecting information more specifically related to the enterprises – their start-up, the sector of activity, the innovation strategies and so on (Table 3.2).

The first thing to note is that the sample covers a large time-span, in practice two centuries (the nineteenth and the twentieth), even though the bulk of the individuals were active in the post-Unification period (in other words from 1861 onwards). Among these entrepreneurs, 331 (about 85 per cent of the total) should be considered 'pure': so we can define those who owned and directly managed their firm, while 59 (15 per cent) were less easily defined actors. The latter category includes at least three groups of individuals: first, those who kept the position of manager/director in the enterprise founded by them and later sold (for instance Ettore Conti, who created Imprese Elettriche Conti); second, managers/directors who were among the founders of important concerns, of which they owned a small or a minority share (such as Giuseppe Colombo, among the founders of the Edison Co.); and, third, dynamic managers who *de facto* acted like real entrepreneurs either in public companies or in state-owned enterprises (for example Guido Donegani in Montecatini or Eugenio Cefis in ENI).

Table 3.2: Descriptive Statistics.

	Frequency	%
Who is Who		
Enterpreneur/owner	48	12.3
Enterpreneur/manager	59	15.1
Enterpreneur/owner & manager	283	72.6
Gender		
Male	383	98.2
Female	7	1.8
Age of First Entrepreneurial Activity		
< 20	49	12.8
21–5	94	24.5
26–30	86	22.4

	Frequency	%
31–5	74	19.3
36–44	58	15.1
> 45	23	6.0
Missing values = 6		
Area of Birth		
Centre	71	18.4
Abroad	22	5.7
North-east	74	19.2
North-west	153	39.7
South	65	16.9
Missing values = 5		
Year of Birth		
Before 1830	49	12.6
1831–50	63	16.2
1851–70	79	20.4
1871–90	82	21.1
1891–1910	76	19.6
After 1910	39	10.1
Missing values = 2		
Religion		
Atheist	3	0.8
Catholic	373	95.9
Protestant	3	0.8
Hebrew	9	2.3
Other	1	0.3
Missing values = 1		
Involvement in Politics		
Yes	113	29.0
No	277	71.0
Level of Involvement in Politics		
Local level	67	59.8
National level	27	24.1
International level	4	3.6
Local & national level	14	12.5
Missing values = 278		
Honour of Cavaliere del Lavoro		
Yes	99	25.4
No	291	74.6
University Teaching		
Yes	15	3.9
No	375	96.2
Affiliation to Employers Associations		
Yes	143	36.7
No	247	63.3
Affiliation to Masonry		
Yes	6	1.5
No	384	98.5

	Frequency	%
Financial Public Support		
Yes	33	8.5
No	357	91.5
Social Class		
Low (farmer/labourer)	29	8.5
Medium (small entrepreneur, merchant & craftsman)	202	59.2
High (large entrepreneur, freelance, noble)	110	32.3
Missing values = 49		
Father's Main Activity		
Farmer	6	2.1
Labourer	11	3.9
Manager	11	3.9
Technician	5	1.8
Craftsman	35	12.3
Entrepreneur	129	45.3
Freelance	22	7.7
Employee	11	3.9
Merchant	55	19.3
Missing values = 105		
Father's Employment Status		
Employee	79	27.7
Self-employee	206	72.3
Missing values = 105		
Family Job Relationships		
Yes	224	57.4
No	166	42.6
Partner's Social Class		
Low (farmer/labourer)	2	3.4
Medium (small entrepreneur, merchant & craftsman)	23	39.0
High (large entrepreneur, freelance, noble)	34	57.6
Missing values = 331		
Job Relations with Partner's Family		
Yes	30	7.7
No	360	92.3
Education Level		
Illiterate	14	4.6
Primary education	28	9.2
Middle school	39	12.8
High school	96	31.5
Laurea degree	122	40.0
Post-laurea degree	6	2.0
Missing values = 85		
Field of Laurea		
Laws	29	23.4
Economics	17	13.7
Other arts	9	7.3

	Frequency	%
Engineering	42	33.9
Chemistry/pharmacology	11	8.9
Other sciences	16	12.9
Missing values = 266		
Education Abroad		
Yes	59	15.1
No	331	84.9
Experience Abroad		
Yes	150	38.5
No	240	61.5
Typology of the First Activity		
Farmer	2	0.5
Labourer	37	9.9
Manager	46	12.3
Technician	43	11.5
Craftsman	28	7.5
Entrepreneur	108	28.8
Freelance	32	8.5
Employee	49	13.1
Merchant	30	8.0
Missing values = 15		
Apprenticeship		
Yes	54	13.9
No	336	86.2
Typology of the First Activity		
One-man company/informal company/unknown	125	32.1
Società di persone	189	48.5
S.R.L. (limited company)	9	2.3
S.P.A. (public limited company)	53	13.6
S.P.A. quotate	5	1.3
Società cooperative	9	2.3
Starting Sector		
Agriculture, hunting and silviculture	21	5.4
Extraction	8	2.1
Manufacture	250	64.1
Energy-using products, gas appliances	10	2.6
Construction	15	3.9
Trade, servicing for cars, goods	43	11.0
Transport, storage and communications	9	2.3
Financial services	27	6.9
Property, renting, IT, services	2	0.5
Other public, social and personal services	5	1.3
Main Macro-Sector		
Agriculture, hunting and silviculture	20	5.1

	Frequency	%
Extraction	8	2.1
Manufacture	261	66.9
Energy-using products, gas appliances	10	2.6
Construction	17	4.4
Trade, servicing for cars, goods	28	7.2
Transport, storage and communications	7	1.8
Financial services	31	8.0
Property, renting, IT, services	2	0.5
Other public, social and personal services	6	1.5
Number of Sectors (at the Same Time)		
2	101	51.3
3–4	74	37.6
> 4	22	11.2
Missing values = 193		
Relations with Banks		
Yes	135	34.6
No	255	65.4
Ways of Company Acquisition		
Founder	173	52.7
Inheritor	132	40.2
Purchaser	23	7.0
Missing values = 62		
Innovative Entrepreneur (Schumpeterian)		
Yes	284	72.8
No	106	27.2
Product Innovation		
Yes	121	31.0
No	269	69.0
Process Innovation		
Yes	142	36.4
No	248	63.6
New Sale Markets		
Yes	181	46.4
No	209	53.6
New Markets of Production		
Yes	76	19.5
No	313	80.5
Missing values = 1		
New Raw Material		
Yes	27	6.9
No	363	93.1
New Organizational Models		
Yes	77	19.7
No	313	80.3

	Frequency	%
Level of Innovation		
None	106	27.2
Low	100	25.6
Medium	148	38.0
High	36	9.2

A majority of our sample of entrepreneurs come from the north-west region (153, corresponding to roughly 40 per cent of the total), the area which was the forerunner of Italian industrialization; almost 20 per cent (74 entrepreneurs) came from the north-east, the region bound to become one of the most important sectors of the third and fourth dimensions of Italian capitalism (districts and pocket multinationals). Such a destiny was to be shared with central Italy, which registers similar values (71 entries, corresponding to 18.5 per cent). The south and the islands (65 individuals, corresponding to 16.9 per cent of the total) stay at the bottom, whilst a fair number (22 and 5.7 per cent) were foreign entrepreneurs.[14]

A fundamental question of the theory of entrepreneurship is how the entrepreneurial activity began: in other words, whether the entrepreneur created the new activity from scratch, or whether he (or she) inherited the activity or acquired it from someone else. Our evidence does not offer a neat answer. Even though information on this subject is not complete, it appears all in all exhaustive enough: it covers 328 cases, that is 84.1 per cent. At a very aggregate level the start-ups of entrepreneurship can be divided almost equally in two classes: the first groups 173 individuals (53 per cent) who were founders of a new firm, the second 155 (47 per cent) who acquired it: 132 (40.2 per cent) by inheritance, 23 (7 per cent) by purchase.

Sex does appear to have had a crucial role in Italian entrepreneurship. In fact the value corresponding to the total amount of female entrepreneurs is quite negligible: just seven. This, however, should not surprise social scientists at home, most familiar with the social, cultural and institutional backwardness of the country. Also unsurprising is the age at which the greatest part of our sample began their entrepreneurial activity: about 60 per cent of them did it before their 31st birthday, with a concentration in the 21–30 age group. Our finding that a little less than 30 per cent of the sample (112 entrepreneurs) was born before 1850 deserves some reflection. It is an important piece of information if conjugated with the previous one: there is a 60 per cent probability that these 112 entrepreneurs started their activity before 1880, the date at which the new technologies of the Second Industrial Revolution began to be introduced in Italy. This seems to suggest that they should be classified as 'traditional', meaning with this that they almost certainly pertained to the trajectory of the First Industrial Revolution.

As far as the social class of origin is concerned, we have information covering 341 entries of 390. The greatest part of them (202, corresponding to 67.7
per cent of the coverage) came from the middle class – a category in which we
registered artisans, small entrepreneurs, retailers and shopkeepers; a fair number
(110 or 32.3 per cent) from the upper class – great entrepreneurs, professionals,
well-born individuals – and just 29 (8.5 per cent) from the lower classes: 6 peas-
ants and 23 factory workers. A convincing specification concerning the origins
of the entrepreneurs is the one related to the profession and the level of education of their fathers.

With regard to the first point, fathers' prevailing activity, this can be
divided in two main categories: dependent or independent activity. Evidence
covers about 73 per cent of the sample: 28 per cent (79 in absolute values) are
located in the dependent category, which registers humble occupations such
as workers, labourers, ploughmen and also managers and technicians. In the
second group – independent activities – there are 206 entries (72 per cent of
the collected data), with a clear majority of entrepreneurs (45 per cent) who
most likely handed their assets onto their sons, followed from afar by traders
(19.3 per cent) and artisans (12.3 per cent). As for the level of education of the
fathers, unfortunately only scattered information has been collected (71 cases of
390): 72 per cent of these show high level of education (41 per cent a university
degree and 21 per cent a high school degree). Returning to our entrepreneurs
a legitimate question is whether the first working activity might be indicative
of their future entrepreneurial destiny. According to the 375 answers that have
been collected this does not come out so clearly, if we take into account the two
larger categories – dependent or independent activity (self-employment) – in
which they have been portioned: 45 per cent of them belong to the category of
the dependent employees. Yet if we get into more detail we discover that 108
(28.8 per cent) began their working career as entrepreneurs, 30 as shopkeepers
or merchants, 28 as artisans and 89 (23.7 per cent) as managers or technicians.
Conversely only 39 (10.4 per cent) came from more humble activities (country
or city labourers) whereas 32 (8.5 per cent) took their first footsteps in the
liberal professions.

It has to be underlined that education comes out as probably the most
interesting and crucial variable in the description of our sample and by far the
most surprising. The sample offers a good quantity of information concerning
the basic data, related to the level of schooling: it has been registered for 305
cases, that is 78.2 per cent. A large share of them – 224 (73.5 per cent) – had a
high level of formal education: 122 (40 per cent) could boast a university degree
(laurea) and 6 (2 per cent) a post-doctoral degree, whereas 96 (31.5 per cent)
possessed a high-school degree. Conversely only 14 entrepreneurs – less than 5
per cent of the entries – were illiterate whereas 28 (9.2 per cent) had attended

just the elementary school and 39 (12.8 per cent) were educated to middle-school level. Regarding the specific areas of schooling we have a clear preference for the techno-scientific curricula: 56 per cent of the graduated students *vis-à-vis* 23.4 per cent of law students, 13.7 per cent of business students and just 7.3 per cent of humanities. Among the 68 entrepreneurs with a techno-scientific formation a clear preference (42, i.e. 61 per cent) had been given to engineering, with 11 (16 per cent) studying chemistry and 16 (23 per cent) other fields. Additionally, in 59 cases (15.1 per cent) the curriculum of formal education had been at least partly carried out abroad.

It is interesting that often the process of human capital formation did not stop with formal education. A good part of our entrepreneurs (150 out of 390, i.e. almost 40 per cent) had training experience abroad, mostly in more industrialized countries (about 90 per cent out of the 140 recorded cases): since the 1880s this had become quite a familiar tradition among young Italian entrepreneurs, particularly (but not exclusively) in the case of wealthy and/or already consolidated entrepreneurial dynasties. Finally, an indirect test of the medium-high average education of the 390 entrepreneurs is that only 54 of them (less than 14 per cent) undertook workshop apprenticeship, which is a more or less prolonged period of training on the job.

It is well known that another central feature of the historical and theoretical debate on entrepreneurship is the role of family. Our survey offers some interesting evidence on this point. Let us first consider marriage: the family of one of the two partners can add to the activity of the other in terms of wealth, capital, material and immaterial assets. Therefore the social class to which the partner belongs can be indicative of possible further 'acquisitions' to the family of the entrepreneur. Unfortunately information about this point is much scattered in our database (it covers only 15 per cent of the total entries). Yet the result seems to converge with the conventional wisdom: 98 per cent of the entries (that is 57 entrepreneurs out of 59) married partners coming from high-medium classes: more specifically 34 (57 per cent) married the offspring of well-born, entrepreneurial or outstanding professional families and just 2 those of country or town workers. A further aspect to be considered is whether the entrepreneur had work relations with his (or her) own family, which is a very much debated issue in the literature on family business.[15] Our survey does not offer an unambiguous answer: 224 out of 390 entrepreneurs (57.4 per cent) maintained job relations with members of their families; much fewer (only 30, i.e. 7.7 per cent) with members of their partner's family.

Further information about the background of the sample concerns religion, political commitment, affiliations and honorary rewards. As for the first point, 373 out of 389 entries (96 per cent) were Catholic while Jewish and Protestant formed a small minority. The great majority – 277, i.e. 71 per cent – was not involved in politics: of the politicized minority (113) almost 60 per cent had commitments at the local level, 24.1 per cent at the national level, 12.5 per cent both at the local and national level and less than 4 per cent at the international level. Such evidence is indirectly confirmed by the restricted number of entrepreneurs (33 individuals or 8.5 per cent) who during their activity could avail themselves of the financial support of the state. With regard to affiliations, the majority (247, that is 63.3 per cent) belonged to entrepreneurial associations while only a very small number (6) was affiliated to freemasonry. Finally, a good number of our entrepreneurs (99, that is 25.4 per cent) would see their entrepreneurial activity rewarded with their appointment to the honour of knighthood (*Cavaliere del lavoro*).

The second broad category of information includes the basic evidence concerning the companies. One set of data is related to the juridical forms which characterize the enterprises at their start-ups: here individual firms (125, corresponding to 32.5 per cent of the total) or limited/commercial partnerships (189, that is 48.5 per cent) largely prevailed. Conversely limited liability companies – 9, i.e. 2.3 per cent – and joint-stock companies – 58 (14.9 per cent), 5 of which quoted on the stock exchange – were a clear minority. The widespread family business form which characterizes the sample seems to be consistent with the extensive preference for self-financing showed by the data concerning the bank–firm relationship: 255 (65.4 per cent) entrepreneurs did not show clear links with the bank system.

Another interesting point to be clarified concerns the start-up sectors of the various business initiatives. Manufacturing firms were the clear majority (64.1 per cent), followed at a long distance by commercial (11 per cent), financial (7 per cent), agricultural (5.4 per cent) and building (3.9 per cent) initiatives. Out of the 250 enterprises which started their activity in the manufacturing sector, about one-third belonged to traditional sectors such as the textile/apparel industry (50, i.e. 13 per cent), food, beverage and tobacco (38, i.e. 9.7 per cent), leather and shoes (9, i.e. 2.3 per cent); lumber (8, i.e. 2.1 per cent) and paper, pulp and publishing (18, i.e. 4.6 per cent). Conversely fewer (75, i.e. 19 per cent) were modern industries: chemicals, synthetic fibres and rubber attracted 20 start-ups (5.1 per cent), metallurgy 24 (6.2 per cent), engineering 31 (8 per cent), electromechanics and electrical equipment 14 (3.6 per cent).

Not very different values (except for the commercial initiatives) are shown by the evidence concerning the macro-sectors in which the core activity of the sample of firms specialized after their start-ups. The manufacturing sector stays again clearly at the top (67 per cent), followed by the financial one (8 per cent), the commercial (7.2 per cent), the agricultural (5.1 per cent) and the building (4.4 per cent). Such outcome is consistent with the one related to the sector mobility of the firms in the sample, or, in other words, the versatility of our entrepreneurs.

In fact, as far as macro-sectoral mobility is concerned, less than 10 per cent of them abandoned their initial area of activity to move into a new one. The mobility within macro-sectors offers only slightly different results as the percentage of change grows to about 15 per cent.

Quite dissimilar, however, is the evidence concerning the presence of multi-sectoral activities. The sample is almost equally divided between entrepreneurs who concentrated their operation in just one sector (193, i.e. 49.5 per cent) and those who were active in various sectors at the same time (197, i.e. 50.5 per cent). We have more detailed evidence for 197 cases: 101 entrepreneurs were active in two sectors at the same time, 74 in 3–4 sectors, 22 in more than 4 sectors, with a sample average of 2.98.

Finally a few sentences must be devoted to describe an important part of our database, the one concerning innovation. Innovation capacity – as known – is one of the key factors of entrepreneurial success. In order to follow Schumpeterian suggestions and to avoid too narrow an approach, we have selected six different kinds of innovative capacity. The first two are the traditional proxies: innovation product and innovation process; then we have picked up the entrepreneur's ability to innovate with regard to sale markets and production markets within and outside the country. Finally we have considered the introduction of new raw materials in the process of production and of new organizational models in the firm. The results obtained are quite surprising. If we consider as an innovative entrepreneur the individual who has at least one positive answer to the six variables related to innovation, we have 284 individuals (72.8 per cent) who can be attributed to such a typology. Yet this outcome is probably too optimistic with regard to Italian entrepreneurship. Therefore the modality innovation deserves some further specification. For instance, if we take into consideration each variable, 31 per cent of our sample introduced product innovation and 36.4 per cent process innovation. The capacity to move towards new sale markets concerns 46.4 per cent of the entire sample, but much less (23 per cent) outside Italy and even less (16 per cent) outside Europe. As for new markets of production, a phenomenon not very common in the past, we have positive answers in 19.5 per cent of the total. The introduction of new raw materials regards only 7 per cent of the total and the introduction of new organizational models about 20 per cent.

We then collected all the answers and attributed one point to each positive answer: thus we obtained a score between 0 (all negative answers) and 6 (all positive answers). In this way we produced a more reliable proxy of innovation, which allows us to distinguish among 'no innovation' (27.2 per cent of the total), 'low level of innovation' (25.6 per cent), 'medium level of innovation' (38 per cent) and 'high innovation' (9.2 per cent).

Methodology: The Multidimensional Analysis

To develop a taxonomy of Italian entrepreneurs we have carried out some multidimensional analyses: first Multiple Correspondence Analysis (MCA), then Cluster Analysis (CA) on the factors obtained from the MCA.[16] Eighteen active variables have been selected for the MCA, while other variables have been used as illustrative ones: these are mainly related to the status and personal characteristics of the entrepreneur or do not offer a primary contribution to the explanation (see Table 3.3).

Table 3.3: List of Variables used for the MCA.

Active Variables	Illustrative Variables
Entrepreneurial typology	Place of birth (area)
Social class	Age
Educational level	Religion
Father's educational level	Direct involvement in politics
Father's main activity	Honour of *Cavaliere del lavoro*
Family job relationships	University teaching
Typology of the first activity	Noble
Indirect involvement in politics	Member of aristocracy
Affiliation to employers' associations	Affiliation to masonry
Form of enterprise	Financial public support
Modalities of acquisition of the company	Job relations with the partner's family
Sector of activity	Experiences abroad
Relations with banks	Age of first entrepreneurial activity
Innovative entrepreneur	Main sector of activity (not aggregated)
Product innovation	Business strategies
Process innovation	Innovation level
New sale markets	
New markets of production	

Thirty-five Eigen values had been identified by the MCA, each of which can account for a very low proportion of inertia because of the high number of categories involved in the analysis. That is the reason why the proportion of inertia each Eigen value accounts for was calculated using the correction of Benzecrì, which takes into account the number of categories involved.[17] Thanks to this correction, the first 4 Eigen values account for the 97 per cent of the variance, and that is the number of dimensions considered in analysing the phenomenon of Italian entrepreneurship.

The significant active variables for each dimension (subdivided in the left and right quadrant) have been selected every time they account for a proportion of inertia higher than the average inertia, which is when the contribution of each variable is higher than the total of inertia (100) divided by the number of active variables (18). The items of the significant active variables belong to a dimension when their contribution is high and the values of the squared cosine, which represent the quality of the graphical representation, are around 0.20 (see Tables 3.4–7). Concerning the illustrative variables, their categories are significant for one dimension when the value test is higher than 2.0 (absolute value).[18]

On the basis of the corrections suggested by Benzecrì, the first dimension turns out to account for 55 per cent of the inertia (according to the correction of Benzecrì) and is characterized (see Table 3.4), in particular, by active variables (left quadrant) concerning *the activity in manufacturing, the propensity to innovate* (mostly product innovation) and *the ability to open new sale markets.* Other active variables are *being owner and manager at the same time, having a job relationship with their own family, being scarcely connected to the banking system.* On the other hand, in the right quadrant, we have some symmetrical active variables (in respect to those of the left quadrant), particularly regarding innovation, and some other variables such as financial activities. We have called this dimension 'entrepreneurial spirit' because most of the variables which characterize the dimension are relative at the capacity/incapacity to develop entrepreneurial activities through new ideas, even with/without the direct support of the family.

Table 3.4: Dimension 1: 'Entrepreneurial Spirit'.

Left Quadrant

Categories of Active Variables	Contribution	Squared Cosine
Owner and manager	2.2	0.39
Family job relationships	2.7	0.27
Manufacture	2.0	0.28
No relation with banks	2.3	0.29
Innovator	2.1	0.36
Product innovation	3.5	0.19
New sale markets	5.1	0.38
Supplementary Categories	*Test Value*	*Distortion*
No direct involvement in politics	−5.5	0.16
Cavaliere del lavoro	−2.4	2.25
Age of first job < 20	−4.3	5.58
Age of first job 21–5	−3.9	2.43
Food	−4.2	6.16
Textile	−3.0	5.71
Machinery	−3.1	3.67
Other manufacture	−3.1	10.11
Integration	−2.1	3.08
Integration and diversification	−3.8	5.32
Medium innovation	−8.8	1.18
High innovation	−6.3	7.95

Right Quadrant

Categories of Active Variables	Contribution	Squared Cosine
Manager	14.6	0.62
No family job relationships	4.5	0.29
Financial activities	11.9	0.46
State-owned enterprise	9.0	0.34
Relation with banks	5.2	0.30
No innovator	6.5	0.33
No product innovation	2.0	0.28
No process innovation	1.6	0.19
No new sale markets	5.2	0.44
Supplementary Categories	*Test Value*	*Distortion*
Born abroad	2.7	13.65
Age 75–84	2.3	1.62
Hebrew	2.6	34.80
Direct involvement in politics	5.1	1.85
No *Cavaliere del lavoro*	5.5	0.11
University teacher	4.2	20.48
Masonry	3.7	52.70
Public support	3.1	8.76
Age of first job 31–5	2.1	3.35
Age of first job 36–44	4.2	4.56
Age of first job > 45	5.9	13.01
Energy	5.1	31.22
Financial activity	14.4	9.39
Other activities	2.4	20.48
Other strategies	6.5	0.92
No innovation	13.5	2.04

The second dimension, as shown in Table 3.5, accounts for almost 28 per cent of the inertia and is clearly linked to the entrepreneurial family tradition. Among the active variables (in the left quadrant) we have: *belonging to the upper class, having a job relationship with members of the family, inheritance of the firm, being an independent worker since the first job* and, most interesting, *high level of formal education.* On the other hand (in the right quadrant) we have belonging to the lower classes, low education level, not having family job relationships and low level of education of the father. We have called this dimension 'entrepreneurial stability' in the sense that the active variables which characterize this dimension are mainly relative to social status.

The third dimension, as shown in Table 3.6, accounts for 10 per cent of the inertia and is strictly relative to innovation. There are three active variables in the left quadrant concerning *innovation*. The active variables in the right quadrant are the negative counterparts of most of the innovation variables. Also the *high educational level* appears to be significant. Consequently, we have called this dimension simply 'innovation'.

Table 3.5: Dimension 2: 'Entrepreneurial Stability'.

Left Quadrant

Categories of Active Variables	Contribution	Squared cosine
High class	6.8	0.29
Father self-employed	5.5	0.39
Family job relationships	3.5	0.28
High education level	0.9	0.04
First job self-employment	5.4	0.30
Inheriting	9.6	0.44
Supplementary Categories	*Test value*	*Distortion*
Cavaliere del lavoro	−3.6	2.25
Public support	−2.8	8.76
Job relationships with the partner's family	−2.7	9.74
Job experience abroad	−2.0	1.05
Agriculture	−2.2	15.11
Commercial services	−3.6	10.51
Diversification	−3.5	2.54
No innovation	−4.7	2.04

Right Quadrant

Categories of Active Variables	Contribution	Squared Cosine
Low class	7.8	0.24
Father with low level of education	7.2	0.22
Father employee	6.1	0.23
No family job relationships	5.1	0.27
Low education level	8.1	0.27
First job employee	5.1	0.34
Founding	3.6	0.20
Supplementary Categories	*Test value*	*Distortion*
Born in the north	3.9	0.42
No direct involvement in politics	3.0	0.16
No *Cavaliere del lavoro*	6.3	0.11
No public support	3.1	0.00
No job relations with the partner's family	2.7	0.00
No experience abroad	2.7	0.38
Started working 31–5	2.1	3.35
Machinery	3.0	3.67
Other strategies	4.0	0.92
Medium innovation	3.2	1.18

Table 3.6: Dimension 3: 'Innovation'.[19]

Left Quadrant

Categories of Active Variables	Contribution	Squared Cosine
High education	5.0	0.16
Innovator	3.2	0.33
Product innovation	8.6	0.27
Process innovation	4.3	0.15
Supplementary Categories	*Test value*	*Distortion*
Born in the north	2.8	0.42
Age > 85	3.8	3.24
Cavaliere del lavoro	3.2	2.25
University teacher	2.5	20.48
Public support	3.6	8.76
Experience abroad	4.1	1.05
Chemistry/mining/carbon	2.9	3.60
Machinery	3.7	3.67
Other manufacture	2.3	10.11
Integration and diversification	2.2	5.32
Medium innovation	7.7	1.18
High innovation	7.2	7.95

Right Quadrant

Categories of Active Variables	Contribution	Squared Cosine
Owner	10.2	0.25
Not innovator	8.1	0.24
No product innovation	3.8	0.32
No process innovation	2.4	0.16
No new sale markets	2.4	0.12
No new market production	1.1	0.19
Supplementary Categories	*Test value*	*Distortion*
Other religion	−2.2	321.22
No direct involvement in politics	−2.1	0.16
No *Cavaliere del lavoro*	−4.8	0.11
No public support	−3.0	0.00
No experience abroad	−4.5	0.38
Building	−4.1	17.95
Commercial services	−5.1	10.51
No innovation	−11.5	2.04

The fourth dimension, as shown in Table 3.7, accounts for almost 4 per cent of the inertia. Despite its low contribution to variance, this factor has to be taken into consideration because of a few aspects which appear useful in explaining the characters of Italian entrepreneurship. The only two active variables in the left quadrant are related to *lobbying activity*: the first with politicians, the second through participation in various kinds of association. At the same time we have symmetrical active variables in the right quadrant. We have called this dimension 'political and lobby commitment'.

Table 3.7: Dimension 4: 'Political and Lobby Commitment'.[20]

Left Quadrant		
Categories of Active Variables	*Contribution*	*Squared Cosine*
Indirect involvement in politics	11.8	0.29
Employers' association	11.9	0.33
Supplementary Categories	*Test value*	*Distortion*
Age 75–84	2.3	1.62
Direct involvement in politics	3.0	1.85
Cavaliere del lavoro	3.4	2.25
Chemistry/mining/carbon	3.4	3.60
Building	2.3	17.95
Integration and diversification	3.0	5.32
Right Quadrant		
Categories of Active Variables	*Contribution*	*Squared Cosine*
No indirect involvement in politics	6.2	0.43
No employers' association	8.2	0.44
Medium class	6.4	0.25
Supplementary Categories	*Test value*	*Distortion*
Born abroad	−2.4	13.65
No direct involvement in politics	−6.0	0.16
No *Cavaliere del lavoro*	−7.5	0.11
No public support	−3.3	0.00
No job relation with partner's family	−2.6	0.00
No experience abroad	−2.5	0.38
Extraction	−3.7	39.28
Other activities	−5.9	20.48
Other strategies	−3.2	0.92
No innovation	−2.1	2.04

The Results of the Cluster Analysis

MCA describes the main features of the data as they appear in the space spanned by the four principal dimensions. In order to synthesize the phenomenon and to highlight the main groupings of individuals with respect to their most significant profiles, a Cluster Analysis (CA) has been carried out in the dimensional space spanned by the four significant axes. The CA performs the classification of the entrepreneurs: it takes into account the factorial coordinates which characterize them on the four dimensions of the MCA in order to calculate the distances among individuals and aggregate them according to a technique that minimizes the variance within classes and maximizes the variance among classes.

The CA reveals five clusters. All the items in each cluster were selected according to their value within the cluster (MOD/CLA), as compared to their value in the global population (GLOBAL), as well as to the percentage of people characterized by the modality within the cluster (CLA/MOD).[21] Each cluster, defined according to significant groupings of responses, is identified by the objective characteristics of the individuals involved. The five clusters, shown in the dendogram of Figure 3.1 where they are listed according to their relative position, have been named as follows: 1. Schumpeterian entrepreneurs; 2. first-generation entrepreneurs; 3. defensive entrepreneurs; 4. Well-established entrepreneurs; and 5. entrepreneurial managers.

Figure 3.1: Dendogram Showing Five Main Clusters from the Classification of Profiles.

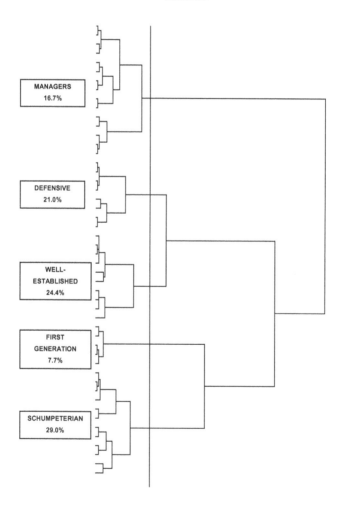

The first cluster (Table 3.8) – the larger – includes 29 per cent of the entrepreneurs: we have called them 'Schumpeterian' entrepreneurs, because their prevailing peculiar modalities roughly refer to the characteristics attributed by Schumpeter to his innovative entrepreneur.[22] First, the individuals within this cluster were all private entrepreneurs (MOD/CLA = 100 per cent), whereas the cluster contains (CLA/MOD) 31.6 per cent of all the private entrepreneurs of the sample. About 68 per cent of the cluster's individuals were direct founders of their firm, *vis-à-vis* the value of 44.4 per cent shown by such modality in the population and that of 44.5 per cent corresponding to the share of the cluster in the sample. Besides, the 90.3 per cent of the people in the cluster show the modality owner + manager and this corresponds to about 36 per cent of all the entries similarly characterized.

Second, about 96.5 per cent of the entrepreneurs in the cluster are classified as innovative, a modality which actually distinguishes (GLOBAL) about 72 per cent of the population: of this about 39 per cent stays in the cluster. The attribute 'high innovative' connotes only 9.23 per cent of the sample: 52.8 per cent of them stay in this cluster within which 16.8 per cent of the entries are labelled in such a way. Product innovation characterizes the strategy in the cluster of 63.6 per cent of all entrepreneurs labelled with this modality (which are 31 per cent of the total), process innovation about 43 per cent out of 36.4 per cent: yet respectively 68.1 per cent and 54 per cent of the people in the cluster are to be identified accordingly. As a further confirmation of this tendency almost 88 per cent of the entrepreneurs within this cluster are manufacturers while the cluster contains almost 38 per cent of the share of manufacturers (about 67 per cent) of the sample.

Third, 69.9 per cent of the people in the cluster comes from the middle class *vis-à-vis* the share of 51.7 per cent in the population; the majority of the population does not have any political commitment either direct (82.3 per cent) or indirect (92.9 per cent) versus respectively 71 per cent and 69.7 per cent of the entire sample and a cluster's share of 33.6 per cent and 38.6 per cent on total entries. Moreover 86.7 per cent of the people in the cluster do not entertain close relations with banks (versus 65.4 per cent of the total) and this corresponds to a 38.4 per cent cluster's coverage of this modality. Finally about 77 per cent of the cluster is not affiliated to entrepreneurial associations (versus 63.3 per cent in the sample). This confronts with a CLA/MOD value of 35.2 per cent.

The second cluster (Table 3.9) is the thinner as it includes only 7.7 per cent of the whole population. Its tag – first-generation entrepreneurs – wants to symbolize at best the features of the founders of new enterprises in a backward local

Table 3.8: Cluster 1: 'Schumpeterian Entrepreneurs' (29%).

Modalities	Test Value	% of Cluster Within Modality (CLA/MOD)	% of Modality Within Cluster (MOD/CLA)	% of Modality Within Sample (GLOBAL)
Product innovation	9.83	63.64	68.14	31.03
Innovator	7.61	38.93	96.46	71.79
No individual political involvement	6.78	38.60	92.92	69.74
New sale markets	6.10	44.20	70.80	46.41
Founding	5.95	44.51	68.14	44.36
No relation with banks	5.82	38.43	86.73	65.38
Manufacture	5.72	37.93	87.61	66.92
Medium innovation	5.39	45.27	59.29	37.95
Owner & manager	5.19	36.04	90.27	72.56
First job employee	4.55	39.02	70.80	52.56
Medium class	4.51	39.11	69.91	51.79
Process innovation	4.44	42.96	53.98	36.41
Purchasing	4.40	73.91	15.04	5.90
Private enterprise	4.26	31.56	100.00	91.79
Machinery	3.82	49.28	30.09	17.69
Other Manufacture	3.67	62.07	15.93	7.44
No employers' association	3.53	35.22	76.99	63.33
No direct political involvement	3.09	33.57	82.30	71.03
High innovation	2.99	52.78	16.81	9.23
Medium education	2.47	37.40	43.36	33.59
Father employee	2.35	40.51	28.32	20.26
Commercial services	−2.64	7.14	1.77	7.18
Father medium educated	−2.68	0.00	0.00	4.10
High education	−2.86	19.20	21.24	32.05
Direct political involvement	−3.09	17.70	17.70	28.97
State-owned enterprise	−3.13	0.00	0.00	5.13
Father self-employed	−3.40	21.36	38.94	52.82
Employers' association	−3.53	18.18	23.01	36.67
Commercial services	−3.57	5.26	1.77	9.74
Financial activity	−4.18	0.00	0.00	7.95
Financial activities	−4.18	0.00	0.00	7.95
Manager	−4.33	6.78	3.54	15.13
No process innovation	−4.44	20.97	46.02	63.59
First job self-employed	−4.76	16.47	24.78	43.59
Inheriting	−5.64	11.36	13.27	33.85
High class	−5.68	9.09	8.85	28.21
Relation with banks	−5.82	11.11	13.27	34.62
No new sale markets	−6.10	15.79	29.20	53.59
Indirect political involvement	−6.78	6.78	7.08	30.26
No innovator	−7.61	3.64	3.54	28.21
No innovation	−8.55	0.94	0.88	27.18
No product innovation	−9.83	13.38	31.86	68.97

environment, such as the one which characterized large areas of Italy for most of its economic history. As a matter of fact about 97 per cent of its members were new founders: this compares with the 44.4 per cent share of the same modality within the sample and a cluster's share of 16.8 per cent. A good share of the people in the cluster are owners of their assets (63.3 per cent). Many fewer are the ones who can be qualified as owner/manager (36.7 per cent), a percentage remarkably lower than the population's share of such modality (72.6 per cent). This specification seems to suggest that the entrepreneurial performance during the first generation did not reach the level of a managerial organization and that can be indirectly confirmed by the highest percentage (90 per cent) of the people in the cluster who do not have direct bank connections as compared to a fairly lower value for the entire population (65.4 per cent).

Table 3.9: Cluster 2: 'First-Generation Entrepreneurs' (7.7%).

Modalities	Test Value	% of Cluster Within Modality (CLA/MOD)	% of Modality Within Cluster (MOD/CLA)	% of Modality Within Sample (GLOBAL)
Low education	8.93	48.98	80.00	12.56
Father low educated	8.88	73.08	63.33	6.67
Low class	8.00	62.07	60.00	7.44
Owner	6.86	39.58	63.33	12.31
Founding	6.21	16.76	96.67	44.36
First job employee	3.45	12.20	83.33	52.56
Building	3.14	35.29	20.00	4.36
No relation with banks	2.96	10.59	90.00	65.38
Father employee	2.83	16.46	43.33	20.26
No *Cavaliere del lavoro*	2.43	9.62	93.33	74.62
Cavaliere del lavoro	−2.43	2.02	6.67	25.38
Manager	−2.52	0.00	0.00	15.13
Medium education	−2.84	2.29	10.00	33.59
Relation with banks	−2.96	2.22	10.00	34.62
First job self-employed	−3.47	2.35	13.33	43.59
Father self-employed	−3.63	2.91	20.00	52.82
High education	−3.75	0.80	3.33	32.05
High class	−4.01	0.00	0.00	28.21
Owner & manager	−4.11	3.89	36.67	72.56
Inheriting	−4.59	0.00	0.00	33.85

As for the social origin, 60 per cent come from the low-class *vis-à-vis* a value of 7.4 per cent for the entire population, whereas the cluster contains 62.1 per cent of the individuals labelled by the same modality; almost four-fifths show a low level of formal education, a modality which in the population accounts for less than 13 per cent, while the cluster covers about 49 per cent of it. Similar evidence (MOD/CLA = 63.3 per cent, CLA/MOD = 73 per cent) can be found for the category 'father's low level of education', quite rare (6.8 per cent) in our sample. Moreover the high percentage (83.3) of those in the cluster who began as employees – versus 52.6 for the entire population – seems to suggest that the phenomenon of self-employment might have been a significant component of the socio-economic determinants of Italian entrepreneurship.

The third cluster (Table 3.10) incorporates 24.4 per cent of the entrepreneurs. As its label – well-established entrepreneurs – already suggests, here converges the elite of the entrepreneurs. First, the cluster contains about half of the people having upper-class origin, a modality which within the cluster characterizes 54.7 per cent of its members as compared to 28.2 per cent of the entire population. Second, 64.2 per cent of the cluster inherited the business, a characteristic shared – as already mentioned – only by 33.9 per cent of the sample; on the contrary just 31.6 per cent of the well-established entrepreneurs are to be considered founders, as compared to a sample percentage of 44.4 per cent. More than half of the individuals in the group (versus less than one-third) were politically involved and more than two-thirds were members of industrial and/or employers associations (versus 36.7 per cent in the population). Third, 64.2 per cent of the people in the cluster (versus about 44 per cent in the sample) began their entrepreneurial career as independent workers; their fathers were for the most part (76.8 per cent versus 52.8 per cent) autonomous workers. Moreover a large share of them (86.3 per cent versus 57.4 per cent) had job relations with members of their families.

Further specifications of the cluster highlight that all of them were private entrepreneurs and that a good share had been appointed to the honour of *Cavalieri del lavoro* (40 per cent versus 25.4 per cent in the population).

The fourth cluster (Table 3.11) includes 21 per cent of the entrepreneurs. We have called it defensive entrepreneurs because its prevailing modalities are almost the opposite of the ones characterizing the first cluster. First of all, the defensive entrepreneurs do not innovate or innovate very little: the label 'no innovator' fits 74.7 per cent of the people in the cluster (whose share in this modality covers 59.1 per cent of the total) while the same modality is rare enough in our population (28.2 per cent). Moreover just 1 per cent of them has been highly innovative, a modality which characterizes almost 10 per cent of our population: in particular they seem stubbornly resistant to innovation in products (98 per cent versus 69 per cent in the sample), in new sale markets (90.8 per cent versus 53.4 per cent), in new product markets (95.4 per cent versus 80.3) and in processes (92 per cent versus 63.6 per cent).

Table 3.10: Cluster 3: 'Well-Established Entrepreneurs' (24.4%).

Modalities	Test Value	% of Cluster Within Modality (CLA/MOD)	% of Modality Within Cluster (MOD/CLA)	% of Modality Within Sample (GLOBAL)
Employers' association	7.42	46.15	69.47	36.67
Inheriting	6.93	46.21	64.21	33.85
Family job relation	6.76	36.61	86.32	57.44
Innovator	6.55	32.50	95.79	71.79
New sale markets	6.32	39.23	74.74	46.41
High class	6.26	47.27	54.74	28.21
New market product	6.18	53.95	43.16	19.49
Father self-employed	5.39	35.44	76.84	52.82
Owner & manager	5.34	31.10	92.63	72.56
Indirect political involvement	5.19	42.37	52.63	30.26
First job self-employed	4.54	35.88	64.21	43.59
Medium innovation	4.44	37.16	57.89	37.95
Private enterprise	3.76	26.54	100.00	91.79
Cavaliere del lavoro	3.53	38.38	40.00	25.38
Process innovation	3.37	34.51	51.58	36.41
Manufacture	3.34	29.50	81.05	66.92
Integration & diversification	3.04	43.14	23.16	13.08
Experience abroad	2.69	31.85	52.63	40.26
Integration	2.65	36.71	30.53	20.26
Father medium educated	2.56	56.25	9.47	4.10
Father highly educated	2.33	44.83	13.68	7.44
Age of first job 21–5	2.33	34.04	33.68	24.10
Food	2.33	40.00	18.95	11.54
No experience abroad	−2.69	19.31	47.37	59.74
State-owned entrepreneur	−2.73	0.00	0.00	5.13
Founding	−2.79	17.34	31.58	44.36
Low education	−3.31	6.12	3.16	12.56
Father employee	−3.36	10.13	8.42	20.26
No process innovation	−3.37	18.55	48.42	63.59
Medium class	−3.48	16.83	35.79	51.79
No *Cavaliere del lavoro*	−3.53	19.59	60.00	74.62
Financial activity	−3.68	0.00	0.00	7.95
Financial activities	−3.68	0.00	0.00	7.95
Other strategies	−3.99	14.29	25.26	43.08
First job employee	−4.14	15.61	33.68	52.56
Manager	−4.97	1.69	1.05	15.13
No indirect political involvement	−5.19	16.54	47.37	69.74
No new sale markets	−6.32	11.48	25.26	53.59
No new market product	−6.37	16.93	55.79	80.26
No innovator	−6.55	3.64	4.21	28.21
No family relation	−6.76	7.83	13.68	42.56
No employers' association	−7.42	11.74	30.53	63.33
No innovation	−7.56	0.94	1.05	27.18

Most of them were independent since the beginning (about 72 per cent as compared to 44 per cent in the sample), and were children of independent workers as well (77 per cent versus 52.8 per cent). The majority comes from the central/southern regions because the value of the modality 'north born' is more minor than the one in the sample (43.7 per cent versus 58.2 per cent). A fair share of defensive entrepreneurs seems to be devoted to commercial activities (17.2 versus 7.2 per cent): actually the cluster's share in the modality was well over the majority (53.6 per cent). A good part inherited the business (64.4 per cent versus 33.9 per cent), in which other members of the family were inserted (81.6 per cent versus 57.4 per cent).

Table 3.11: Cluster 4: 'Defensive Entrepreneurs' (21%).

Modalities	Test Value	% of Cluster Within Modality (CLA/MOD)	% of Modality Within Cluster (MOD/CLA)	% of Modality Within Sample (GLOBAL)
No innovation	10.44	60.38	73.56	27.18
No innovator	10.40	59.09	74.71	28.21
No new sale markets	8.29	37.80	90.80	53.59
No product innovation	7.39	31.60	97.70	68.97
No process innovation	6.64	32.26	91.95	63.59
Inheriting	6.55	42.42	64.37	33.85
First job self-employed	6.05	37.06	72.41	43.59
Family job relation	5.24	31.70	81.61	57.44
Father self-employed	5.12	32.52	77.01	52.82
No new market product	4.30	26.52	95.40	80.26
Commercial services	3.58	53.57	17.24	7.18
Farming/extraction	3.58	53.57	17.24	7.18
Agriculture	2.59	50.00	11.49	5.13
Diversification	2.58	32.97	34.48	23.33
Commercial services	2.36	39.47	17.24	9.74
Owner & manager	2.34	25.44	82.76	72.56
Low class	−2.58	3.45	1.15	7.44
Founding	−2.74	15.61	31.03	44.36
Born in the north	−2.98	16.74	43.68	58.21
Machinery	−3.04	8.70	6.90	17.69
Father low educated	−3.06	0.00	0.00	6.67
High innovation	−3.13	2.78	1.15	9.23
Manufacture	−3.98	16.09	48.28	66.92
New market product	−4.24	5.26	4.60	19.49
Manager	−4.64	1.69	1.15	15.13
No family relation	−5.24	9.64	18.39	42.56
Father employee	−5.75	1.27	1.15	20.26
Process innovation	−6.64	4.93	8.05	36.41
First job employee	−7.03	8.29	19.54	52.56
Product innovation	−7.39	1.65	2.30	31.03
Medium innovation	−7.94	2.70	4.60	37.95
New sale markets	−8.29	4.42	9.20	46.41
Innovator	−10.40	7.86	25.29	71.79

The fifth cluster (Table 3.12) includes 16.7 per cent of the population. It has been denominated entrepreneurial managers in order to emphasize the managerial functions performed by its components, who often were more talented administrators than entrepreneurs. In fact 89.8 per cent of the entries classified as 'manager' stay in this cluster: 81.5 per cent of the people in it were managers, versus a corresponding value of 15.1 per cent for the entire population. Furthermore 95 per cent of the managers working in state-owned enterprises were in the group: within it not much lower (83.3 per cent) was the share of those working in business, partly private and partly public. The second most relevant characteristic is that the percentage of the modality 'owner' is much lower in the cluster than in the sample (3 per cent versus 12.3 per cent) and that only 4.2 per cent of all the owners belong to the cluster. On the other hand, these individuals: 1. were involved in financial activities much more than the remaining population (38.5 per cent versus 8 per cent); 2. had much closer connection with the banking system (75.4 per cent versus 35 per cent); and 3. began their career mostly as employees (78.5 per cent versus 52.6 per cent). In addition almost 97 per cent of them did not have job relations with member of their family, as compared to a sample value of 42.6 per cent. About 8 per cent of them were Hebrew, corresponding to about 55 per cent of all the Hebrews in the population.

Table 3.12: Cluster 5: 'Entrepreneurial Managers' (16.7%).

Modalities	Test Value	% of Cluster Within Modality (CLA/MOD)	% of Modality Within Cluster (MOD/CLA)	% of Modality Within Sample (GLOBAL)
Manager	14.27	89.83	81.54	15.13
No family relation	10.20	37.95	96.92	42.56
Financial activities	8.18	80.65	38.46	7.95
State entrepreneur	7.83	95.00	29.23	5.13
Relation with banks	7.27	36.30	75.38	34.62
No new sale markets	6.23	27.27	87.69	53.59
High education	5.82	33.60	64.62	32.05
Private/public enterprise	4.91	83.33	15.38	3.08
Energy	4.88	90.00	13.85	2.56
First job employee	4.56	24.88	78.46	52.56
No product innovation	4.35	21.93	90.77	68.97
No innovation	4.34	31.13	50.77	27.18
Other strategies	3.97	25.60	66.15	43.08
Age of first job > 45	3.87	52.17	18.46	5.90
No innovator	3.83	29.09	49.23	28.21
Father employee	3.63	31.65	38.46	20.26

Modalities	Test Value	% of Cluster Within Modality (CLA/MOD)	% of Modality Within Cluster (MOD/CLA)	% of Modality Within Sample (GLO-BAL)
Direct political involvement	3.10	26.55	46.15	28.97
No new market prod	3.10	19.49	93.85	80.26
University teacher	3.10	53.33	12.31	3.85
Hebrew	2.40	55.56	7.69	2.31
No process innovation	2.36	20.16	76.92	63.59
Process innovation	−2.36	10.56	23.08	36.41
Father low educated	−2.44	0.00	0.00	6.67
Medium education	−2.47	9.92	20.00	33.59
Textile	−2.51	4.17	3.08	12.31
Owner	−2.51	4.17	3.08	12.31
Integration & diversity	−2.68	3.92	3.08	13.08
Food	−2.91	2.22	1.54	11.54
New market product	−3.05	5.26	6.15	19.49
No university teacher	−3.10	15.20	87.69	96.15
No direct political involvement	−3.10	12.64	53.85	71.03
No masonry	−3.24	15.63	92.31	98.46
Age of first job 21–5	−3.51	5.32	7.69	24.10
Age of first job < 20	−3.82	0.00	0.00	12.56
Innovator	−3.83	11.79	50.77	71.79
First job self-employed	−3.90	8.24	21.54	43.59
Product innovation	−4.35	4.96	9.23	31.03
Medium innovation	−4.49	6.08	13.85	37.95
Father self-employed	−4.92	7.77	24.62	52.82
Founding	−5.25	5.78	15.38	44.36
Manufacture	−6.17	8.05	32.31	66.92
New sale markets	−6.23	4.42	12.31	46.41
No relation with banks	−7.27	6.27	24.62	65.38
Inheriting	−7.38	0.00	0.00	33.85
Private enterprise	−9.69	10.06	55.38	91.79
Family job relation	−10.20	0.89	3.08	57.44
Owner & manager	−10.64	3.53	15.38	72.56

As for the level of education, 64.6 per cent of them (versus 32.1 per cent in the population) were highly educated, and 12.3 per cent (versus 3.9 per cent) taught in the university, that is 53.3 per cent of the university professors in the population, while a share larger than in the sample (46.2 per cent versus 29 per cent) was involved in politics. Finally it is worth noting that the cluster's entrepreneurial managers were active particularly in financial activities – as already mentioned – and in the energy industry (respectively about 81 per cent and 90 per cent of all the entries characterized by such modalities), that is to say in modern sectors which required complex organizations calling for large bureaucracies; on the contrary traditional activities such as food and textiles were largely under-represented in the cluster (2.2 per cent and 4.2 per cent of total population).

Conclusions

The general aim of our research was to describe the main features of Italian entrepreneurship over the long haul, in order to evaluate which have been the crucial socio-economic determinants which can explain its historical evolution. This has been made possible by the availability of a new data set built over a significant sample of entrepreneurs.

Our contribution is composed of two main parts. In the first one, a descriptive analysis of the main peculiarities of the country's entrepreneurship has been performed on the basis of a few standard variables traditionally used in economic analysis. In the second part, the descriptive approach has been refined by means of a methodology – Multiple Correspondence Analysis and Cluster Analysis – usual by now in standard statistics, yet not very familiar to students in economic and/or business history. This has allowed us to single out from a large set of variables a few entrepreneurial typologies of the history of Italian capitalism.

The features which emerge from such analysis – as provisional as it is – only partly confirm what has been so far reconstructed by the economic and business historiography: in fact a few interesting novel aspects emerge. Among what comes out neatly confirmed are the supposed prominence of northern entrepreneurs, the strong relations both with one's own and one's partner's families, the almost total absence of female entrepreneurs and an entrepreneurship rooted in the middle class. Among the novelties, the most surprising aspect is the good level of formal education, which shows that a clear majority of our sample (60 per cent) have a medium/high degree and almost one-third have a university degree.

The cluster analysis has allowed us to divide our sample into five groups, each of them characterized by its original entrepreneurial typology: 'Schumpeterian entrepreneurs' (which groups about 29 per cent of the population), 'first-generation entrepreneurs' (8 per cent), 'defensive entrepreneurs' (21 per cent), 'well-established entrepreneurs' (24 per cent) and 'entrepreneurial managers' (17 per cent).

We see this result as a necessary step towards two further objectives of our research programme: first, these typologies – their characteristics, modalities, backgrounds etc. – can furnish new pieces to complete the puzzle of the process of economic growth in Italy and, second, they offer the possibility to make comparisons with the basic characters of the entrepreneurship of other countries.

4 ENTREPRENEURSHIP: A COMPARATIVE APPROACH

Gabriel Tortella, Gloria Quiroga and Ignacio Moral

'The crucial theoretical problem [of the social sciences] is understanding the process of human learning'.[1]

Introduction

The role of the entrepreneur in economic development is well established since Schumpeter published his *Theory of Economic Development* almost a century ago (1911) and perhaps since Von Thünen wrote his *Isolated Estate* in 1826.[2] One could even go back to Cantillon in 1755 and Adam Smith in 1776.[3] Cantillon's definition of the entrepreneur is of remarkable modernity, as we will see later on. Entrepreneurial studies have been proliferating lately and a question which is cropping up often is: what moves entrepreneurs? Of course we know that the profit motive is the chief drive but our question here is a little more refined: what makes a successful entrepreneur? In other words: is it just a matter of genes, or drive, or calling, or are there more general factors (social, psychological) which move people to become entrepreneurs; and not only this: what makes entrepreneurs successful? We will argue (as Cantillon does, by the way) that almost everybody has played the role of entrepreneur at some moment or other. The question is, why are some successful and others not? What makes some behave in a certain way and others differently?

About these and somewhat related topics there has recently been debate among Spanish economic historians. One of us wrote years ago about 'the weakness of the Spanish entrepreneurial spirit'.[4] Other writers have debated this statement. García-Sanz, for instance, criticized it while apparently not in total disagreement.[5] Other authors seemed to agree at least in a general way. Carreras and Tafunell, for instance, have written that 'there has never been in Spain a "managerial revolution"'.[6] Many others could be cited.

Carreras and Tafunell have tried to explain the reasons for the rarity of big business and other peculiarities of Spanish enterprise. They adduced three main explanations: first, small market size; second, lack of comparative advantages in sectors where big business thrives; and, third, lack of a 'real entrepreneurial culture' and the lateness with which business schools appeared.[7] Let us say in a few words that the first explanation is unconvincing. If narrowness of the domestic market were an explanation for the absence of big business, how could we justify the existence of big multinationals in Switzerland, Sweden or the Netherlands? The second explanation is not very convincing either: why should oranges and fruits, minerals or olive oil, all products in which Spain has a natural advantage, not be conducive to big business? There are multinationals in food products, in drinks and spirits, in cork, in minerals and in other products which Spain exports or has exported. The only plausible and intriguing explanation is the third one. Cultural factors, among them the educational system, are worth studying further. For unknown reasons, Carreras and Tafunell reject that education should have something to do with the weakness of the entrepreneurial spirit in Spain. Thus, in a synthesis in a volume on Spanish entrepreneurial history, they state that (our translation): 'Educational retardation cannot be considered as an obstacle to the appearance of entrepreneurs, since it is conceivable that tradition and on-the-job learning could be adequate channels for attaining the knowledge needed to carry out entrepreneurial initiatives'.[8] One is surprised by the total lack of evidence offered to support so radical an assertion. We hope to be able to show in the following pages that education has indeed an influence on entrepreneurial callings and on the ways they developed.

There is no doubt that the topic is complex. There is a continuous feedback between economic growth at large and the entrepreneurial spirit. As we hinted before, entrepreneurship developed considerably in Spain during the last century. Tortella himself has written: 'It cannot be doubted that the entrepreneurial spirit has not been lacking in twentieth-century Spain'.[9] Even so, another specialist in the topic has written: 'Spain has become a fully developed country from the theory's point of view, while lagging seriously behind other major countries in terms of technological and marketing expertise'.[10]

It should be added that this discussion is not limited to Spain. In many other countries the issue of the economic role of education and of its impact upon the formation of the entrepreneurial spirit is going on and perhaps nowhere as much as in England. Among the most notable are the writings by Aldcroft, Coleman, Fox, Jeremy and Sanderson.[11] It is interesting that while in England, the cradle of the Industrial Revolution and still one of the economic leaders of the world, scholars debate bitterly about 'Education and Britain's Growth Failure',[12] as one of Aldcroft's articles is entitled, the problem should be declared non-existent by leading Spanish scholars.

This is not an exclusively Spanish problem, however. There is an established scholarly tradition which sustains, on very shaky evidence, that education has little to do with economic growth. American scholars such as David Mitch and Harvey Graff belong to this school and in Italy Renato Giannetti also holds this opinion.[13] This in spite of several recent articles which empirically support the contrary view, in the tradition of the classical article by Schultz,[14] such as, for instance, Bania, Eberts and Fogarty, Bates, Evans and Leighton, Praag and Cramer or Wong.[15] We are not going to go into this complex discussion here, and refer to a book edited fifteen years ago.[16] Let us go back from this excursus into the actual research we have been carrying out.

Method and Sources

Our main sources are biographical dictionaries, whose number, fortunately, is increasing every day. So far we have processed the data of 288 Spanish and 1,712 British businessmen culled from the books by Torres Villanueva, Vidal Olivares and Cabana for Spain and Jeremy and Jeremy and Tweedale (which we will call JI and JII for short) for Britain.[17]

For Spain were have therefore three volumes. Those of Vidal Olivares and Cabana are regional and deal with Valencian and Catalan businessmen respectively, while Torres Villanueva studies 100 Spanish businessmen, presumably the most distinguished, whose activity took place in the twentieth century. Vidal Olivares's and Cabana's volumes also include nineteenth-century biographies and all three of them are supposed to deal with the most distinguished individuals in their respective regions and periods. The Spanish subsets, therefore, are rather distinct. The 'Spanish' group is limited to the twentieth century but, being a subset from a wider population than those of the regional dictionaries, it offers a richer variety of sectors of activity, whereas Catalan and Valencian biographies are more concentrated upon consumer industries: food and textiles.

The *Dictionary* of David Jeremy (JI) offers some 1,300 biographies of British businessmen grouped into five volumes. Its time span is 1860–1980; this is the period when the entrepreneurs were active; some were born even before 1800. The selection criterion is territorial: these were businessmen operating in England and Wales; Scotland and Ireland are therefore excluded. This does not mean, however, that there are no individuals from these areas; there are, provided they worked mostly in England and Wales; the same goes for foreigners such as Americans (United States and Canada) and Germans, of whom there is a fair number, Italians, etc. The same author's (with Geoffrey Tweedale) *Dictionary of Twentieth-Century Business Leaders*, what we will call JII, offers 750 biographies of twentieth-century British business leaders, of which 209 are included in JI.

We have so far extracted a sample of 1,712 biographies from the Jeremy books (JI and JII) and 288 from the Spanish books (not 300 because there is some overlap). In the British sample we have made a distinction between those businessmen who acted rather as managers than as pure entrepreneurs (i.e., as salaried employees rather than risk-takers). In the Spanish case we have sometimes separated the 101 elite twentieth-century entrepreneurs from the regional businessmen because there are reasons to assume that these are two distinct subsets. We have also selected two elite groups (i.e., those we consider as the most distinguished and accomplished) among British businessmen, 100 for the nineteenth century (1830–1918) and 102 for the twentieth (1919–80). The criteria utilized in the selection of the English elite samples have been social prominence, economic achievement, technical achievement and versatility.

Our samples show certain limitations of which we are conscious. The first and fundamental problem is that devising an unbiased sample of entrepreneurs is impossible. We are dealing in both cases with a distinguished group of entrepreneurs-businessmen whose careers and successes were doubtless above average. One difficulty in this connection lies in that the border between entrepreneurs and non-entrepreneurs is wide and blurred. First, the distinction that we have made between managers and entrepreneurs is uncertain (although undeniable). Second, even the definition of entrepreneur is imprecise. Many scholars consider that what defines an entrepreneur is the willingness to take risks and the ability to adapt to (and take advantage of) unexpected situations. Yet this can also be said about many professions, such as surgeons, boat skippers, aeroplane pilots, policemen, truck drivers, even orchestra conductors. Furthermore, a vast majority of people have undertaken entrepreneurial activities at some point in their lives, i.e., have engaged in some kind of business. Just making decisions about one's estate is an entrepreneurial activity: buying or selling a house, contracting a mortgage, borrowing or lending, all these are entrepreneurial activities which most adults (and some teenagers) assume with greater or lesser frequency. We are interested in full-time entrepreneurs, but even these are difficult to tell apart from part-time entrepreneurs and frequently in our samples we find individuals who became entrepreneurs gradually and, in some cases, intermittently. We must, therefore, not only define the entrepreneur as a risk-taker and somebody able to take advantage of and adapt to unexpected situations, but also somebody who obtains profit by combining factors of production within the framework of a market. Purely professional activities, however profitable, are not entrepreneurial. This is why we think that a pure manager is not a real entrepreneur, but rather a professional. Let us say *en passant* that these notions are not new. Richard Cantillon characterized the entrepreneur as the person whose customers paid extra to avoid the risk and the bother of storing the merchandise they were going to consume in the future; thus the income of entrepreneurs was uncertain (*gages incertains*), and this is why they were so often bankrupt.[18] Third, what makes an entrepreneur well known is success. You do not find entrepreneurial biographies of failed businessmen (unless they have been involved in titillating scandals); most often failed businessmen abandon business. So the fact of being studied already presupposes a measure of success, of being above average. Simple continuity in business already implies success.

In consequence of all this, we do not worry too much about sample bias. We think that 'average entrepreneur' is an elusive concept and, after all, we are not trying to understand the average entrepreneur, but rather what makes a successful entrepreneur, since we believe that entrepreneurial success is conducive to social welfare. If we want to know what makes horses run we should study thoroughbreds rather than 'the average hack'.

For these reasons we have frequently made comparisons between our 101 twentieth-century Spanish entrepreneurs and the two similar groups of elite English entrepreneurs, 100 for the nineteenth century and 102 for the twentieth.

The variables we have selected for the following exercises are as follows. First, studies: secondary, vocational, apprenticeships, college-level and university studies; within college and university studies we have taken into account field of study (law, medicine, engineering, etc.); we have also tried to take into account not only quantity (years studied) but also quality (for instance, in England public schools are supposed to be superior to grammar schools at the secondary level and we have considered them separately). Second, family relations: whether there is a business saga, business-related marriage, to what extent family background has determined the business activity of our entrepreneurs, etc.; we have also introduced other variables, such as the degree of entrepreneurial self sufficiency (self-made, heir and two intermediate categories) and a time variable.

For us the main explanatory variable is education, although not the only one. Family-related variables may also be used as explanatory, and some social indicators, such as religion, country or region of origin, may be so used also, although our problem with religion now is that this variable does not apply in the Spanish case. Our main dependent variable refers to entrepreneurial performance: versatility (sector and number of sectors – such as banking, textiles, food, electricity, etc.), plus other not strictly professional, such as political and other social activities. Since the ability to adapt, according to Schultz, Kirzner, Casson and Godley and many others),[19] is one of the key abilities of entrepreneurs, versatility is one of our key indicators of quality of the entrepreneurial factor, as adaptation often will entail transferring factors from one sector to another. Finally, we have also considered that belonging to our elite samples is an indication of entrepreneurial success and have considered it as a second dependent variable in some of our econometric exercises.

Descriptive Analysis

Our first table reflects the educational levels of entrepreneurs (Table 4.1). If we add those without studies and those about whose studies we have no information in percentages we find that 34 per cent of Spaniards probably had no studies above primary school (since the most probable is that 'don't know' means 'no studies') compared to 22 per cent of Englishmen in the JI sample and 15 per cent of twentieth-century English businessmen (JII). However, the picture changes if we take university-level studies into account. If we include unfinished university studies, over half (52.1 per cent) of Spanish entrepreneurs had attended institutions of higher education whereas only 30.6 per cent of English (JI) had. Even the JII sample of twentieth-century Englishmen exhibits a lower proportion of university trainees (48.1) than the Spanish sample. If we excluded those who had not finished their university studies, the proportions would not vary appreciably: 49.7 for Spain, and 26.9 for JI and 45.9 for JII.

In raw terms English entrepreneurs have been commonly depicted as having relatively low levels of formal education until quite recently. This was already pointed out in a pioneering study by De Miguel and Linz,[20] who compared a Spanish sample with samples of English, American and French businessmen. They found that Spanish and French entrepreneurs had higher standards of formal education than their Anglo-Saxon counterparts. The same has been observed more recently by Cassis[21] in a comparison of French, British and German businessmen. The French had the highest levels, then the German and the British came last. However, Cassis concluded that the differences in educational levels between British, French and German business elites had little effect on business or economic performance. He argued that the differences among educational systems were less than usually thought.

This is one of the big differences between Spanish (more generally, Continental) and British entrepreneurs: whereas Spaniards went to the university, Englishmen had more practical methods of training in mind. This may be due to the character deliberately humanistic and anti-utilitarian of English universities, especially the top ones, until well into the twentieth century, as contrasted with French and German universities, more inclined to experimental sciences and to being in contact with industry. John Stuart Mill, no less, in an inaugural as rector of St Andrews University in 1867 said the following:

> There is a tolerably general agreement about what a university is not. It is not a place of professional education. Universities are not intended to teach the knowledge required to fit men for some special mode of gaining a livelihood. Their object is not to make skilful lawyers and physicians or engineers, but capable and cultivated human beings.

Table 4.1: Educational Level of Spanish and English Entrepreneurs.

	Spanish		Spanish Elite		Valencian		Catalan		English JI		English JII		English Elite 20th Century		English Elite 19th Century	
	No.	%	No.	%	No.	%	No.	%	No.	%	No.	%	No.	%	No.	%
No Studies	64	22.22	13	12.87	39	34.21	15	14.29	169	14.31	57	7.60	12	11.76	14	14.00
Unknown	33	11.46	11	10.89	13	11.40	17	16.19	93	7.87	54	7.20	4	3.92	5	5.00
Apprenticeship	35	12.15	10	9.90	14	12.28	14	13.33	201	17.02	61	8.13	14	13.73	26	26.00
Articled Apprenticeship	–	–	–	–	–	–	–	–	154	13.04	73	9.73	10	9.80	11	11.00
Secondary Education	6	2.08	2	1.98	3	2.63	1	0.95	148	12.53	99	13.20	14	13.73	16	16.00
Public School	–	–	–	–	–	–	–	–	55	4.66	45	6.00	6	5.88	4	4.00
Engineer/Architect	47	16.32	23	22.77	6	5.26	22	20.95	65	5.50	61	8.13	9	8.82	2	2.00
Law	40	13.89	23	22.77	12	10.53	11	10.48	30	2.54	40	5.33	2	1.96	1	1.00
Economics	31	10.76	10	9.90	14	12.28	11	10.48	24	2.03	39	5.20	9	8.82	–	0.00
Sciences	13	4.51	3	2.97	6	5.26	6	5.71	53	4.49	23	3.07	4	3.92	7	7.00
Cross-Disciplinary and Unknown University Studies	–	–	–	–	–	–	–	–	93	7.87	127	16.93	6	5.88	9	9.00
Unfinished University Studies	7	2.43	2	1.98	4	3.51	4	3.81	43	3.64	17	2.27	7	6.86	2	2.00
Miscellany	12	4.17	4	3.96	3	2.63	4	3.81	53	4.49	54	7.20	5	4.90	3	3.00
Total	288	100	101	100	114	100	105	100	1,181	100	750	100	102	100	100	100

Mill admitted that there was a social demand for engineers and 'industrial arts', but he thought these matters should be taught elsewhere, not at universities.[22] Continental universities did not emphasize this distinction: the polytechnic institutes (Spanish *escuelas especiales*, French *écoles polytechniques*, German *Hochschulen*, American institutes of technology: MIT, Caltech) were considered part of the universities, although somewhat autonomous, or akin to universities. This reticence on the part of English universities to embrace technological institutes until relatively recently has been acerbically criticized by British specialists (Sanderson, Aldcroft, Coleman). Alfred Marshall, however, bemoaned the passing away of learning 'by imitation', as he described apprenticeship.[23]

In any case, the proportion of English businessmen having gone through apprenticeship was 28.2 per cent in the JI sample, more than double the Spanish case, 12.2. The proportion was also higher in the JII sample: 17.9 per cent. Furthermore, many English apprenticeships were 'articled', i.e., they entailed practical studies in factories or firms and ended up in the acquisition of a title or degree, very frequently in engineering, but often also in other fields such as accounting or actuarial science. In fact, those articled apprenticeships were not very different from the studies in polytechnic schools on the Continent.

The other English speciality was the public schools. These elite institutions of secondary education are considered by some as closer to universities than to ordinary secondary ('grammar') schools. In many cases they have been considered as entrance doors to the best universities. In other cases their prestige was considered sufficient by their alumni to substitute for a college education, especially by those vowed to business and politics. Some 4.7 per cent of English businessmen in our JI sample and 6.0 per cent in JII studied in Public schools and did not go on to college. Among elite businessmen the proportion was 4.0 per cent in the nineteenth century and 5.9 per cent in the twentieth.

Regional disparities among Spanish businessmen were considerable; unfortunately the only regional biographies we have processed so far relate to Catalonia and Valencia. The differences among these two groups and with the Spanish elite group are considerable. The Valencia group had a distinctly lower level of university studies: only 39.5 per cent, whereas the total Spanish average was 52.1. The Catalans were slightly above the average (55.2) and the Spanish elite group clearly above: 64.4, i.e., almost two in three elite businessmen had university studies. What is remarkable about Spanish businessmen is how low was the proportion of those who had secondary studies but did not go on to college or university: about 2 per cent. There are at least two reasons for this: 1. almost no vocational study programmes were – or are – available; and 2. access to university studies has always been easy and inexpensive for Spain's middle classes.

As to the degree of self-sufficiency of businessmen (Table 4.2), we have established four categories: self-made, heirs, nearly self-made and nearly heirs. On one extreme are those entrepreneurs who created a successful firm or product by themselves or almost; on the other extreme are those who inherited an ongoing concern from close relatives; in most cases these entrepreneurs made the firm larger or more profitable, or branched out into other sectors, etc.; but they started out with a clear advantage: we call them heirs; then we have two intermediate gradations: nearly self-made, those who had some help from relatives but created something different and fairly new; and those who received substantial family help but introduced considerable quantitative or qualitative changes. We have not had too much trouble classifying our subjects. Spanish entrepreneurs relied more on family networks than English: for the large samples, 49 per cent of Spanish entrepreneurs were self-made, and 57 per cent of the English in the JI sample and 65 per cent in the JII (all in all, 60 per cent of English entrepreneurs were self-made).

In the elite groups the English proportion was also slightly higher; 51 (53 per cent for nineteenth-century entrepreneurs, 50 per cent for twentieth-century) against 48 per cent for Spaniards. What is remarkable, but not surprising, is that among English managers (not entrepreneurs proper) the self-made were 78 per cent. These were people who owed their success to their skills; their level of studies was clearly higher than the average; as we said, these people were a mixture of entrepreneur-cum-professional. As to Spanish regional variations in the proportions of self-sufficiency, they are not remarkable. Valencians are slightly above average, Catalans more clearly below. One reason why this should be so is that Catalan industrialization preceded Valencian by almost a century, so that most Catalan entrepreneurs in the sample are already second generation, whereas many Valencians are beginners.

Conversely, the proportion of heirs is larger among Spaniards than among English: 31 per cent versus 26 per cent in the JI sample and 24 per cent in the JII. This would seem natural, since Latin societies tend to have stronger family ties. The picture gets more blurred, however, if we focus upon elite groups: Spanish elite entrepreneurs received substantially less help from their families (heirs were less than one-quarter, 23.8 per cent), whereas elite English entrepreneurs received about the same proportion of family help as in the larger sample: 29 per cent for elite heirs in the nineteenth century, 25 per cent in the twentieth. If we aggregate 'heir' and 'nearly heir' it turns out that, while in the large samples the proportion of heirs and near heirs was higher in the Spanish case (40.6) than in the English (37.5), the reverse is true for the elite samples: of the elite twentieth-century Spanish group only 35.6 per cent received substantial family help, whereas the proportions were 41.0 per cent for the English nineteenth-century sample, 42.2 for the twentieth-century one.

Turning to the economic sectors (Table 4.3) in which our agents worked, the percentages of entrepreneurs from each national sample who worked in the vari-

Table 4.2: Degree of Self-Sufficiency of Spanish and English Businessmen.

	Spanish		Spanish Elite		Valencian		Catalan		English JI		English JII		English Elite 20th Century		English Elite 19th Century	
	No.	%	No.	%	No.	%	No.	%	No.	%	No.	%	No.	%	No.	%
Self-Made	141	48.96	48	47.52	59	51.75	46	43.81	673	56.99	484	64.53	50	49.02	53	53.00
Heir	90	31.25	24	23.76	41	35.96	33	31.43	304	25.74	179	23.87	26	25.49	27	27.00
Nearly Heir	27	9.38	12	11.88	5	4.39	12	11.43	140	11.85	49	6.53	17	16.67	14	14.00
Nearly Self-Made	30	10.42	17	16.83	9	7.89	14	13.33	64	5.42	38	5.07	9	8.82	6	6.00
Total	288	100	101	100	114	100	105	100	1,181	100	750	100	102	100	100	100

ous sectors are quite different. To start with, Spanish entrepreneurs were more concentrated in a few sectors, while the British were more evenly distributed. Then, the large Spanish sample shows a rather traditional sector distribution: banking, agriculture, textiles, building & real estate, chemistry and commerce are the main sectors where Spanish businessmen worked; by contrast, British entrepreneurs were concentrated in transportation, metallurgy & machine building, commerce, automobile & aeronautics, banking, textiles and communication & show business. Aside from banking and commerce, which hardly denote either modernity or tradition, the main sectors for Britain (transportation, metallurgy & machine building and automobile & aeronautics) are typical of an industrial economy, while of the main Spanish sectors only textiles and chemistry are genuinely industrial, with textiles typical of the early industrial stages. Spanish industrialists seem to be highly specialized in textiles; there are, however, a couple of surprises: chemistry concentrated a higher proportion of Spanish than of British entrepreneurs, while there is more concentration in mining in Britain than in Spain. The truth is that chemicals have traditionally been a strong industry in Spain (and let us not forget that we are dealing with percentages, not absolute numbers). As to mining, although the mineral richness of Spanish soils is (or rather, was) proverbial, two facts explain the largest concentration of British entrepreneurs: first, the basis of British metallurgy was iron and coal mining; and second, many large Spanish mining companies were the property of Britons. Aside from these occasional exceptions, it is obvious that the occupational structure of entrepreneurs reflected the higher technical structure of the British economy. Even the relatively larger size of British communication & show business reflects the greater weight of the press and the publishing sector in Britain.

Comparing elite groups the conclusions are similar, although with some interesting nuances. Spanish elite businessmen are even more concentrated than those of the larger sample, and that mainly in three sectors: banking goes up from 14.2 to 18.4 per cent; food stays around 14 per cent; and building stays around 10.5 per cent. The textile sector, by contrast, goes down considerably, from 11.3 to 4.5. Commerce goes down considerably also, from 6.1 to 2.3, and, though in lesser proportions, so do consumer industries and communication & show business. In exchange, other sectors become more crowded: mining does so in a most clear way, attracting 5.0 per cent of elite entrepreneurs, contrasted with 1.9 in the larger sample. The same happens in iron & steel (from 2.9 to 5.0), chemistry (from 7.1 to 8.4), power and electrical equipment (which combined go from 5.2 to 6.7) and insurance (from 1.5 to 3.4). On the whole these changes confirm a well-known fact: Spanish big businessmen in the twentieth century inclined towards banking and heavy industry in a much greater degree than those of the lower echelons, who preferred consumer industries.

Table 4.3: Economic Sectors in which Entrepreneurs Worked (%).

	All Spanish	Spanish Elite	Valencians	Catalans	English JI (n = 1,181)	English JII (n = 750)	English Elite 20th Century	English Elite 19th Century
Agriculture & Food	13.60	13.97	16.67	12.08	5.82	7.12	9.21	6.34
Automobile & Aeronautics	1.72	1.68	1.61	2.42	7.25	6.34	10.53	3.52
Banking	14.18	18.44	9.68	12.56	7.12	8.12	6.58	5.63
Commerce	6.13	2.23	7.53	6.76	7.52	6.34	7.89	9.86
Communication & Show Business	4.41	3.91	4.30	5.31	6.21	6.23	11.84	6.34
Building & Real Estate	10.34	10.61	15.59	5.80	5.23	4.34	4.61	2.11
Consumer Industries	3.07	3.35	5.91	0.97	4.84	3.56	6.58	1.41
Power	4.21	6.15	1.08	5.80	4.58	4.34	1.97	1.41
Electric Equipment	0.96	0.56	–	1.93	2.16	3.11	1.97	2.11
Metallurgy & Machine Building	5.17	5.03	2.69	8.21	9.48	5.67	5.92	14.79
Mining	1.92	5.03	–	0.48	3.73	3.23	1.97	6.34
Chemistry	7.09	8.38	4.84	9.66	4.71	4.67	7.89	6.34
Insurance	1.53	3.35	–	1.93	1.57	2.11	1.97	0.70
Services	4.60	2.79	7.53	1.93	3.53	2.11	4.61	4.23
Iron & Steel	2.87	5.03	1.61	1.93	4.25	4.89	1.97	12.68
Textiles	11.30	4.47	12.90	16.43	6.54	5.90	3.29	8.45
Transportation	5.75	4.47	7.53	3.86	10.07	12.35	7.89	6.34
Miscellany	1.15	0.56	0.54	1.93	5.42	9.57	3.29	1.41
Total	100	100	100	100	100	100	100	100

English elite businessmen exhibit a more nuanced and complex picture. Here again, as in the larger sample, they show less sector concentration; Table 4.3, furthermore, seems to exhibit a trend towards de-industrialization, something which is not present in Spanish elite entrepreneurs at all. English elite entrepreneurs in the twentieth century seem to veer towards the tertiary sector. Their most populated sector is communication & show business, which goes from 7.0 per cent in the nineteenth-century elite sample to 10.8 per cent in the twentieth-century elite group; second comes automobile & aeronautics (from 3.5 to 10.5), a very large increase but largely due to the fact that these industries are typical of the twentieth century and almost unknown in the nineteenth. Another expanding sector is food and agriculture while the concentration in such traditional sectors as metallurgy & machine building, iron & steel and textiles goes down. In exchange, consumer industries go up. This sector includes home appliances and furniture, office machines and scientific and photographic instruments. Chemistry was the only heavy industry sector where English elite businessmen were more concentrated in the twentieth than in the nineteenth century. Other sectors whose attraction for English elite entrepreneurs went up in the twentieth century are insurance, services (law, accounting and tourism are the largest subsectors), and transportation. The relative fall in commerce obviously does not mean that the sector's output went down, but probably that English retailing was not as innovative and dynamic in the twentieth century as it had been in the nineteenth.

Comparison of the Spanish elite sample with the British elite samples of the nineteenth and twentieth centuries also yields interesting results. The Spanish concentration in banking is remarkable. We have already commented on that: it must be pointed out that the elite sample shows even more concentration in that sector than the larger sample. Compared to the English twentieth-century elite, the Spanish elite almost triples the degree of concentration in banking. The second largest sector for the Spanish elite was agriculture & food processing; it was a considerable sector in Britain too, and growing. In both countries this sector must have a traditional element (weightier in Spain, no doubt) and another element related to retailing and modern food processing, and the trend must be the growth of the second at the expense of the first. Another sector which is disproportionally larger in the Spanish sample is building & real estate. This must be related to the fact that the Spanish population grew in the twentieth century at a faster rate than in the nineteenth and also experienced a marked improvement in its standard of living. The Spanish twentieth-century business elite was much more concentrated in heavy industry than the wider sample: such is the case of power, chemistry, mining and iron & steel. By contrast, British elite entrepreneurs tended to abandon their traditional heavy industry sectors: such is the case with iron & steel, metallurgy & machine building and mining. Another traditionally very strong industry, British textiles, also declined from the nineteenth to the twentieth century. The trend towards a tertiary-sector economy in Britain is visible in the growth of services, insurance, transportation and, above all, communication & show business (mostly publishing and cinema). The comparison of the elite samples, therefore, again shows the weight of traditional industries in Spain and the tertiarization of the British economy in the twentieth century. If we disaggregated further than the tables show, we would see that there was a larger proportion of twentieth-century British elite businessmen in tourism (included in services) than Spanish.

The contrast between the elite samples is therefore rather eloquent. In twentieth-century Spain big business gravitated towards banking and heavy industry; in England it veered towards the tertiary sector and deserted heavy industry. The obvious explanation for this is the different degree of maturity of both economies. England was becoming post-industrial while Spain was industrializing.

Our evidence also reflects the correspondence between areas of study, with special attention to university, and sectors of activity. It shows the polarization in the studies of Spanish entrepreneurs: 33.7 per cent had no secondary or university studies (or we have no information); at the other end, 52.1 per cent had university studies. Only 14.2 per cent had gone to secondary school or taken apprenticeship but had no university studies. This was in contrast with British entrepreneurs, where there was a large 'middle stratum'. Between the 22.2 per cent of English entrepreneurs with 'no studies' beyond primary school or 'unknown' and the 30.6 per cent who went to college or university, there was almost half (47.2 per cent) who had secondary studies or had taken an apprenticeship.

Polarization again obtains for the Spanish elite sample, only here the weight of university studies is more considerable (64.3 per cent), and that of lower education smaller (23.8) while the intermediate stratum is a paltry 1.9 per cent (plus 9.9 per cent who took apprenticeships). In contrast both English elite samples show a substantial proportion of businessmen with secondary education and no university or college studies (43.1 per cent for the twentieth-century sample, 57.0 for the nineteenth-century one).

In the wider Spanish sample (Table 4.4), the second largest group was that of 'no studies', and those businessmen tended towards the traditional sectors: food, textiles, building & real estate and commerce, in addition to banking. As to those who had been apprenticed and therefore had not gone to university but had had professional training, they again flocked towards the less technically sophisticated sectors: textiles, commerce and food, in addition to banking, which was a sort of 'joker card' sector. Commerce is also somewhat of a *portmanteau*, in that it may span from high-level international trade-cum-finance activities to just plain peddling. Those with university studies are even more concentrated in banking, agriculture & food and real estate, but their presence in chemicals, communication & show business, textiles, transportation and iron & steel is (with the exception of textiles) much stronger than that of the other groups. The textile sector is more the preserve of those with lower levels of education. Engineers are more concentrated in more technical sectors such as power and electrical equipment, chemistry and metallurgy & machine building, although also in building & real estate (not too surprising, since the group includes road and bridge engineers and architects) and in banking and agriculture & food. The other large group of Spanish entrepreneurs with university studies is that of lawyers and economists. This is a versatile group: bankers predominate, but agriculture & food is a strong second, followed by building & real estate, with textiles, transportation and services somewhat behind. Obviously, social science students tended to be jacks-of-all-trades. The other groups were rather small, so just a brief comment should suffice: it seems logical that those with degrees in sciences should concentrate in chemicals.

Our data shows that the average versatility of Spanish businessmen was 1.8 sectors per person. Engineers were above average, although in the lawyers' and economists' case, slightly below, the difference was probably not significant. Somewhat surprisingly, the other groups that are clearly above the average are those with other, not specified, university degrees (another *portmanteau*) and those who did not finish their studies, although these are not much above average. All in all, however, figures support our initial assumption: university studies make entrepreneurs more versatile, and also better able to tackle sectors that are more complex technically. This does not seem very surprising to us, but not much quantitative evidence of this sort has been gathered before. And, as we saw in the introduction, these results should surprise some scholars.

English entrepreneurs (Table 4.4) seem to have been less versatile than the Spanish, for an average of 1.3 sectors for each individual. Those lacking university or secondary studies are concentrated upon commerce, transportation and textiles, very traditional sectors in England. As in the Spanish case, their versatility is below average. In general, the versatility of English businessmen is clustered around the average, with a few exceptions: those who did not finish their university studies were clearly less versatile than the average, while those who graduated from public school and those who studied sciences were clearly more versatile; those who studied economics and commerce were also about one percentage point above average. Public school students clustered around four sectors: banking, commerce, transportation and metallurgy. There is no clear pattern here, save their versatility and their strong specialization in banking (29 per cent). Those who took apprenticeship, articled or not, veered heavily towards metallurgy & machine building, with automobile & aeronautics as a strong second and transportation in third place. No surprise here. Other sectors that those who had been apprenticed tended to were building & real estate, textiles, power and electrical equipment and commerce. The pattern here is a clear preference for the technical and mechanical industries. For those who graduated from college or university without a distinct specialization no clear pattern is discernible either: transportation, textiles, mining and banking are the main sectors, but there is a wide spread.

Turning to our elite samples, some contrasts are telling: for instance, almost one-quarter of our elite Spanish entrepreneurs had studied law, while of the 202 English elite entrepreneurs only 3 did, a paltry 1.5 per cent. In exchange, 30 per cent of elite English entrepreneurs had taken up apprenticeship, as contrasted with 10 per cent of the Spanish. Another clear contrast is the proportion of elite entrepreneurs who took up secondary studies only: 14.9 per cent of the English. If we add those who attended public schools, the combined percentage is 19.8 per cent. By stark contrast, the proportion of Spanish elite entrepreneurs who did secondary studies only is 2 per cent. We commented on this before.

As expected, most of the elite Spaniards with no university training (including the ones we have no information about) gravitated towards more traditional sectors: food, building, textiles and banking. By contrast engineers, while also prominent in banking and building, were almost equally conspicuous in power and electrical equipment, metallurgy & chemicals. It is interesting that engineers should be relatively numerous in communication & show business. There are three of them in this sector, as many as in mining. This is due to a curious coincidence: one of the three in communication & show business (Pau Salvat i Espasa) was the scion of a dynasty of book publishers who studied architecture (he designed the firm's building) but in the end followed the family tradition; another (Nicolás Urgoiti) was an engineer who started out working for a paper mill and became a newspaper publisher. Lawyers, on the other hand, flocked to banking (over half of them) and insurance. A little more surprising is that four of them should be in iron & steel.

Elite English entrepreneurs were more evenly distributed. Banking was less prominent than among Spaniards and technical sectors more so. Those with no university or secondary education (or 'no information') were 17 per cent of the total. They gravitated towards commerce and communication & show business, but also towards iron & steel. A good example is William M. Aitken, Lord Beaverbrook, of Canadian origin, a self-made man with no university studies (he failed a Latin exam) who became a press tycoon in England. There are no comparable press magnates in Spain, although in our sample Urgoiti, Godó (of a textile and newspaper dynasty) and Luca de Tena were the founders of newspapers, two of them still extant. Other sectors which attracted non-educated English elite entrepreneurs were general services and textiles. Of the one-third (66 individuals) of English elite entrepreneurs who undertook university studies one-quarter

Table 4.4: Spanish and English Entrepreneurs, Education Levels and Economic Sectors.

	Spanish						English					
	No Studies/Unknown	Apprenticeship	Secondary Education	Public School	University Studies	Total	No Studies/Unknown	Apprenticeship/Articled Apprenticeship	Secondary Education	Public School	University Studies	Total
Agriculture & Food	30	5	3	–	33	71	27	29	20	15	46	137
Automobile & Aeronautics	3	1	–	–	5	9	18	58	13	3	44	136
Banking	24	6	2	–	42	74	20	15	21	23	80	159
Commerce	12	8	1	–	11	32	42	30	28	14	38	152
Communication & Show Business	5	1	–	–	17	23	31	21	31	5	47	135
Building & Real Estate	17	4	–	–	33	54	24	40	16	5	24	109
Consumer Industries	6	4	1	–	6	16	23	20	9	7	38	97
Power	3	2	1	–	16	22	11	24	7	1	49	92
Electric Equipment	–	–	–	–	5	5	6	11	7	3	23	50
Metallurgy & Machine Building	7	4	1	–	15	27	29	72	16	9	49	175
Mining	2	2	–	–	6	10	12	17	6	8	36	79
Chemistry	5	4	–	–	28	37	15	14	20	2	45	96
Insurance	1	–	–	–	7	8	6	10	7	7	9	39
Services	9	4	–	–	11	24	17	28	4	4	15	68
Iron & Steel	3	–	–	–	12	15	22	23	5	4	38	92
Textiles	29	11	2	–	17	59	39	38	23	4	30	134
Transportation	10	3	–	–	17	30	45	49	38	16	81	229
Miscellany	–	1	–	–	5	6	20	26	19	3	82	150
Total	166	60	10	–	286	522	407	525	290	133	774	2,129
Entrepreneurs	97	35	6	–	150	288	323	441	229	92	627	1712
Average	1.71	1.71	1.67	–	1.91	1.81	1.26	1.19	1.27	1.45	1.23	1.24
Standard Deviation	9.27	2.66	0.75	–	10.83	21.31	11.06	16.26	9.53	5.76	20.32	45.89

(24 per cent) never finished. By contrast, 101 (50 per cent) had secondary studies, apprenticeship or went to public schools. Of these, 65 took up technical professions, in sectors such as metallurgy & machine building, automobile & aeronautics, power and electrical equipment, transportation, chemistry and iron & steel. Of the total elite group this was about one-third (32.2 per cent). This contrasts with 13 (6 per cent) among those with lower levels of education who undertook work in those sectors. The proportion of those who took occupation in those technical sectors among the college or university educated was 23.3 per cent (47 individuals). From this standpoint, in the English elite, entrepreneurs with secondary education seem to be the most technologically inclined, and those with higher studies a little less, while those with no, or only elementary, education seem to belong to a different population with much lower technical propensities or abilities. The same seems to obtain in banking, commerce and tourism. Banking seems to have attracted the educated much more, whereas commerce and tourism seem clearly the domain of the less educated.

To what extent did university education make a difference in England? Not much when compared with secondary education. The university-educated seem to have been more specialized in automobile & aeronautics, banking, iron & steel and chemistry than the other groups and clearly less in Food. In automobile & aeronautics and in banking the more education the more participation seems to have been the rule. But, to repeat, among English elite entrepreneurs the great divide seems to have been between those with only primary education (or less) and the others. Among the Spanish elite the cleavage is between the university-educated and the rest, because there was hardly any middle ground.

To reiterate once more, these impressionistic but stubbornly consistent conclusions seem quite commonsensical and self-evident but, as we have seen, are far from being widely shared. Elite entrepreneurs both in England and in Spain had higher levels of education than the average. In addition versatility and the choice of more technically sophisticated sectors also seem to be a function of the level of studies and of the fields of study. The main difference between the two countries was that secondary education was much more effective in England than in Spain, so many successful entrepreneurs in England just completed this level of education.

One possible objection which could be posed to our finding that successful entrepreneurs have a higher educational standard than the average (or than those less prominent or successful) is that the relation may be just the inverse, i.e., the causation might not run from studies to performance, but rather in the other direction; or, at least, that there might be a reciprocal causation. The possibility exists that those entrepreneurs who have higher-level studies may often belong to prosperous families and, therefore, they may owe both their success and their high-level studies to a third factor: family income or status.

In order to contrast this alternative hypothesis we have analysed our 'self-made' sample to see whether the level of studies was significantly different from the rest. Since the self-made entrepreneurs do not owe their success to their families' wealth, in this case the role of family income as independent or causal variable should be excluded. Therefore, if family income or status were determinant, the level of studies of the 'Self-made' should be significantly lower.

An X^2 test showed that the difference in the level of studies between self-made entrepreneurs and the rest was not significant among all our samples of entrepreneurs, both English and Spanish. Family income or status, therefore, does not seem to account for entrepreneurial versatility.

Econometric Analysis

We start with the analysis of a variable that would express a degree of entrepreneurial success. According to the definitions of entrepreneurship which we cited before, economic versatility (or adaptability) could be considered as one of the essential qualities of entrepreneurship. We assume that the more versatile an entrepreneur is, the more successful or, at least, the better prepared he is to be successful.

After a series of failed trials with linear regression, we decided to try the logit method, since most of our variables are of the binary nature to which logit is best adapted. Our dependent variable, therefore, will be the number of sectors in which our subjects had been active. It has been made binary by considering that the entrepreneur was versatile if he operated in more than one sector and not versatile if he operated in only one sector.

We group these independent variables into three categories: time, education and self-sufficiency. These groups can be decomposed into several groups of variables collected into our database as follows:

– Time: birth (year of birth; this is the only continuous, non-binary variable).

– Education: no studies (or only primary studies) and unknown; apprenticeship; articled apprenticeship; secondary school; public school; sciences, engineering or architecture; economics or law; and rest of university studies (various fields or unfinished university studies).

– Self Sufficiency: self-made entrepreneur; heir (inherited an ongoing business), nearly self-made and nearly heir.

All these variables have been more fully discussed above. The only one not discussed is year of birth. We have included this variable because we wanted to know whether as time passed entrepreneurs became more or less versatile. There are reasons in favour of both possibilities. They could become more versatile as their years and quality of schooling lengthened and improved. They could become less so as economic complexity increased and specialization became more necessary for good performance. An example will suffice: we found that in England carpenters or cabinetmakers often ended up designing aeroplanes, as did automobile engineers. The somewhat surprising role of carpenters in the early years of aviation was due to the fact that the first fuselages were made of wood. As materials and design improved, however, only aeronautical engineers designed aeroplanes. In this case, versatility would decrease with time and correlation would be negative.

Our model then would be as follows:

Probability $(Y = 1)$ = Probability (versatile entrepreneur = 1) =

$$\frac{\exp \left(\beta_0+\beta_1 Nac+\beta_2 Engl+ \beta_3 ApprMed+ \beta_4 Publ+ \ldots + \beta_7 Heir+ \beta_8 Self \right)}{1+\exp \left(\beta_0+ \beta_1 Nac+\beta_2 Engl+ \beta_3 ApprMed+\beta_4 Publ+ \ldots + \beta_7 Heir+ \beta_8 Self \right)}$$

Our initial sample is a set of 1,181 English entrepreneurs (only JI). And the results would be as summarized in Table 4.5 (first column).

The most significant educational variables are public school (significant at the 99 per cent level) and economics/law (90 per cent level). They tell us that the most versatile entrepreneurs were those who had attended public school and, with a smaller probability, those who had studied economics or law. Further tests will show that the public school variable is quite robust (so much so that we can only subscribe to Berghoff's conclusion, that 'the hypothesis of the negative influence of public schools on late nineteenth-century economic growth must be rejected *in toto*'):[24] while economics/law is considerably less so. As to what we have called entrepreneurial self-sufficiency, our results show that moderately self-sufficient entrepreneurs (nearly self-made and nearly heir) were more versatile than self-made or heirs. These results are quite logical. By our definition heirs tended to stick to the business and the sector they inherited; self-made individuals probably also stuck to the business they built and therefore tended to stay in that same sector.

Although not significant, it is interesting to note that three variables have negative values: apprenticeship, articled apprenticeship and secondary education. We interpret this as a strong indication that college- or university-level studies contributed to entrepreneurial versatility, something that is suggested by the positive sign of sciences/engineer/architect and rest of university studies, in addition to economics/law. This will be confirmed in further tests. The apprenticeship variables, however, have positive signs and become significant in other, more refined tests, as we will see. The birth variable appears to be minuscule and not significant, but this will also change somewhat in further tests.

A first refinement of our analysis will be to introduce multinomial logit in order to be able to distinguish between 'moderately versatile' (active in 2 sectors) and 'highly versatile' (active in 3 or more sectors) entrepreneurs. The results are in Table 4.5 (second column).

Here again in both cases public school has high values and significance: public school graduates were among the moderately and the highly versatile. The relative novelty is that while economics or law graduates were moderately versatile, scientists and architects emerge now as highly versatile with a strong coefficient and good significance (95 per cent). For the rest, the comments about the straight logit model seem valid here. As a final consideration, the predictive value of our model seems more than acceptable with more than three-quarters of the cases correctly predicted in both simple and multinomial models.

A possible objection to our assumptions could be about the meaning of versatility as measured by number of sectors of activity. It could be said that working in several sectors might indicate failure rather than success, since it is possible that a businessman failing in a sector would move to a different one in hope of better luck. This could be a sort of 'forward escape' phenomenon (what the French call *fuite en avant*). We know this to be a rather infrequent case among the individuals in our sample, but we may agree that just 'number of sectors' seems too crude a measure, especially if not complemented with a different type of measure or variable. This is one reason why we decided to build our elite groups or sub-samples. We had already made an elite sample of Spanish entrepreneurs in the Torres Villanueva book of the 100 entrepreneurs of the twentieth century. We would gather two similar samples of around 200 English businessmen in order to facilitate comparison; although the Spanish group belonged to the twentieth century only, since the English economy was far more advanced, comparison with nineteenth-century Englishmen seemed to us perfectly legitimate and justified. The criteria utilized in the selection of the English elite samples were mentioned before. The building of these samples would not only permit comparison; it would also provide us with a second variable indicating entrepreneurial success and very amenable to the logit model. Inclusion in our elite samples would be an alternative variable indicating success.

Our next test would, therefore, use inclusion in our two English elite samples (a total of 202 individuals) as a dependent variable; the large sample would be that of 1,181 entrepreneurs. The independent variables would be the usual ones. The results are in Table 4.5 (fourth column).

Although again our educational variables seem to have considerable effect upon the success of English entrepreneurs, there are some notable changes in this new test. For one thing, the fit is much better than in the 'versatility' tests: almost 92 per cent of the predictions are correct. For another thing, birth turns out to be highly significant now, although it also has a negative sign and a low coefficient. This would seem to indicate that English entrepreneurs were a little less successful in more recent times, something that we find difficult to interpret.

May this mean that the age of the grandest English entrepreneurs was the heroic nineteenth century? Perhaps the main novelties, however, are the solid coefficient and high significance of apprenticeship and the negative sign and lack of significance of economics/law. These are novel but not too surprising. Apprenticeship has a strong tradition in England and a crucial role in the formation of entrepreneurs, who may not be very versatile but often became highly successful in their fields of specialization. As to graduates in economics and law, their case seems to be the reverse: versatile, but not as well-rounded in their role of businessmen. Public school again has a strong and highly significant coefficient and the same is the case of scientists and architects. Another group of university- and college-educated businessmen, including those who did not obtain a degree (rest of university studies), has a respectable positive coefficient which is significant at the 90 per cent level. By contrast, the various degrees of self-sufficiency seem to have no appreciable effect upon entrepreneurial success. All in all, this model seems to confirm quite categorically that university and college training is a powerful lever to entrepreneurial success according to the two definitions of it we have used, versatility and overall distinction.

Our next step in the utilization of our elite samples will be to compare English and Spanish entrepreneurs. We return to our versatility model: dependent variable is again number of sectors per businessman and the independent variables are the usual except for three variations: one, public school, has been eliminated because, as we know, public schools do not exist in Spain; two, articled and non-articled apprenticeships have been aggregated because there are no articled apprenticeships in Spain. The aggregate variable now is called apprenticeship. As result of these changes our English sample is reduced to 189 individuals (those who did not attend public school); the Spanish sample is composed of 101 individuals; total sample size, therefore, is 290. The third variation is that we have added the variable English which denotes whether the entrepreneur was English or Spanish. It is worth mentioning that since here we are dealing with elite entrepreneurs the 'forward escape' phenomenon which could affect versatility as a positive entrepreneurial trait could be totally discarded. The results are in Table 4.5 (final column).

Our first finding is that the English variable is neither high nor significant, which undoubtedly means that the differences between English and Spanish entrepreneurs regarding versatility are not very important. Its sign is negative, though, which accords with our finding through descriptive analysis that English entrepreneurs were less versatile than Spanish. Birth is even lower and less significant, and also negative. The apprenticeship coefficient is high and significant at the 95 per cent level. It is also negative. This agrees with our earlier findings that businessmen who went through apprenticeship tended to stick to their speciality and were not very versatile, although this did not prevent them

Table 4.5: Econometric Results.

Dependent Variable	Logit with all English Entrepreneurs	Multinomial with all English Entrepreneurs		Logit with English Elite	Logit with English and Spanish Elite
		2 Sectors versus 1	3 Sectors versus 1		
	Y = 1 works in two or more sectors; Y = 0 works in one sector	Y = 1 works in one sector; Y = 2 works in two sectors; Y = 3 works in three or more sectors		Y = 1 belongs to elite group; Y = 0 belongs to the rest	
Sample Size	1,181	1,181	1,181	202/1,181	189/101
Constant	-1.5988710	-2.8545013	0.22770436	82.747151‡	5.1982335
English	–	–	–	–	-0.29682249
Birth	3.5047717e-005	0.00060670174	-0.0018858109	-0.046419344‡	-0.0032788158
No Studies/Unknown	Reference group in 'studies'				
Apprenticeship	-0.27342438	-0.11874345	-1.0749997*	0.66438734†	-0.77288163†
Articled Apprenticeship	-0.28107408	-0.38215011	-0.0094928665	0.25369633	–
Secondary School	-0.010434710	0.0039628607	-0.060878961	0.56778958	0.39608676
Public School	0.96588428‡	0.89770483†	1.1912513†	1.1963696†	–
Sciences/Engineer/Architect	0.37520838	0.20592752	0.81821008†	1.0955430†	0.72456247*
Economics/Law	0.57453743*	0.64065550*	0.28970883	-0.60990338	0.62676281
Rest of University Studies	0.13321616	0.17571579	-0.040910759	0.79620120*	–
Heir	Reference group in 'kind of entrepreneur'				
Self-Made	0.27027580	0.19135534	0.57822555	0.089347366	0.59493965*
Nearly Self-Made	1.2502198	1.0759166‡	1.8157885‡	0.25919766	1.6287862‡
Nearly Heir	0.65088357‡	0.59871671†	0.86631934*	0.13679747	1.0409395†
Likelihood Ratio Chi-Square	41.8713	1555.9754		119.8564	32.5662
% Correctly Predicted	76.7993	76.1219		91.6173	66.2069

* = significance at the 10% level; † = significance at the 5% level; ‡ = significance at the 1% level.

from achieving distinction. Sciences/engineer/architect has a positive sign and is significant at the 90 per cent level. Economics/law, although lower and non-significant, has a positive sign. It compares well with secondary, confirming our impression that college education favours versatility. As to the degrees of entrepreneurial self-sufficiency, it seems again that heirs were the least versatile, followed by self-made individuals. This is also consistent with our previous findings. The model, however, has lost predictive power relative to our earlier 'versatility models', no doubt due to diminished homogeneity when mixing English and Spanish businessmen.

Final Considerations

Our results are far from conclusive. It is our immediate purpose to enlarge our Spanish sample so as to make it more homogeneous and thereby facilitate further comparison with the English sample. However, it is encouraging that the data gathered and processed so far seem to confirm our rather simple and commonsensical hypotheses that education has a beneficial influence upon entrepreneurial activity and that college and university education (with the addition of public schools) improve the versatility and overall performance of entrepreneurs. In other words, nurture is an important part of entrepreneurship. Nature can be improved upon.

5 DYNASTIES AND ASSOCIATIONS IN ENTREPRENEURSHIP: AN APPROACH THROUGH THE CATALAN CASE

Paloma Fernández-Pérez and Núria Puig

Introduction

Recent literature on entrepreneurship stresses the fundamental role played by networks in achieving innovation, competitiveness and internationalization. Networks with an impact on entrepreneurship in a territory often are of two kinds: an individual entrepreneur with other entrepreneurs and firms, and a group of firms establishing networks with other firms and institutions.[1] Dynasties are examples of the first type and associations of firms of the second type of networking.[2] Some dynasties have played a determinant role in promoting innovation in some economic sectors and regions of the world, as the Wendels, Haniels and Falcks in the iron and steel industries of Europe, or the Fords and the Toyodas in the organization of the car industry in America and Asia. As economic historian David Landes has outlined, scholars have generally underestimated the role of dynasties in the advance of entrepreneurship in both developed and underdeveloped economies.[3] Associations of entrepreneurs, on the other hand, have often performed a key role as rather stable networks that help reduce information and knowledge transfer costs among small and medium enterprises or that help large corporations monopolize some markets. Academic literature usually studies both kinds of networks in separate ways, but economic and business history reveals that often both have played a combined role in promoting entrepreneurial spirit in a territory in the long run. Our chapter offers empirical data and analysis about the role dynasties and associations have performed in fostering entrepreneurship in Catalonia during a period of more than a century. With this contribution we want to highlight the importance of social capital construction to understanding the history of entrepreneurship.

It is precisely in order to shed light on the role played by dynasties in the creation of social capital and the accumulation and transfer of entrepreneurship that this section starts by looking at the role played by dynasties in the long term, from the late nineteenth century through the late twentieth century, in the Spanish region of Catalonia. Spanish economic historians have stressed the historical leadership of this region in the Spanish industrialization process. Moreover, hundreds of biographies have revealed the existence of many Schumpeterian innovative entrepreneurs in the region, able to see opportunities and gather resources to establish businesses in a wide variety of economic activities. There is, however, comparatively less work, with a cross-sector approach, on the social and institutional dynastic networks that made entrepreneurship such a historically available, and adaptive, resource in this region. Interestingly, in Catalonia a considerable number of Schumpeterian dynasties have managed to transfer entrepreneurship from generation to generation, thus leaving a valuable bequest for the future of the region. Many of these dynasties are indeed leading the internationalization process of many Spanish firms in quite a successful way. We will place the Catalan dynasties in a theoretical framework that takes into account the social capital of the region as a factor that helped to build the networks through which information, goods and persons have flowed over time. Ultimately, we want to add evidence on the role of dynastic networks in the endowment of entrepreneurship in this territory since the last third of the nineteenth century.

Dynasties are usually visible in politics, and often political analysts and journalists have studied the complex ways through which some dynasties have determined the economy and politics of a country or region for generations. Dynasties have also been studied in economic and business research, particularly in the world of finance since the Middle Ages and in the iron and steel industries since the Industrial Revolution. The Fuggers, the Rothschilds, the Wendels, the Falcks, the Thyssens or the Ybarras or Gironas are only a few well-known examples. However, dynasties are often analysed as isolated case studies, and economists and historians have not in general analysed in a collective way their contribution to regional or national entrepreneurship and economic growth. As Harvard professor David Landes has outlined, the prevalent economic thought prefers to ignore family firms as a serious material of study and usually deals with them as a kind of obsolete and irrelevant type of firm.[4] This viewpoint may offer dangerously misleading conclusions, because many dynasties have performed an outstanding role in advancing innovation in developing countries and in creating enduring brands that have improved a country's image in world markets. The performance of a dynasty would be determined by two dominant factors: the entrepreneurial activity in which it is involved, and the way a particular society perceives such activity.

The few available books of entrepreneurial dynasties during the twentieth century usually highlight a few well-known cases. The key issue is if we can go beyond cases and anecdotes and build a more collective approach to the role played by dynasties in the endowment of entrepreneurship in a territory. More particularly, the question we address here is if we can identify dynastic factors in the analysis of entrepreneurship in a region for which we have relative wealth of published biographical information of entrepreneurs: Catalonia.

Our first hypothesis is that the accumulation of entrepreneurial dynasties facilitates knowledge exchange, networking, accumulation of social capital and therefore potential to create more entrepreneurship outside the dynasties, around them, in the territory where they perform their economic activity. By entrepreneurial dynasty we understand an extended family linked by blood or spiritual ties whose members have created and maintained regionally embedded businesses of diverse kinds during several generations. Our second hypothesis is that entrepreneurial dynasties provide endowment of entrepreneurship in a given territory only if they are able to combine three factors: historical specialization in some market niches, associative skills for knowledge exchange and lobbies for collective action. Figure 5.1 illustrates this.

Figure 5.1: Factors of Dynastic Entrepreneurship.

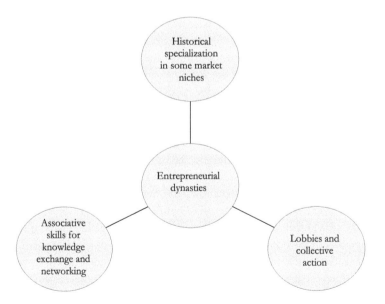

Very rarely have economic or business historians taken into account the historical contribution of dynastic business groups to the formation of entrepreneurship and social capital in Spain with a cross-sector macroeconomic perspective. This is particularly true in Catalonia, perhaps as a legacy of the democratic transition in the twentieth century, in which great fortunes were ideologically identified as the backbone of Franco's four-decade-long military dictatorship. Indeed it is a big contrast in comparison with recent work done on the contribution of dynasties to European, American and Asian capitalism in the last two centuries, in which dynasties are identified with innovation and progress in key sectors of the first and second technological revolution.[5] We believe that the time is right to start revisiting our own business history and acknowledge the role played by enduring entrepreneurial families (regardless of their political ideology and activity) to wealth creation.

This study benefits from accumulated published studies about entrepreneurs in Catalonia and identifies the most enduring dynastic business groups and entrepreneurial families. Catalan dynasties are placed in a four-generational framework that allows understanding of their timing, specialization and growth strategy. The relationship of dynasties to regional economic history provides arguments to illustrate the three determinants that in combination have allowed a strong contribution of dynasties to a rich endowment of entrepreneurship in Catalonia: 1. historical specialization in market niches (consumer goods, metal-mechanical and pharma-chemical industries); 2. accumulated skills to associate for training, networking and knowledge-exchange purposes (with a strong role played by nineteenth-century associations, chambers of trade, entrepreneurial associations and business schools); and 3. accumulated skills to develop collective action while adapting and trying to shape changing political and market environments.

Jordi Nadal, Francesc Cabana, Angels Solà and Gary McDonogh, among many other relevant authors, have offered good general approaches and excellent biographies about entrepreneurship in the industrial, commercial and banking sectors of the region in the nineteenth century and a good deal of the twentieth century.[6] Pere Pascual has also recently published with Jordi Nadal an extensive study about the copper manufacturing family of Lacambra (200 years in the business). Insightful studies are also available about large landowning families in Catalonia by Jordi Planas. He has studied how the Instituto Agrícola Catalán de San Isidro, founded in 1851, gathered 100 large landowners who successfully lobbied for tax reduction between the end of the nineteenth century and first decades of the twentieth century. Miquel Gutiérrez has published on the paper-making families of Capellades in Anoia and their long-lasting competitive advantages in this sector until modern times. Francesc Valls has studied the contribution of wine producers to the Catalan textile industry. Of course we cannot forget the pioneering studies of Josep Maria Benaul on the woollen entrepreneurs of the Vallés district and Esteve Deu's studies on long-lasting innovative entrepreneurs in the metal-mechanic sector in this Vallés district.[7] All these studies are major landmarks in our knowledge about entrepreneurship embedded in districts in Catalonia.[8] Instead of focusing on particular sectors as the historiography has frequently done in the last decades, we here try to go a step further to offer a cross-sectoral analysis.

An Empirical Examination of Catalan Entrepreneurial Dynasties

A relatively recent research about 400 family firms in Catalonia in 1999, with a turnover of more than 1.2 million euros, showed that of a total sample of 7,899 firms with sales of more than 1.2 million euros and legal residence in Catalonia, 65 per cent were family-owned and controlled and their employment was 57.1 per cent of the sample and sales 54.9 per cent of the sample.[9] The most important sector in which these family firms developed their activities was metal manufacturing (more than 70 per cent of the firms of this sector in Catalonia were family firms), followed by the chemical sector (53 per cent of the firms of this sector in Catalonia were family firms). Only 6.8 per cent of them had given full executive responsibilities to outsiders. More family control usually ran parallel to decreasing dimension and sales, and usually less family control was linked to bigger size and sales. Regarding longevity, 32 per cent were founded after 1970, 41.4 per cent between 1940 and 1969, 15.9 per cent between 1910 and 1939 and 10.8 per cent before 1910. The contrasts with average percentages for Spain (according to the sample of Gallo in 1989) were striking, as in this Spanish sample the percentages of firms were 75 per cent in first generation, 16 per cent in second generation, 8 per cent in third generation and 1 per cent in fourth or more generations.[10] However, percentages regarding generation ownership and control among the 107 members of the Spanish Instituto de la Empresa Familiar (IEF) were closer to the Catalan ones: first generation 13 per cent, second 42 per cent, third 21 per cent and fourth or more 24 per cent.[11] Catalan family firms at the end of the twentieth century performed in a similar way compared with North American family firms in terms of longevity: in 1997 in the United States 32 per cent of family firms were on first generation of family control, 41 per cent on the second one, 16 per cent on the third one, and 11 per cent on fourth or more.[12]

Our study, which focuses more precisely only on 'historical' family firms with at least two family generations in control of the firm, demonstrates and confirms that there is a large number of historical family firms in Catalonia. Of a total number of 84 Catalan large family firms, 15 were born before the twentieth century, 18 during the first third of the twentieth century, 43 during Franco's regime and 8 after 1975. The tables provided in the appendix to this chapter present data for the year 2005 about 84 family firms (55 of them internationalized) with legal residence in Catalonia, with at least 40 million euros turnover and some members of at least the second generation of the family with managerial respon-sibilities (a sign of their willingness to keep working in the family business).[13] Half of them were founded before the Spanish Civil War, which means a big success of endurance in the territory despite the political and economic turmoil suffered by entrepreneurs since that time. Many also started their internationali-zation strategies before the war, though of course the big rush to conquer foreign markets took place after Franco's death as conditions drastically improved with democracy and integration in European institutions. There are many examples of medium family firms that internationalized between the late nineteenth cen-tury and the early 1930s, in specialized regionally embedded market niches like paper-making, alcoholic beverages, food production and cork or book manufac-turing. Latin America and France were the preferred destinations of this Spanish foreign activity, and some even tried the United States market.

From the late eighteenth century through the mid-twentieth century, Catalo-nia led the industrialization process in Spain. This leading position was based on a set of institutional reforms introduced in the fifteenth century as well as on its strategic position in the western Mediterranean. As a result, Catalan agriculture soon became market-oriented. Not only at a national scale, since the demand for Catalan wines and spirits soared through the seventeenth and eighteenth centu-ries in the shadow of the American empire. All this favoured the accumulation of capital as well as the dissemination of mercantile attitudes and aptitudes across the region. It was on this favourable soil that the first attempts to introduce Eng-lish technical and commercial innovations took place.

As in most parts of Europe, in Catalonia the first industrialization wave focused on consumer, labour-intensive industries such as textiles, metal and food. It developed under a strong foreign influence. Most of the enterprises that led the take-off of the Catalan industrialization between *c.* 1840 and *c.* 1890 were family owned and managed. The effects of this first generation of 'modern' entrepreneurs on the Catalan business and social structure were and remain huge.[14] As Catalo-nia became Spain's workshop and most advanced region, its economy increased its dependence on the textile (cotton and wool) industry (Nadal has stated that by the end of the century Catalonia produced 90 per cent of cotton, 63 per cent of wool, 55 per cent of silk, and 44 per cent of linen textiles in Spain)[15] and the business landscape was dominated by small and financially weak firms. The various crises (American Civil War, Great Depression, Spanish–American War) that took place during this period proved that this concentration was risky. As a result, Catalan entrepreneurs became increasingly risk-averse and protectionist. Collective research published on Catalan entrepreneurs shows that, notwith-standing this, a number of entrepreneurial families managed to diversify and build powerful business groups. An outstanding example of this is the Comillas group, created by the López and Güell colonial families, well studied by historian Martin Rodrigo. By the turn of the century, Comillas investments included not only textiles, but banking, shipping, insurance, tobacco, telecommunications and cement, among others. Its founders, Antonio López and Joan Güell, reached a prominent position in the Spanish political economy and society of the time. Around them we have identified a large number of families that played an important role in the modernization of the textile, food, metal and chemical industries of the nineteenth century: Bonaplata, Planas, Muntadas, Ferrer-Vidal, Serra-Bertrand, Batlló, Puig-Fabra, Marqués, Sedó, Rosés, Torras and Rivière, among others. Supported by Basque industrialists (specializing in iron and steel) and Castilian large landowners (specializing in wheat), these early entrepreneurs succeeded in shaping a highly protectionist framework in 1891 and 1906. During the subsequent six decades, the Catalan industry, sheltered from foreign competition by an increasingly protectionist legal framework, focused mainly on the domestic market.

It was in this sort of setting that the second industrialization wave took hold and a second generation of modern entrepreneurs and entrepreneurial dynasties emerged. Many of the already mentioned families kept on playing an important role in the Catalan economy. But there was a new batch of entrepreneurs, many of whose firms have actually survived and become large and international. This is the case of Raventós-Codorniu, Ferrer-Freixenet and Torres (wine); Uriach and Esteve (pharmaceuticals); Puig (perfume); Torras (paper); Godó and Salvat (publishers); Roca (metal); Rivière (steel wire); Roviralta (construction); and Cottet (optics). All of them are present in our database of the largest Catalan historical family firms.[16] Historical background of this second generation of entrepreneurs, active between the period 1890–1935, includes the impact of the colonial crisis and the Great War and the fall of early Catalan banks. In the 1930s Catalan business (its largest firms) was dominated by family firms, business groups (many of them multi-family groups) and foreign multinationals. The latter played a relevant role in the implementation of the Second Industrial Revolution and created many business opportunities for those Catalan families (old and new) able to execute business projects. Besides Comillas and some of the old names we find new families working in partnership with Ford, Nestle, Coca-Cola, American Standard, Bayer or Hoechst, as well as others working on their own.

Available biographies add qualitative information about the internationalization paths of Catalan family firms, eventually illuminating the process of creation of their competitive advantages. For instance, Pau Miquel i Costas opened his first distribution establishment in La Habana in 1880, the Mateu family opened the first subsidiary of their car factory Hispano Suiza in France in 1912, the Jorba family established the significant retail store Maison Jorba in Brussels in 1919, the Salvat family of publishers spread their exports throughout Latin America in the first decade of the twentieth century, Daniel Carasso established the first French factory of the Catalan family firm Danone in Lavallois Pret in 1932, agreements with foreign partners to transfer modern technology were signed by the Vilà family of textile industrialists with French partners in 1923. Perfume manufacturers like Myrurgia of the Monegal family used to hire French technicians to update their designs and marketing techniques in the 1920s. And the cork producer Joan Miquel i Avellí managed to transform his Manufacturas de Corcho (founded in 1916) into the European leader of cork manufacturing in 1929. Whereas some of these and similar firms disappeared after the war, many others were acquired along with their brands and know-how by surviving firms, and others like Miquel i Costas have endured as remarkable family firms able to adapt flexibly to new times.[17] In the Catalan case, the modernization of the textile, food, metal and chemical industry during the nineteenth and early twentieth centuries was carried out to a large extent by a few prominent families. It was the case of Bonaplata, Planas, Güell, López-Güell, Muntadas, Ferrer-Vidal, Serra-Bertrand, Batlló, Puig-Fabra, Marqués, Sedó, Rosés, Torras and Rivière, among others.[18] Many of the firms that have survived and grown large and international were born precisely in this region.

Roca, a world leading sanitary equipment manufacturer, is a case in point.[19] The small iron workshop of Ignasi Soler, established in Manlleu in 1830, was transformed several times during the nineteenth century to adapt first to steam power and to provide auxiliary services to the textile industry and house appliances demand, and afterwards by the end of that century to electric power and new urban demands. From repairing local horseshoes they were able to repair power looms and steam machines of the nearby villages and then learnt to build iron radiators for the Spanish market. The second and third generation of the Roca family of Manlleu learnt new techniques by travelling during their youth to Barcelona for apprenticeship in the best and most innovative metal mechanic manufacturing houses, many of them founded by foreigners like Casa Alexander or Talleres Pfeiffer. At the beginning of the twentieth century and right before the First World War some members of the fourth generation travelled to France and managed to be employed in the French subsidiary of the American Radiators Corporation (ARCo), the world leading manufacturer of iron and steel radiators and sanitary ceramic equipment. Martin and Matias led the production after massive imitation of the American products observed in France while their sister Angela managed the book accountancy and younger brother Josep Roca Soler attended high technical studies in two of the few innovative centres established in Spain in electronics and engineering: Instituto Electrónico de Sarrià and Escuela de Ingenieros of Barcelona. The new generation was able to juxtapose their different abilities and skills for new purposes. Their differentiating strategy regarding Spanish competitors was to combine innovation with technical service, and for this reason in 1929 they established a cooperation agreement with the big American corporation from which they learnt the new path of industrial activity: ARCo. This agreement meant sharing ownership (51 per cent for the American corporation), but led them to leadership in the Spanish market of radiators and sanitary ceramic equipment during almost all of the twentieth century. Today, they continue this strategy of cooperation abroad and are world leaders in this sector of activity.

The outbreak of the Spanish Civil War in 1936 put an end to the implementation of the Second Industrial Revolution. Even more harmful were the effects of the autarkic policy displayed in the next two decades, as it forced many small and middle-sized firms to integrate vertically and rely on low quality, expensive raw materials. At the same time, however, the new framework created opportunities for those entrepreneurs and family firms, old and new, able to survive and link their destinies with the new political order. Again we find a third generation of family entrepreneurship in the region that is best exemplified by the Carulla and Lara families. As a matter of fact, Table 5.2 in the appendix reveals that many of the surviving firms were founded under Franco's rule, a fact that suggests that extreme protectionism might have provided an advantage for many firms, limiting foreign and eventually also domestic competition. Tables in the appendix show further that surviving Catalan family firms still keep a strong industrial profile, with a remarkable specialization in food processing, chemicals and pharmaceuticals. This is consistent with the economic transformation undergone in the previous period and with Catalonia's industrial atmosphere. But it is also consistent with the sort of stimulus created by the otherwise irrational industrial policy of the 1940s and early 1950s. Interestingly, in technically complex industries such as chemical and pharmaceutical industries, autarky soon became rhetoric and domestic firms managed to get the necessary technological assistance from foreign firms. Catalan family firms kept on excelling at this, in some cases building on pre-war links, in others establishing new links. The overall business atmosphere, however, was suffocating (corruption dominated import licenses and the distribution of industrial inputs, for instance), so that both international contacts or skills and political connections became crucial to found a firm or keep it going. Anna Solé's preliminary results of her database on post-war surviving industrial firms in Catalonia show the pain suffered by larger firms in capital-intensive industries and the relatively massive survival of small and medium firms in the consumer goods industries and construction.[20]

Not many post-war family firms had the means or political influence needed to succeed in the poor yet protected Spanish market. A few examples will show how they found their own way into this market. Lluis Carulla started manu-

facturing concentrated soup cubes – introduced in Spain by the Swiss firm
Maggi – in 1937 under the Gallina Blanca brand, a process well studied by Javier
Moreno.[21] At the same time, the Catalan firm successfully adapted foreign ideas
and techniques to improve and diversify its production. Extensive radio – and
later, also television – advertising to reach the fragmented and badly connected
Spanish consumers soon became characteristic of the firm.[22] Andreu Costafreda
Montoliu, a baker since 1928 who struggled through the war and early post-war
period, soon realized that this sector of small and medium family firms could
only grow through collective action. In 1945 he created Compañía Auxiliar de
Panificación SA to represent better and legally to defend bakers of Barcelona as
well as providing them with social protection. He would later on found Panrico, one of the largest family firms in the second half of the twentieth century,
sold in 2006 to a British venture capital firm.[23] Another good example is Planeta, one of the ten most important publishing corporations of the world. José
Manuel Lara, a Sevillian established in Barcelona after the Civil War, bought the
small publishing firm Editorial Tartessos in 1944 and started the publication of
best-sellers written by American and Spanish authors, beginning in 1952 what
would become one of the most important marketing tools of the Spanish-speak-
ing publishing world, the Planeta novel prize.[24] A different example is Mier, a
firm founded by the two Asturian brothers Pedro and Ramón Mier Allende as
a radio shop in Barcelona in the late 1940s (Radio Lyra), the firm performed
radio repairs, and during the 1950s and 1960s slowly developed innovative car
antennas bought by foreign multinationals and auxiliary products for radio and
television. During the 1960s and 1970s the excellent relationships of the Mier
brothers with foreign world leaders in telecommunications (Philips, Fuba), their
promotion of associations in their sector and their stable links with Catalan
technical universities helped them become one of the few Spanish family firms
providing auxiliary products for the European AirSpace Agency (ESA) in 1985.
After the 1950s and during the 1960s they flourished in construction, printing
and publishing, food and beverages, soap and perfumery and light metallurgy.

Those firms that either established enduring relationships with foreign
partners or ventured into foreign markets in spite of the prevailing adverse circumstances became leaders at home. It is the case in the 1960s and early 1970s
of the above-mentioned firms Panrico (Costafreda family) and Gallina Blanca
(Carulla family) and the continuous efforts in this direction of early internationalized family firms such as the sparkling wine manufacturer Freixenet (Ferrer
family). Also the efforts to build brands and internationalize were remarkable in
the perfume (Puig family) and pharmaceutical (Esteve family) industries in Catalonia.[25] Growth required new strategies and structures, like in the managerial
corporations. Organizational routines, lay-outs and new distribution channels
started to appear and adapt to the new realities of increased complexities in pro-

duction and distribution. However, professionalization of the management took place slowly in comparison with the managerial corporations and with a strong component of family individuals. This process in the most capital-intensive family firms could lead to conflicts with shop-floor employees and with non-family managers. New organizational routines often came through technology transfer from abroad, which was increasingly possible after 1959 through partnerships with foreign firms. This strategy allowed growing family firms to modernize layouts without losing ownership and control. This happened since the 1960s for instance in Agrolimen with the American Purina in the food industry, Rivière with Belgium firm Bekaert in steel wire manufacturing, Mier Comunicaciones with German firm Fuba, and many others in the chemical and engineering sectors. These agreements provided, depending on each case, improvements in technology, marketing and management. Another strategy to get professional managers among the family members of big family firms in the 1950s and 1960s was the promotion and support of private business schools (Esade and IESE in Barcelona, created in 1958). Only rarely in these years did senior family managers send their offspring abroad to receive high technical and professional training, though when this happened it helped technology transfer, as it was the case in Rivière or in CELSA, which bought Rivière in 1999.

At a regional level, during the 1950s–70s, Catalonia remained home to many of the most outward-looking family firms of the time. Some of those already mentioned performed well during the early phase of the dictatorship: Freixenet, Codorniu, Roca, Rivière, Torras, Ribera, Myrurgia. Others transformed themselves successfully: Uriach, Esteve, Andreu, Puig, Torras, Roca. Others built their firms from scrap: Planeta, Carulla, Ferrer, Almirall, Pujol-Ficosa, Rubiralta-Celsa. Many adapted American techniques of productivity gains from textbooks or Spanish engineers trained abroad who worked in the public and private sector, as well as from the modernizing institutions that proliferated throughout these years inside and outside Spain, particularly consulting firms and business schools. This does not mean that privileges and nepotism were being replaced by meritocracy. But the dissemination of modern management ideas and techniques undoubtedly helped many entrepreneurs and heirs to improve their firms' performance. The spread of modern marketing and advertising techniques is a case in point. Note that brands are essential in the industries where family firms are hegemonic. Conditions for their development improved dramatically after 1959, as the Spanish government gave its autarkic policy up and opened the door to foreign investment under the advice of international institutions. Thus the third generation of family firms and enterprising families that we have identified was strongly influenced by the timid yet irreversible liberalization of the Spanish market, and many of those firms had first-hand, positive or negative, experience of foreign competition. One should not underestimate, finally, the role of Spanish massive emigration and European rising tourism in the updating of many Catalan family firms between the 1950s and 1970s.

The industrial crisis of the 1970s, along with the political uncertainty unleashed by Franco's death in 1975, posed many challenges to Catalan family capitalism. The textile industry, which still represented a large part of it, was hit hard. In fact, the textile crisis has constituted the background of Catalonia's economic development from then to the present day. On the other side, the creation of a Catalan administration eager to support Catalan entrepreneurship, Spain's integration into the European Union in 1986 and the many opportunities brought about by globalization, can be viewed as positive. It was within this new institutional environment that Catalonia, and the whole of Spain, experienced the longest and most intense period of economic progress and a fourth generation of family firms emerged. Interesting as they might be, most of them are not included in our sample, as they had not yet undergone their first succession process in 2005. But there are some interesting examples, like Ficosa, Arbora, Tarradellas, Bon Preu, Corporacion Age or Lamigraf. Even more interesting is the way in which older firms and families have consolidated their strong position in the domestic market while seizing the opportunities of globalization.

Relatively Neglected Determinants of Entrepreneurship: Dynasties and Social Capital

The concept of social capital was developed in the late 1980s by social scientists in several fields willing to understand the role of civil society in modernization processes. By analogy with notions of physical and human capital, social capital refers to features of social organization such as networks, norms and social trust that facilitate coordination and cooperation for mutual benefit.[26] In a recent survey of the role of networking in American business, historian Pamela Laird has shown that social capital, defined as access to the circles that control and distribute information, training and opportunities, is an important ingredient of modern capitalism. Business, indeed, is a social process and as such cannot be understood without being aware of and examining the social dynamics that pull some people while pushing others out of business opportunity.[27] These dynamics are embedded in the societies where entrepreneurship arises and develops. In many cases, the mechanisms through which social capital works are not visible, but in others they become embodied in commercial or professional associations. Trust and engagement are two facets of the same underlying factor: social capital. Shared expectations and goals keep formal and informal networks going. From a business historical perspective, the interesting questions about social capital are related to the social capitalization process (how it arises and develops in a particular region or country) and its impact on entrepreneurship and business performance.

Social capital used for business purposes has concentrated and is still concentrated in Europe around a few cities and districts. Extensive literature in economic history has provided theory and examples about the formation of industrial districts in Europe and about the institutions that have created economic agglomeration effects, and an 'industrial' atmosphere of knowledge exchange, in the last two centuries.

Usually human and social capital formation has been studied from the shop floor of the factories or from the individual platform of particular Schumpeterian entrepreneurs difficult to replicate. However, networks of entrepreneurs make up also, collectively, a good deal of a regional system of human capital creation. How can we study in the long term the identity and role of such networks? Dynasties, to start with one good example, were a platform of entrepreneurial networking during a century in Catalonia, as we have seen in the previous section. Associations of entrepreneurs and firms were, also, another important focus of entrepreneurial networking that favoured social capital formation in the long term in the region.

We do not have much statistical data about associationism of entrepreneurs in Spain with a long-term perspective. However, for this study we have used registers of associations for the city of Barcelona, available in the main Spanish cities since the 1869 and 1887 legislation ruling associations in the country, a source of information that has not been exploited so far for business history research. Our study makes a first attempt at using this source to get a glimpse at the evolution and intensity of networking among entrepreneurs in the main industrial region of Spain during a century, by focusing on the case of the city of Barcelona and its associations of entrepreneurs during the years 1870 to 1969 (Table 5.1 in appendix). The registers of associations included information obtained at the city level of all kinds of associations, which has required a close reading of the information in order to find only associations among entrepreneurs and companies. The conclusions of this information are interesting: 1. most of these associations were created by small and medium enterprises (SMEs, a neglected subject in the Spanish literature about associationism); 2. only a minority were promoted by medium or relatively large firms; and 3. their main official goal was to protect and foster their business and 'class' interests.

The most important years of registration and creation of associations of entrepreneurs in Barcelona were between the last two decades of the nineteenth century and the outbreak of the Spanish Civil War in 1936, in close relationship with: new legislation that allowed and promoted associationism; the final crisis of the guild traditions of associationism; the rise of the labour unions and socialist ideologies among workers; a strong protectionist commercial policy at home and abroad; and the crisis of traditional markets and firms provoked by the spread of technologies and transport systems of the Second Technological Revolution. In these times of big turmoil and uncertainty associations may have played a strong role in creating social capital that could have benefited information transfer and contacts to design a new entrepreneurial landscape in the city. Table 5.1 in the appendix shows the expansion of associations of entrepreneurs in this context and the enormous brake in this formation of social capital that the Francoist dictatorship meant with its extremely regulatory legislation.

A strong and enduring associationist experience among entrepreneurs in a dynamic economic region or city reveals a high accumulation of intangible assets from which firms benefit, according to literature about districts, clusters and social capital.[28] It is not at all surprising that another important intangible asset like brands, from which firms greatly benefit in the long term to differentiate their products in highly competitive markets, have also been historically highly concentrated in total numbers and in *per capita* figures in this region since 1850 until at least mid-twentieth century.[29]

Dynasties and associations have paved the way to collective action in the region in the past and also in recent times. The organization of the interests of Spanish family firms has been led to a large extent (and very effectively) by a group of Catalan firms.[30] They had international experience and contacts and the strong support of the regional government. The lobby of large Spanish family firms, with its origin in Barcelona, led by interests of Catalan policymakers and entrepreneurs facing the challenge of integration in Europe, has actively promoted the world's most important network of university chairs in family firm studies, with 36 chairs where 200 university professors collaborate to teach on average 1,800 students a year in the whole of Spain by the end of 2008. Furthermore, institutions such as the business school IESE, founded in Barcelona in 1958, the many more or less formal Catalan clubs that exist around the world and public institutions aimed to promote the internationalization of Catalan firms within the Catalan government and the chambers of trade and industry, among other institutions, have given support to the networking and lobbying activities of Catalan dynasties of entrepreneurs.

Is the contribution of entrepreneurial dynasties and associations of entrepreneurs to the creation of social capital, in Catalonia, an exception in the Spanish context? Further studies about these entrepreneurial networks, for other regions, will help provide some answers.

Appendix

Table 5.1: Associations of Entrepreneurs and Firms in the City of Barcelona, 1870–1969.[31]

Years	Inhabitants Barcelona City	New Associations Registered in the City (all kinds)	New Associations Registered in the City (of firms and entrepreneurs only)
1870–9	248,943	105	0
1880–9	272,481	1,589	11
1890–9	509,589	1,333	58
1900–9	533,000	2,116	153
1910–9	587,411	2,027	302
1920–9	710,335	2,264	607
1930–9	1,005,565	2,143	210
1940–9	1,081,175	549	2
1950–9	1,280,179	601	1
1960–9	1,557,863	241	0
Total		12,968	1,344

Table 5.2: The 84 Largest Catalan Historical Family Firms in 2005.[32]

Group Name	Families	Date of Foundation	Sector	Turnover (€m)	Employees
FCC	Koplowitz	1900/1992	Construction	7,090	67,562
Celsa (I)	Rubiralta (1st–2nd)	1967	Metal	2,757	5,753
Caprabo	Carbó	1959	Retailing	2,300	19,100
Roca (I)	Roca	1880/1929	Construction (sanitary equipment)	1,669	16,000
Catalana Occidente (I)	Serra	1864	Insurance	1,502	2,824
Cirsa (I)	Lao (1st–2nd)	1968	Gambling	1,155	11,000
Colega	Daurella	1951	Food & beverages	1,125	1,411
Puig (I)	Puig (3rd)	1914	Perfume	962	5,250
Almirall (I)	Gallardo (2nd–3rd)	1944	Pharmaceuticals	962	3,200
Planeta (I)	Lara (2nd)	1949	Communication	960	4,725
Miquel Alimentació	Miquel	1925	Food & beverages	836	3,700
Ficosa (I)	Pujol-Tarragó (2nd)	1976	Motor	824	6,550
Esteve (I)	Esteve (3rd)	1929	Pharmaceuticals	818	2,469
Panrico (I)	Costafreda (2nd)	1960s (sold 2006)	Food & beverages	731	8,284
Damm	Coll	1876/1910	Food & beverages	656	1,785
Condis	Condal	1961	Food & beverages	652	4,650
Arbola Holding	Carulla	1978	Chemicals	650	125
Comsa (I)	Miarnau	1934	Construction	642	1,030

Group Name	Families	Date of Foundation	Sector	Turnover (€m)	Employees
Copisa	Cornadó	1961	Construction	637	627
Molins (I)	Molins	1929	Construction (concrete)	594	2,485
Borges (I)	Pont (3rd–4th)	1896	Food & beverages	540	1,082
Grifols (I)	Grífols (2nd)	1940	Pharmaceuticals	524	3,443
Colomer (I)	Colomer (2nd)	1924/2000	Perfume	486	2,310
Uniland (I)	Rumeu/Fradera	1896/ 1901/1973	Construction (concrete)	472	1,301
Tarradellas (I)	Tarradellas (2nd)	1983	Food & beverages	424	950
Emte	Sumarroca	1961	Construction	400	2,020
Freixenet (I)	Ferrer-Bonet	1861	Food & beverages	379	1,323
Nutrexpa (I)	Ferrero	1940	Food & beverages	327	1,333
Bon Preu Sau	Font	1974	Retailing	315	1,918
Godó	Godó	1881	Communication	311	1,500
Editorial Prensa Ibérica	Moll	1872	Communication	309	na
Mecalux (I)	Carrillo (2nd)	1969	Construction (logistics)	292	2,170
Ferrer (I)	Ferrer-Salat (2nd)	1947	Pharma	274	1,174
Agrolimen (I)	Carulla (2nd)	1937	Food & beverages	261	520
Chupa Chups (I)	Bernat	1958 (sold 2005)	Food & beverages	260	1,170
Gallo (I)	Espona	1946	Food & beverages	226	436
Vall Companys	Vall Companys	1967	Food & beverages	221	89
Ros Roca (I)	Roca (3rd)	1953	Engineering	218	11
Codorniu (I)	Raventós	1872/1926	Food & beverages	198	1,006
Soler y Palau (I)	Soler Palau	1951	Engineering	190	515
Grupo de Estampación Sabadell	Bonet	1965	Engineering	186	1,165
Habitat (I)	Figueras (2nd)	1953	Real estate	180	156
Torres (I)	Torres	1870	Food & beverages	176	800
Frigicoll	Coll	1967	Retailing	175	323
Hesperia (I)	Castro (2nd)	1971	Tourism	171	3,300
Alimentaria de Guissona	Alsina	1959	Food & beverages	168	174
Superficies de Alimentación	Sorli	1979	Retailing	165	1,130
HUSA (I)	Gaspart (2nd)	1930	Tourism	162	2,800
Lacer (I)	Andress	1949	Pharmaceuticals	160	600
Lípidos Santiga	Soler	1968	Textiles	159	106
Miquel y Costas (I)	Miquel	1725	Paper	157	913
Uriach (I)	Uriach (5th)	1838	Pharmaceuticals	153	753

Group Name	Families	Date of Foundation	Sector	Turnover (€m)	Employees
Simón (I)	Simón	1916	Electrical equipment	145	930
Indo (I)	Cottet y Colomer	1902/ 1937–8	Optics	144	1,722
Corporación Age	Boada/Gummà/ Masferrer	1981	Construction	143	1,025
Colomer Munmany (I)	Colomer	1792	Leather	140	913
Aceros Bergara (I)	Boixareu	1945	Metal	132	102
Titán (I)	Folch	1917	Chemicals	137	624
Synthesia Española	Zuloaga	1964	Chemicals	127	203
Vichy Catalán (I)	Renat/Casa/Murla/ Montalat/Lluansí	1901	Food & beverages	122	725
Campí y Jové (I)	Campí y Jové (2nd– 3rd)	1923	Chemicals	120	82
Basi (I)	Basi (2nd–3rd)	1948	Fashion	111	415
Noel (I)	Bosch	1940	Food & beverages	109	449
Cuatrecasas (I)	Cuatrecasas (3rd)	1926	Legal services	106	350
Pronovias (I)	Palatchi (2nd)	1922/1968	Textiles	103	23
Ausa (I)	Perramón	1956	Machine manufacturing	98	353
Comexi (I)	Cifra	1954	Machine manufacturing	85	252
Abressa (I)	Dude	1971	Construction (concrete)	85	40
Espuña (I)	Espuña	1947	Food & beverages	79	459
Goma Camps	Goma Camps	1941	Paper	77	275
Sacresa	Sanahuja	1960s	Real estate	75	69
Sedatex (I)	Pich	1886/1940	Textiles	75	160
Colortex	Taberner	1967	Textiles	75	686
Lamigraf	Colomer/Ibáñez	1975	Paper	70	205
Casademont (I)	Casademont (2nd)	1960s	Food & beverages	69	485
Prefabricados Prensados	Pujol	1979	Construction (concrete)	68	78
Alier	Alier	1934	Paper	68	259
Murtra (I)	Murtra	1897/1922	Textiles	67	316
Palex (I)	Knuth (3rd)	1955	Chemicals	65	126
Inoxcrom	Vaqué	1964	Paper	61	581
Galerías Tarragona	Tarragona	1965	Furniture	55	374
AC Marca (I)	Marca	1922/1999	Chemicals	52	254
Chocovic (I)	Rius	1977 (1872 Arumí)	Food & beverages	45	120
Kettal	Alorda	1964	Furniture	40	500

(I) = Internationalized.

Table 5.3: Date of Foundation of the 84 Largest Catalan Historical Family Firms in 2005.[33]

Date	Number of Firms	% of Total
Before 1900	15	17.85
1900–39	18	21.42
1940–75	43	51.19
After 1975	8	9.52

Table 5.4: Main Specialization of the 84 Largest Catalan Historical Family Firms in 2005.

Sector	Number of Firms	% of Total
Food and Beverages	21	25.00
Chemicals and Pharmaceuticals	14	16.66
Construction and Real Estate	13	15.47
Industries Other than Food and Chemicals (textiles, paper, metal, machinery, furniture, optics, motor,	20	23.80
Total of Primarily Industrial Firms	68	80.95
Retailing	4	4.76
Communication	3	3.57
Engineering	3	3.57
Other	6	7.14

Table 5.5: Catalan Historical Internationalized Family Firms in Spanish Perspective, 2005.[34]

Region	Number of Firms	Founded Before 1936–9	Founded 1940–75	Founded after 1975	Dominant Field	Internationalized before 1936	Internationalized 1940–86	Internationalized after 1986
Catalonia	55 (37.67%)	28	26	1	15 FB / 12 CP / 7 C / 5 TF	4	16	35
Madrid	21 (14.38%)	6	11	4	4 C / 4 PC	0	7	14
Valencia	11 (7.53%)	2	8	1	6 C	1	2	8
Andalusia	10 (6.84%)	5	5	0	4 FB	3	3	4
Basque Country	9 (6.16%)	7	2	0	–	1	2	6
Aragon	7 (4.79%)	4	3	0	–	0	2	5
North Castile	7 (4.79%)	2	5	0	6 FB	0	0	7
Balearic Islands	6 (4.10%)	2	3	1	5 T	0	2	4
Galicia	6 (4.10%)	4	2	0	5 FB	0	4	2
South Castile	5 (3.42%)	2	3	0	5 FB	0	1	4
Rioja	3	0	3	0	–	0	0	3
Asturias	2	1	1	0	–	0	2	0
Murcia	2	2	0	0	2 FB	0	0	2
Cantabria	1	1	0	0	–	0	1	0
Navarre	1	0	1	0	–	0	0	1
Spain	146	66 (45.20%)	73 (50%)	7 (4.79%)	46 FB / 18 CR / 17 CP / 9 TF / 7 T / 6 E / 5 PC	9 (6.16%)	42 (28.76%)	95 (65.06%)

FB = Food and beverages; CP = Chemicals and pharmaceuticals;
C = Construction; TF = Textiles and fashion;
PC = Press and communications; T = Tourism; E = Engineering.

6 ENTREPRENEURIAL CULTURE OR INSTITUTIONS? A TWENTIETH-CENTURY RESOLUTION

James Foreman-Peck and Peng Zhou

Introduction

What does a favourable culture contribute to entrepreneurship, compared with other influences, such as appropriate institutions? Entrepreneurial business often provided outlets for the energies and enterprise of national and religious minorities who were blocked from rising through the state apparatus. Max Weber instanced Poles in Russia and eastern Prussia, Huguenots in France under Louis XIV, Nonconformists and Quakers in England, and Jews for two thousand years.[1] For Weber it was the (institutional) barrier, not the culture, that explained the entrepreneurial precocity of these minorities. His most famous supposed positive cultural influence on business and economic development, the Protestant Ethic, was something extra, he maintained.

Virtually the converse of the Protestant Ethic, the 'cultural critique' of British capitalism looks instead at how culture *constrained* entrepreneurship. For the later nineteenth century Martin Wiener proposed that British culture encouraged 'gentrification', exactly what Protestants, or at least Puritans, would never accept, for it entailed enjoying their wealth.[2] A pervasive anti-industrial and anti-business culture especially transmitted through middle-class education was supposedly responsible for Britain's 'industrial decline' in these years.[3]

There is more evidence for David Landes's assertion that culture makes all the difference to economic development.[4] He focuses on expatriate entrepreneurial performance; Jews and Calvinists throughout much of Europe, Chinese in East and South-East Asia, and Indians in East Africa, when thwarted by 'bad government' at home or, more generally, by poor institutions. By moving away from the constraining institutions or government, but taking their culture with them, expatriates' cultural inheritances were allowed to flourish.

Landes's European examples may consist of groups prevented from rising through conventional paths to power and prestige choosing business as an alternative, without necessarily any cultural predisposition to entrepreneurship. Economic migrants are not subject to this objection, but at least two potential problems remain with Landes's analysis.

The first is that culture is not necessarily autonomous or exogenous to economic activity or to institutions. As Landes points out, Thai culture for instance has responded to economic growth in the reallocation of time away from monastic apprenticeship towards making money.[5] Perhaps because of obvious cultural changes in Britain over the quarter century from 1980, the 'cultural critique' is now less popular. British culture, and entrepreneurial culture in particular, on one interpretation proved malleable with changes in institutions, and the economy responded accordingly. Conversely, when institutions are inimical to entrepreneurship, a nation's culture may be moulded into the same form. If culture is very pliable, how can it explain vigour and contribution to economic development, which must necessarily be a long drawn out process?

The second problem is whether expatriate entrepreneurs are a random selection from their culture. Emigrants may be those with more drive or dissatisfaction than the average of their community. If so, their entrepreneurship abroad may give an upward biased indication of the entrepreneurial orientation of the country of origin. Those that get out may be those who choose not to adjust their expectations and behaviour to the dominant national institutions.

The present chapter offers a resolution of these two difficulties. To address the first, entrepreneurial cultures are measured over the twentieth century independently of institutional influences. Given the great institutional changes of the period, persistence of culture must imply a form of autonomous existence. For the second, migrant entrepreneurs in their adopted country are compared with a large number of other immigrant nationalities, of which they are perhaps no more atypical than the majority of their country of origin. This approach excludes non-immigrants on the grounds that they have not been selected in the same way as migrants.

Having constructed a cross-national index of entrepreneurial culture and a measure of entrepreneurial cultural persistence or autonomy, it is possible to offer a more convincing assessment of the relative contributions of culture and institutions to entrepreneurship. In turn these findings provide some hints about the roles of entrepreneurial culture in economic development. The first section explains the measures of entrepreneurial culture chosen, followed by a description of the data, then the statistical model of entrepreneurship and culture is set out and in the final section the results of the analysis are presented.

Measuring Entrepreneurial Culture

Occupational choices of individuals with exceptional energy, restlessness or ambition depend upon both the institutions and culture of their society, as well as their position in it. The decision to become an entrepreneur, identifying and taking advantage of new or unexploited opportunities, is a high level one that can take a variety of forms. In some circumstances many entrepreneurial types choose crime, terrorism, politics or even lobbying as careers.[6]

Culture can be defined as: 'those customary beliefs and values that ethnic, religious, and social groups transmit fairly unchanged from generation to generation'.[7] The basic idea of an entrepreneurial culture is that shared belief systems, similar ways of earning a living and common educational arrangements could combine to create 'cultures' more or less favourable to entrepreneurship. Translated into individualistic economic concepts, the hypothesis is that cultures can influence time preference, work-leisure trade-offs and risk attitudes. With beliefs that generate lower time preference, a culture will encourage more saving, which could increase the opportunity to start new businesses. Cultures with lower values of leisure are likely to create more entrepreneurs, because successful enterprise requires a great deal of sustained effort. Similar outcomes can be expected in cultures that are less cautious – for start-ups are risky.

A beneficial culture often supposedly induces hard work, high savings and honesty, yielding economic growth. Alternatively the right institutions may have this effect; appropriate tax regimes, secure and clearly defined property rights and an impartial judiciary may encourage effort, thrift and integrity, with the concomitant economic pay-off. Evidence of the importance of institutions for entrepreneurship is that the legal environment and costs of setting up a firm strongly influence differences in business start-up rates between countries.[8]

A strong and persistent entrepreneurial culture does not guarantee successful entrepreneurship, nor does it carry implications for the sectors in which enterprise will be exercised. These depend upon governance institutions, human capital, industrial experience in country of origin, technology and entry barriers, among other considerations. Individuals inheriting a highly entrepreneurial culture are simply more likely to exercise their initiative and ingenuity; how they do this, and with what outcomes, will be determined by institutions and history.

Recent research has begun the attempt to quantify culture's impact upon the contemporary economy in general and upon entrepreneurship in particular. Economies in which more people claim religious convictions apparently tend to grow faster, other things being equal, whereas those with higher proportions of church attendance expand more slowly.[9] An explanation for this association is that church attendance consumes resources, whereas religious convictions motivate. A second cross-country study found that general labour force participation and especially female labour force participation is higher in 'Protestant tradition' countries (including the United Kingdom, the United States, Denmark, Sweden and Norway) when other influences have been controlled;[10] the 'Ethic' apparently still possesses explanatory power.

Another dimension of culture is trust. Religous beliefs are systematically related to how much individuals trust others (in the United States). The chance that a person will found their own firm, self-employment, is also significantly linked to the trust of the individual (again in the United States). Trusting others increases the likelihood of self-employment by 1.3 percentage points (14 per cent of the overall self-employment chance).[11]

How should we measure entrepreneurship that is encouraged or discouraged by culture? We might distinguish between the behaviour or choices of those who were already entrepreneurs and the choice of becoming an entrepreneur.[12] In the first category falls Rubinstein's pioneering 1981 study using non-landed wealth at death.[13] This has the advantage of identifying more and less successful entrepreneurs, but does not control for inheritance or opportunity. It may give undue prominence to the thrifty – and to the successful if the concern is with entrepreneurs as a whole. In any case the most widely used indicator of entrepreneurship is the second category, starting a firm. This is not identical to self-employment (the measure used by Guiso et al. discussed above), for some self-employed may inherit their businesses. Others may simply work on their own account without being in any way innovative, little different from wage labour but without the contractual security. So the practical definition of entrepreneurship adopted is creating a firm that employs people. The contention here is that becoming an employer (in an incorporated business) is an entrepreneurial act in the sense that it involves taking on risk. It also involves being innovative to the extent that setting up any business requires looking for a gap in the market, however narrowly defined. Obviously individuals will show varying degrees of innovativeness and risk-bearing but these need not be considered for the collective concept of culture.

To measure the impact of culture on the firm start-up rate we need to know how those brought up in one country perform in a social and economic environment where institutions and market opportunities are different. Moreover to calibrate the measure we require the performance of persons from a range of different cultures in the same environment. The United States provides a convenient laboratory both to test the persistence of distinctive entrepreneurial cultures over the twentieth century and to compare their performance. We can contrast the propensies of immigrants from different countries to start firms there. This avoids the bias of comparing immigrants with indigenous entrepreneurs. Even though migrants may be exceptional in their originating country, each immigrant group will be exceptional to the same extent unless there are historically unusual 'push' factors that must be identified qualitatively.

We construct two measures of enterprise. The first is simply the chances of a member of the immigrant group being an employer, relative to other groups. The second is the chance of becoming an employer, holding constant a range of other influences on the outcome. To allow for the objection that experience influences opportunities we control for different sectors in which employment or self-employment takes place. Property ownership influences availability of collateral needed to raise finance for start-up firms, while age, gender, marital status, years of residence in the United States, education and naturalization all may determine the likelihood of entrepreneurship. So these are included in the model that estimates the chances of entrepreneurship, other things being equal.[14]

The United States Immigrant Samples

During the twentieth as well as the nineteenth centuries immigrants from a wide range of cultures arrived in the common environment of the United States and some of them started their own businesses. Their different chances of entrepreneurship provide information about the contribution of their origins.

Cultural persistence here is the stability of entrepreneurial propensities between the 1910 and 2000 United States censuses.[15] Although migrants may be selectively recruited in their countries of emigration (migrants who are not 'pushed' could have more 'get up and go'), this will be true of those from every country. Economic costs of movement differ by original location, as does the strength of the push factor, but normally these will only affect the relative volumes of migrant groups. Persecution may be a reason to migrate for large numbers. Yet only when this or other processes select the more or less entrepreneurial from a country does it affect the present 'experiment'.

A root problem is the linking of national categories to national, as against minority, culture. Armenian immigrant entrepreneurs were prominent in many countries at different periods of history without an Armenian 'country of origin'.[16] Again, numbers of Greeks living outside Greece in 1907 were much greater than those within the country and Greek migration from Ottoman-dominated areas, especially for political reasons, was common.[17] Consequently, those migrants recording Ottoman countries of origin may well have been ethnic Greeks before 1914. Minority migration from the Middle East and Turkey was exacerbated by the rise of nationalism there after 1945 as well. Orhan Pamuk wrote in 2005 that the cosmopolitan Istanbul he knew as a child had disappeared by the time he reached adulthood. The riots of 1955 seem to have been an especially good reason to leave; 'More Greeks have left Istanbul over the past fifty years than in the fifty years following 1453'.[18] Further north, migrants registering Russian

Empire country origins in the 1910 United States census are very likely to have been Jews because of the pogroms from the 1880s.

Even when culture is genuinely identified with country of origin, it may not persist over the twentieth century, because of changed conditions in the origin country. In this case the concept has poor explanatory power for long-term entrepreneurship. But there is a considerable body of evidence that particular groups are more entrepreneurial than others at points in time. Turks in Germany were twice as likely to choose self-employment as any other immigrant group there in 2000.[19] This does not seem to reflect a willingness to accept lower rewards because the earnings of self-employed Turks are no different from those of self-employed southern or east Europeans, including immigrants who have become German citizens. Korean/Chinese entrepreneurs starting firms in the United States are distinguished from their non-minority equivalent by their possession of substantially more financial capital.[20] Controlling for firm and owner traits, comparison groups of non-minority and Asian American non-immigrant self-employed borrowers had greater access to loan sources than Korean and Chinese immigrants. But high equity capital investment from the family household wealth offset this disadvantage. In the United Kingdom migrants are more likely to engage in new business activity, although recent ethnic minority migration decreases the odds.[21] Comparing self-employment by the American-born and immigrants in the 1980 and 1990 United States censuses (and therefore including family firms – inheritance of self-employment) yields a substantial positive ethnic effect for Middle East origin, while Mexican and Caribbean origins strongly reduce self-employment chances.[22]

In the present study, we do not compare immigrants with those born in United States but with each other. The American-born are more likely to inherit a family business, which also takes individuals into the employer category. Migrant self-employment through inheritance by contrast is unlikely and is probably in start-ups. The present sample was further restricted to immigrant origins that were quite numerous in 1910 in order to make the comparison over time more consistent.[23] But the highly entrepreneurial Middle East was subsequently disaggregated to examine whether particular sources were driving the result.[24] We exclude 'working on own account' in the early period and 'unincorporated business' in the later period, focusing on employers and incorporated businesses, on the grounds that these categories correspond more closely to the conventional idea of an entrepreneur.

We have excluded agricultural employment from the sample because migrants are likely to experience greater difficulty entering agriculture as entrepreneurs and most agricultural self-employment could not be classified as entrepreneurial. Agriculture provides little understanding of urban industrial entrepreneurship. So with Mexican immigrants for instance, we ask whether they are employers or employees in manufacturing or services; we filter out their propensity to work in agriculture.

Countries of origin of immigrants to the United States at different times depended on a variety of mainly 'push factors'. The 'hungry forties' of the nineteenth century sent large numbers of German and Irish migrants across the Atlantic. Persecution of Jews triggered another wave of migrants from Russia and Poland beginning in the 1880s. Population growth coupled with weak economic development encouraged increasing migration from southern and eastern Europe in the 1890s. A buoyant demand for agricultural labour and proximity increased Mexican immigration in the first decade of the twentieth century.

Cultural differences between these immigrant waves were widely recognized at the time, and reflected in their wages. Hatton's (2000) measurement of immigrant earning power, translated as 'immigrant quality', shows Jews among the highest earners before 1914, with coefficients identical to those of the Dutch and Finnish.[25] Jewish immigrants were also highly entrepreneurial in both London and New York in the generation before the First World War.[26] By contrast migrants from Syria and Turkey recorded the largest ethnic handicap in wage earning. One influence on wages could be legislation by many American states to exclude aliens from practising certain occupations, such as that of physician or lawyer. Nine states required barbers to be American citizens.[27]

A possible explanation for difference in national self-employment patterns, (and perhaps an implication of Hatton and Leigh in 2007) is that 'pioneer immigrants' are less accepted in the employment market and they more often become self-employed.[28] Once the particular migration stream has formed a community integrated into the culture, or better accepted by the host community, they are more likely to slot into paid employment.[29] Here self-employment is casual or insecure and badly remunerated employment. Whereas the entrepreneurial but low-paid migrants from Syria-Lebanon might fit this characterization in 1910, the higher paid but also entrepreneurial Russian-Polish Jews do not. The category of work for immigrants corresponding to this hypothesis is not that of employer, but working on own account and unincorporated business.

Persistence of entrepreneurial propensities over the twentieth century is a vital control for possible influences such as the level of development or income in the country of origin or pioneer immigrant status as determinants of entrepreneurial choice. This is because countries of origin are chosen for the year 2000 that were also substantial sources of migrants in 1910. A pioneer immigrant group in 1910 could not be a pioneer group three generations later. While British migrants in the late nineteenth century may have been less likely to be pushed into entrepreneurship in the United States because of union control of workplaces,[30] this transnational control had disappeared many decades before the end of the twentieth century. A country that was relatively backward in 1910, and therefore whose citizens might have been unable to find secure waged or salaried positions in the United States at the beginning of the twentieth century, was unlikely to be so also in the year 2000.

None of the migrant groups in this study, bar one, was initially 'filtered' for entry by United States legislation. Prior to the First World War and until the Emergency Quota Act of 1921 the only legally restricted group were the Chinese. The Chinese Exclusion Act of 1882 allowed Congress to suspend Chinese immigration, a prohibition that lasted well over sixty years. The Act refused entry to Chinese skilled and unskilled labourers and Chinese employed in mining for ten years, under penalty of imprisonment and deportation. Providing the Chinese had $1,000, they could still enter the United States as 'merchants' however.[31] In 1924 the Immigration Act limited the number of immigrants who could be admitted from any country to 2 per cent of the number of people from that country who were already living in the United States in 1890.

Another major policy change came with the Immigration and Nationality Act of 1965 (becoming law in 1968) which abolished the national origin quotas but introduced Western and Eastern hemisphere quotas. Liberalization continued with the Immigration Act of 1990. After the Act, the United States admitted 700,000 new immigrants annually, an increase of 200,000. The new legislation continued to give preference to immigrants with family members already in the United States. Consequently the past stock of immigrants and quota sizes were extremely influential in determining the country of origin of American immigrants in the years after the Act.[32] However in itself this should not bias the degree of entrepreneurship of migrants relative to those in their country of origin.

The Model of Entrepreneurship and Culture

Entrepreneurial choice usually involves a comparison, on the one hand, of waged employment and rentier income with, on the other, uncertain entrepreneurial income. Entry to entrepreneurial employment typically requires commitment of personal capital, which may need accumulating first. In this case the choice is made over time. During the earlier periods the would-be entrepreneur works for wages and saves. In the later periods, when those who continue to opt for wage work or leisure can live off the interest on their savings, the entrepreneur puts the savings into the business.[33] Cultures that emphasize deferred gratification, that encourage a low rate of time discount, will encourage savings and may boost entry to entrepreneurship by bringing forward the date at which the minimum capital for the business start is achieved.

When everybody is risk averse, a person with a higher income is more willing to take a gamble of a given size. The subjective cost of a given uncertain prospect, relative to the expected value of this pay-off, is lower the larger is the income at which it is offered. The rich are more likely to accept a given bet than the poor, and are therefore more probably entrepreneurial. This argument only holds though when the basis for comparison is the same; that is both the rich and the poor in the comparison have equal access to safe incomes as alternatives to self-employment. Risk attitudes may be culturally influenced and the willingness to make risky choices will also depend upon institutional circumstances – such as bankruptcy legislation and family support networks.

In so far as self-employment is time-consuming, and leisure is a normal good, the rich will be *less* likely to opt for self-employment. This may particularly apply to the children of self-made business people, who either want nothing to do with the family firm or who do not wish to invest the time in it necessary to be as entrepreneurial as their parents. Family socialization must therefore be distinctive and effective if business dynasties are to survive. The net effect of wealth and income on self-employment then depends on the relative impact of this leisure preference and the personal capital requirement for business starts.

The difference in the uncertain well-being from self-employment, $E(U)$, and that from paid employment (V), is:

$$Y^* = E(U) - V.$$

Assuming both RHS terms are linear functions of a characteristics vector X we have:

$$Y^* = X'b + v,$$

where: b is a vector of parameters and v is a normally distributed disturbance term with zero mean and unit variance. Y^* is not observed but the actual occupational choice is. Self-employment is chosen $(Y = 1)$ if $Y^* \geq 0$ and employment $(Y = 0)$ if $Y^* < 0$, both of which outcomes can be seen. So,

$$\Pr[Y_i = 1] = \Pr[Y^*_i \geq 0] = f(X'b).$$

Variables in the X vector include country of origin, as a measure of immigrant culture, the principal interest of this study. But other influences must also be controlled. The need to acquire savings and work experience means entrepreneurship chances at first increase with age and, perhaps as optimism is tempered by experience, eventually diminish.[34] Experience acquired by residence in the United States, is likely to be an essential component of entrepreneurs' information-gathering. The ability to speak English probably facilitates this process, and possibly so also would formal education. The entrepreneur's personal wealth, either as a result of savings or inherited, is typically necessary to provide the equity in the new business – for start-up capital. (Formal education may be correlated with wealth or income, as an income-elastic consumption good.) In the nineteenth century sometimes a motive for founding a firm was to find employment for the progeny of the founder's marriage. More generally families are expensive and self-employment may be perceived as a better way of providing more income than wage employment. If so then marriage boosts entrepreneurship chances.[35] Some migrants intend to return to their country of origin and these are less likely to make the commitment to start a business. To control for this effect we include a 'naturalization' dummy variable. Finally on the entrepreneurial supply side, greater expected rewards of entrepreneurship may increase the likelihood of an individual becoming an entrepreneur.

The opportunities for entrepreneurship depend on industry entry barriers or their absence. At the beginning of the twentieth century the transport sector was dominated by railways and shipping, both of which were capital-intensive. Capital requirements reduced entrepreneurial opportunity. But at the beginning of the subsequent century changing technology, in particular motor road transport, had transformed entrepreneurial opportunities. These possibilities were related to returns to entrepreneurship.

Consequently the probability that an individual will become an entrepreneur can be expressed by a reduced form equation of entrepreneurial supply and 'demand' or opportunities, with expected returns substituted out, as below:

$\Pr[Y = 1] = f$ (*gender, marital status, residence duration, formal human capital, English speaking, sector, age, wealth, culture*).

Results

Average Entrepreneurial Chances

We first consider simple entrepreneurial chances as a measure of entrepreneurial culture. As predicted by Max Weber, United States immigrants from the Catholic group of countries (Table 6.1) in 1910 are near the bottom of the ranking of probabilities, though Wales is lower than Ireland and Italy (as well as China). The highest chances in 1910 are those of the very small Syria and Lebanon group (not shown), then China and Greece, followed by the Russian Empire. In 1910 the Greece and Turkey entrepreneurial ratios are quite similar (t = 1.5853), which could be interpreted as consistent with common ethnicity.

In the year 2000, the top four entrepreneurial groups were those originating from Israel, Syria and Lebanon, Greece and Italy, similar to Australia in 1996.[36] Judged by the criterion of similar entrepreneurial proportions at both dates,[37] Mexico, Cuba, Wales, the Netherlands, Turkey and Japan show stability or persistence of entrepreneurial culture. Greece and Italy increased entrepreneurship probabilities. Overall the chances of entrepreneurship declined from 5.36 per cent in the 1910 sample to 3.38 per cent in the 2000 sample.

Table 6.1: United States Immigrant Entrepreneurship Percentages.[38]

Migrants' Predominant Religion/Culture	Country of Birth	%	
		1910	2000
Protestantism	England	5.80	4.04
	Scotland	5.65	3.32
	Wales	3.43	4.39
	Netherlands	6.75	5.34
Catholicism	Ireland	3.97	5.11
	Italy	3.60	7.82
	Mexico	1.73	1.61
	Cuba	6.02	5.75
Buddhism	China	11.57	4.77
	Japan	2.99	3.49
Greek/Armenian	Syria & Lebanon	–	9.45
Orthodox, Muslim	Greece	7.89	12.02
	Turkey	5.62	6.27
Jewish	Israel	–	10.72
	Russia (Empire, 1910)	6.14	4.33
Total All Immigrant Sample		5.36	3.38

The simple ratio test does not take into account differences among the migrant samples in characteristics that might influence entrepreneurship. So for example those from some countries of migration were more likely than others to be literate and to own their own house, both characteristics that were conducive to entrepreneurship. Consequently such migrants could show relatively high entrepreneurship because of these attributes, whereas purely for cultural reasons they might be less entrepreneurial than those who were poorer or more illiterate.

Much depends on what is assumed culturally determined. It could be contended that education and literacy, like entrepreneurship, depend upon culture. They are not independent variables in the occupational choice model that includes culture. But historical accident and path dependence could nonetheless ensure the independence from culture of the values of variables influencing entrepreneurship at any point in time.

Determinants of Entrepreneurship

Before interpreting the country of origin parameters in the estimates of the above equation, we consider the model controls in Table 6.2. In 1910 a person owning their own property was more likely to be an employer by the same amount as being male; 1.8 percentage points. Residence in the United States longer than 10 years is even more important, adding 2.1–2.4 percentage points, though there is not much evidence of increasing effects beyond a decade. Age increases the chances of becoming an employer up to 59 years old. The rise in probability between the ages of 30 and 60 is also about 1.8 percentage points. Literacy and the ability to speak English add respectively 1.2 and 1.4 percentage points.

Table 6.2: United States Immigrant Entrepreneurship Model: Controls (Logit Marginal Effects of Control Variables).[39]

Variable	Year	Marginal Effect	Standard Error	z
Gender (male = 1)	1910	0.0145	0.0017	8.56
	2000	0.0152	0.0004	39.99
Marital Status (married = 1)	1910	0.0164	0.0016	10.01
	2000	0.0067	0.0004	16.18
6–10 years in US	1910	0.0087	0.0028	3.06
	2000	0.0058	0.0009	6.49
11–15 years in US	1910	0.0165	0.0041	4.04
	2000	0.0097	0.0010	9.81
16–20 years in US	1910	0.0120	0.0035	3.44
	2000	0.0111	0.0011	10.28
21+ years in US	1910	0.0145	0.0033	4.46
	2000	0.0079	0.0008	9.53
Naturalization	1910	0.0150	0.0021	7.03
	2000	0.0025	0.0004	5.85
Literacy (literate = 1)	1910	0.0112	0.0016	7.08
Grade 1–12	2000	−0.0004	0.0010	−0.46
1–3 years of college	2000	0.0024	0.0011	2.16
4+ years of college	2000	0.0046	0.0012	3.98
English Speaking	1910	0.0130	0.0017	7.79
	2000	0.0049	0.0007	7.03
Transportation, Communication and Other Utilities	1910	−0.0102	0.0019	−5.50
	2000	0.0010	0.0009	1.16
Wholesale and Retail Trade	1910	0.0899	0.0052	17.17
	2000	0.0167	0.0007	25.05
Finance, Insurance, Real Estate, Business and Repair Services	1910	0.0360	0.0070	5.12
	2000	0.0143	0.0008	17.76
Personal, Entertainment and Recreation Services	1910	0.0437	0.0043	10.27
	2000	−0.0020	0.0005	−3.58
Age	1910	0.0023	0.0003	8.19
	2000	0.0020	0.0001	24.38
Age Squared	1910	−1.9E−05	0.0000	−6.31
	2000	−1.6E−05	0.0000	−19.66
Own Property	1910	0.0190	0.0019	10.12
	2000	0.0108	0.0004	24.74
Country of Origin Variables in Table 6.3				

Properties of Regressions	Year	Pseudo R^2	Number of Observations
	1910	0.2478	34,035
	2000	0.1091	453,198

The foregoing variables influence the supply of entrepreneurs. Turning to the demand or opportunities, the sector with the lowest entry barrier for entrepreneurship was the wholesale and retail trade – adding 8.7 percentage points to the probability of entrepreneurship, relative to the base case of mining, construction and manufacturing.[40] Transport, communication and other utilities reduced entrepreneurship chances by almost one percentage point relative to the base case. Finance, real estate and personal and professional services added about 4 percentage points.

The marginal effects of the entrepreneurial supply variables are rather smaller on average in 2000 than in 1910. In part this is because the general propensity for self-employment had fallen and perhaps also because of the greater abundance of human capital. Table 6.2 shows that being male increases entrepreneurial chances by 1.1 per cent in 2000, 0.7 percentage points less than in 1910, and marriage boosts self-employment chances by a similar magnitude (in 2000), much less than the 1.6 percentage points at the earlier date. Age at which probability of entrepreneurship is maximized has risen to almost 63, perhaps reflecting greater life expectation. Length of residence in the United States for maximum probability of self-employment increased to 16–20 years in 2000. Property ownership raises entrepreneurship chances by 1.1 percentage points in the later year compared with 1.9 percentage points 90 years earlier, possibly because credit arrangements may have become easier. Education variables at the later date replace 'literacy' in 2000 and so are not directly comparable, but college education increases entrepreneurial chances. Changes in technology boost the attractiveness of the transport, communication and other utilities sector for self-employment. But perhaps organizational changes were responsible for the opposite effect in personal, entertainment and recreation services.

Table 6.3 collects the country of origin logit estimates at the two dates. The highest marginal effects in the relatively free immigration period were those from Syria and Lebanon and Greece. Although migrants from Turkey were on average less likely to be self-employed than those from England, controlling for other influences, the positive marginal effect was higher. As noted above, a substantial proportion of these Middle Eastern immigrants were likely to be Greek or Armenian by language and religion. Migrants from Russia and Poland were less likely to be self-employed than those from the Netherlands, but again controlling for other influence the marginal coefficient was positive and substantial (a 2 per cent effect). As indicated earlier these people from the Russian Empire will have been mainly Jewish.

Unlike Jews and Greeks, migrants from the Netherlands, the archetypal Protestant country, show no greater propensity for or against self-employment as measured by the marginal effect. However the average propensity for self-employment was high and it may therefore be that the estimate of the Protestant Ethic impact is muted by factoring out education and wealth effects which themselves could be influenced by the Ethic.

Table 6.3: United States Immigrant Entrepreneurship Model: Culture
(Logit Marginal Effects of Country of Origin Variables).[41]

Migrants' Predominant Religion/Culture	Country of Birth	Year	Marginal Effect	Standard Error
Protestantism	England	1910	−0.0055	0.0017
		2000	−0.0040	0.0009
	Scotland	1910	−0.0038	0.0026
		2000	−0.0081	0.0015
	Wales	1910	−0.0139	0.0027
		2000	−0.0018	0.0014
	Netherlands	1910	−0.0031	0.0043
		2000	−0.0003	0.0018
Catholicism	Ireland	1910	−0.0110	0.0015
		2000	0.0014	0.0016
	Italy	1910	0.0113	0.0028
		2000	0.0072	0.0012
	Mexico	1910	0.0020	0.0070
		2000	−0.0171	0.0009
	Cuba	1910	0.0214	0.0216
		2000	0.0030	0.0010
Buddhism	China	1910	0.0309	0.0087
		2000	−0.0018	0.0007
	Japan	1910	0.0145	0.0093
		2000	−0.0035	0.0010
Greek/Armenian Orthodox, Muslim	Syria & Lebanon	1910	–	–
		2000	0.0181	0.0022
	Greece	1910	0.1140	0.0202
		2000	0.0222	0.0021
	Turkey	1910	0.0520	0.0156
		2000	0.0105	0.0026
Jewish	Israel	1910	–	–
		2000	0.0270	0.0029
	Russia (Empire, 1910)	1910	0.0215	0.0030
		2000	0.0005	0.0009

Similar remarks apply to English migrants, judged by percentage of self-employed, but the marginal effect is significantly negative, in accordance with Wiener's prediction.[42] In 1910 the Scots were more entrepreneurial than the English according to the logit coefficients, consistent with their disproportionate representation in British business and other elite circles.[43] However, the coefficients are not significantly different.

Some Catholic countries in the sample yield a surprise for Weber's thesis. First, Mexican migrants outside agriculture were rather few in 1910 which may account for the statistically insignificant marginal effect. In 2000 Mexico has the largest negative entrepreneurial marginal effect.[44] Also the lowest proportion of self-employment of the sample is consistent with Weber's thesis. Ireland in 1910 (despite including some Protestants in the group) has a strongly negative marginal effect and a low proportion. In so far as Italy could be said to have a Roman Catholic culture, Italian migrants apparently contradict the Protestant Ethic. The marginal effect is strongly positive (even though the average proportion of self-employed is slightly less than Ireland's). Cuba also becomes significantly entrepreneurial by 2000 (the absence of significant entrepreneurial effect in the earlier year may be due to the small sample). This last finding will be no surprise for students of Cuban migration. By the 1970s there were more than 18,000 Cuban-owned businesses in Dade County, Miami, and supposedly no non-English-speaking immigrant group showed more rapid socio-economic mobility.[45]

As the only group discriminated against by United States immigration legislation in 1910, more than half (52.6 per cent) of the Chinese sample had been in the country for 20 years or more, yet almost half (49.1 per cent) could not speak English. A high proportion of the sample was self-employed (11.25 per cent) but part of this can be accounted for by age and residence, in turn a consequence of the 1882 Act. Controlling for these factors the marginal effect of country of origin is positive and significant (1 per cent level) and adds 2.5 percentage points to entrepreneurship chances, rather more than the predominantly Jewish immigrants from the Russian Empire and Poland. Although much of the qualitative literature emphasizes the discrimination that was responsible for the Chinese not building large business empires in the United States, by 1939 the second highest earner in California was a Chinese immigrant, Joe Shoong, who had begun his career working in a shirt factory and went on to found the National Dollar Stores and the National Shoe Company.[46]

Despite the high proportion of non-English speakers there was no significant effect on entrepreneurship of being both Chinese and English speaking. Entrepreneurship was apparently therefore not a response to inability to speak English and presumably therefore to integrate. But the costs of becoming an entrepreneur might be lower with a larger number of Chinese speakers in a captive labour market, and therefore with lower wages, because of their linguistic deficiencies or discrimination – except that the Japanese did not show such a strong effect.

Japanese migrants were not subject to United States legal discrimination, although at times emigration from Japan was controlled or prohibited. In particular, the 'Gentleman's Agreement' of 1907–8 blocked unskilled Japanese migration to the United States, when the Japanese government agreed not to issue passports to labourers.[47] The proportion of self-employed was the second lowest in the sample (whereas China's was the third highest) and the marginal effect was not significantly different from zero. In the first decade of the twentieth century, the Japanese principally worked as domestic servants or farm labourers, with some operating small family businesses mainly in the western states.[48] The Chinese by contrast were selected by the discriminatory immigration legislation to favour businessmen with capital.

Persistence of Entrepreneurial Culture

A major interest is in the persistence of these entrepreneurial effects, which is assessed by considering a similar specification 90 years later. A statistical test of persistence shows that strictly only Cuba, Italy, England and the Netherlands have similar entrepreneurial coefficients over time.[49] Scotland is stable only at the 10 per cent significance level. Among other things, this means that Ireland and Wales improved entrepreneurial cultures relative to England. By the end of the century Wales and England had apparently acquired similar entrepreneurial cultures.[50] The Scots moved in the opposite direction, becoming significantly less entrepreneurial and the Irish, like the Welsh, were significantly more prone to self-employment in the United States. 'Eirepreneurs' were identified by the Irish press of the 1980s as those using human capital acquired in Ireland, where there were few opportunities at the time, to better themselves in the United States.[51] This is a remarkable shift among the four nations of the British Isles over the twentieth century. The Scottish, the most entrepreneurial of the four in 1910, were the least entrepreneurial in 2000, perhaps directing their energies into politics in the later years.

The 'Catholic' entrepreneurial countries, Italy and Cuba, display stability in different ways; the proportion of self-employed is stable in Cuba and the marginal effect is stable in Italy (comparing Tables 6.3 and 6.1). Mexico is consistently short of entrepreneurship on the simple measure. Marginal effects do not change over the century in the 'Protestant' countries of England and the Netherlands, apparently relatively lacking in entrepreneurship.

Greece and the Middle East continue to dominate the positive entrepreneurial effects, although with smaller coefficients and proportions than in 1910. Second-generation immigrant Greeks were close behind the equivalent Jews in income and above in education, according to the United States censuses of 1960 and 1970. Both migrant groups improved their economic status relative to those born in the United States.[52]

Comparing migrants from Russia and Poland in 2000 with those in 1910 is less appropriate than using Israel for the recent benchmark. The marginal effects turn out similar. As expected if the Jewish element was diluted in the 1910 Russian and Polish numbers, the average entrepreneurial proportion is smaller than that for Israel in 2000.

Judged by the marginal effects in 2000, both Japan- and China-originating migrants changed their entrepreneurial cultures over the twentieth century. After 90 years of rapid economic growth and a variety of immigration legislation, there is a significant and positive effect on entrepreneurship of the interaction between English speaking and Chinese origin (not reported in the table). At 1.3 percentage points this more than offsets the 0.8 percentage point negative impact of Chinese origin *per se* (not shown in accompanying table). The pure English-speaking effect is 0.4 percentage points. A person born in China who did not speak English was 1.2 percentage points less likely to be entrepreneurial than the sample average, whereas one from China who did speak English had about 0.9 percentage point greater chance of entrepreneurship. With no interaction term for Japanese origin, the negative Japanese effect is exactly equal and opposite to the impact of English speaking. The substantial 'linguistic distance' between China and Japan on the one hand and the United States on the other, then may account for the apparent cultural change over 90 years. Taking into account language skills, Chinese entrepreneurialism persists, as does Japanese indifference to self-employment.

Conclusion

In accordance with one aspect of the 'cultural critique', the English were persistently prone to less entrepreneurship than United States immigrant groups in the present sample, once controls for other entrepreneurship influences are included. The Dutch were consistently about averagely entrepreneurial, not as precocious as might be expected if a predominant Protestant religious culture encouraged entrepreneurship. In view of the levels of Gross Domestic Product (GDP) per head attained in 1910 and in 2000, another conclusion must be that entrepreneurial culture was not a fundamental determinant of economic performance. For England was the wealthiest immigrant origin country considered in 1910 and the Netherlands was the runner-up.

Comparison of marginal self-employment propensities of immigrant groups between 1910 and 2000 suggests a number of stable cultural influences. Jews and those from Greece, Turkey and the Middle East were generally more entrepreneurial (defined as being both self-employed and employing other people) over 90 years than other groups. This finding is consistent with the business pre-cocity of Jews and Greeks in nineteenth-century Britain.

Apparently less in harmony with historiography is the evidence for Catholic cultures. On the basis of the nineteenth-century experience, we should look for a 'Catholic Ethic' that diverts attention from economic advance. But whereas the Mexican result matches this hypothesis, the United States evidence indicates that Irish culture apparently changed over the twentieth century, while Italians and Cubans were abnormally entrepreneurial at both reference dates. This last accords with stable Italian and Cuban cultures independent of, or inconsistent with, supposedly anti-entrepreneurial Catholicism.

The Japanese along with the Chinese became less willing to start businesses, perhaps because of the filter of immigration legislation. The Chinese in 1910 were unusually entrepreneurial, probably a consequence of the unique legislative constraints on Chinese migration and naturalization. Language effects may have been particularly important for these two groups and measuring the impact of their cultures on their entrepreneurship propensities. Japanese higher incomes in 1910 and 2000 and lower entrepreneurial index once more confirms the small importance of entrepreneurial culture for economic growth.

That English culture was as 'deficient' in entrepreneurship in 2000 as it was in 1910, and that the Dutch also showed no change, is perhaps a contradiction with the Protestant Ethic. Alternatively the desire to become an employer, rather than a wage worker, might be interpreted as Weber's 'Adventurer's Capitalism', not a reflection of the Protestant Ethic. Consider for instance Samuel Zemur-ray, a Jewish Russian-born entrepreneur in New Orleans, who established the Hubbard-Zemurray Fruit Company in 1910 with plantations in Honduras. Zemurray financed and organized a successful military coup against the Hondu-ran president Miguel Davila in order to obtain tax concessions and grants from his replacement.[53] Had Zemurray stayed in Russia, he was unlikely to have found comparable opportunities for his entrepreneurial talents, and in the United States, business was an obvious occupation for an immigrant. But Zemurray does not show the 'greater economic rationality' of the 'Protestant tradition'.

'Protestant tradition' countries perhaps were less keen on self-employment and on entrepreneurship than on social and political organization. The conclusion that the English in the twentieth century did not have an entrepreneurial culture by comparison with other countries providing immigrants to the United States could be entirely consistent with a strong English entrepreneurial performance in England. All that is required is that other English conditions – organizations and institutions – for beneficial business entrepreneurship were very favourable, as the GDP figures in fact indicate. Conversely, an entrepreneurial culture without such conditions could be positively harmful for economic development, by failing to channel entrepreneurial energies appropriately.

7 ENTREPRENEURSHIP AND CULTURAL VALUES IN LATIN AMERICA, 1850–2000: FROM MODERNIZATION, NATIONAL VALUES AND DEPENDENCY THEORIES TOWARDS A BUSINESS HISTORY PERSPECTIVE

Carlos Dávila

Introduction

Latin America is a space defined in geographic, historic and cultural terms. In current usage, it refers to the Americas south of the United States, covering Mexico, Central America (seven countries), South America (nine countries), Cuba and the Dominican Republic; excluding the Caribbean Antilles, i.e., those territories colonized by France, the United Kingdom or the Netherlands and the Commonwealth of Puerto Rico. Despite its common features: their Spanish colonial past, Spanish as a mother tongue – except for Portuguese in Brazil – Roman Catholicism as the predominant religion and their condition as 'emergent economies', Latin America is a vast area with geographic, economic, social and political diversity expressed in various levels of economic development. The present chapter encompasses Mexico and seven South American nations – Argentina, Brazil, Chile, Colombia, Peru, Venezuela and Uruguay – with particular emphasis on one Andean country: Colombia.

Its purpose is to offer a selective, non-comprehensive survey of the literature dealing with cultural features in their interplay with entrepreneurship in the region for the 1850–2000 period. This literature illustrates both American-rooted psychological and sociological 'modernization' theory, Marxist-inspired 'dependency' theory, national values and business history research. It is examined for clues to the relationship between cultural features and entrepreneurship and its relation to economic development. In addition, the distinctive features and patterns of Latin American entrepreneurship are synthesized and challenges and opportunities confronting future research into the historical explanation of entrepreneurship in this part of the world are delineated. In particular, its potential for aggregate analysis, e.g. through entrepreneurial typologies, as a means to advance the study of entrepreneurship for allowing comparison with ongoing research worldwide is examined.

This chapter is organized into eight sections. After an introduction, the first section summarizes the 'decade of development' (1960s) and 'modernization' theory with its emphasis on the social and cultural factors in economic growth. The second section examines the application of the 'modernization' theory in various Latin American countries during the 1970s and the negative consequences this had on the study of the relationship between cultural features and entrepreneurship. The third section analyses the influence of dependency theory during the sixties and seventies that discouraged the study of business and its actors – entrepreneurs and firms. The fourth section addresses the revival since the mid-1980s of national values theory. It is followed by a section that presents a selective survey of Latin American business history dealing with local and regional culture and entrepreneurship. After this comes a section on studies related to backwardness and substitutes for prerequisites to economic development. The elements towards a synthesis of Latin American entrepreneurship are sketched in the penultimate section which is followed by concluding remarks centred about a proposed analytical scheme for entrepreneurial history.

The Eventful Path of Entrepreneurship in Theory and History in Latin America

Within the renewed academic interest in entrepreneurship theory and history in the international academic communities of both business history and entrepreneurship, there are various reasons to look at the case of Latin America. First, in the post-war period, this part of the world served as a testing ground for diverse disciplinary perspectives on non-economic factors of economic growth, one of them being the role of culture. The results of that experience appear to have been neglected, or a least forgotten. Second, nowadays, placing the Latin American case in a wider international framework may contribute to the recent interest to see the evolution of business history as an academic field in a comparative perspective. In fact, it seems to depart from the experience of the United States wherein a shift of interest from the individual Schumpeterian entrepreneur to the study of Chandler's large-scale company has taken place since the early 1960s; interestingly, four decades later 'entrepreneurial history is now in the process of being reborn.'[1] In contrast, in its recent, brief life span business history in Latin America has focused more on entrepreneurial history – individual entrepreneurs, families, immigrant and related networks – than on the history of individual firms.[2]

Additionally, together with the idea of the 'enterprise culture', since the end of the 1980s there has been a rebirth in some quarters of the thesis about the alleged anti-entrepreneurial values of Latin American culture, and its correlated lack of entrepreneurship, now under the dictum that 'culture matters'. As the present chapter argues, scholars as well as policymakers, entrepreneurship consultants and educators in the region would do well to consult British and American business history's renewed methodological approaches to the history of entrepreneurship, as well as the growing Latin American business research on business history. The Latin American experience shows the theoretical approaches of the 1960s and '70s that were applied to entrepreneurship in this part of the world were seriously flawed in terms of rigorous empirical research. Despite this, the causal mechanisms and relations between culture, entrepreneurship and economic growth are important enough and deserve to be approached from more cogent theoretical and methodological perspectives. The further evolution of research has shown that the work done on the business history of the region urgently needs to link history with theoretical developments in the international business history community.

From the outset it should be stated that Latin American business history is a young academic field whose origins date back to the 1970s; it was preceded by an embryonic development (after 1950) of economic history in almost all countries of the region. Economic history arose as a general field, which gave a central role to economic phenomena in wider explanations of the development of Latin American societies. That centrality receded after the 1970s, 'Economic history, then, became a greater window ... little by little, among the related windows, entrepreneurial history and studies appeared'.[3]

In Latin America, business history has evolved not just under the influence of economic history but also as an interdisciplinary field – a 'no man's land' – in interaction with socio-economic history, social history, economic development literature, sociology and management. Since the beginning of the 1990s business history has experienced important growth in the volume and quality of its academic output, as well as in its degree of institutionalization – that is, presence at international conferences, positions on editorial boards of top journals of the discipline, networking and instruction in business schools. Two recent special issues dedicated to Latin America in two of the discipline's major journals attest it.[4]

This growth has been unequally divided among the countries: Mexico, Argentina and Brazil have received the most attention, followed by Colombia, Uruguay and Chile; these have seen greater development in the new field than the other Andean countries – Peru, Venezuela and Bolivia – as attested by recent surveys of the field.[5]

The 'Decade of Development' in Latin America and 'Modernization' Theory: Entrepreneurship, Social and Cultural Factors in Economic Development

At the end of 1961 the United Nations General Assembly agreed that the decade of the 1960s would be the 'United Nations Development Decade; a programme for international economic co-operation' aimed at advancing economic and social progress for the less developed countries.[6] A few months before, in March 1961, the late American president John F. Kennedy launched the Alliance for Progress, 'a vast cooperative effort' aimed at changing United States policies towards Latin America to 'help create the political, social and economic framework for better living conditions in the hemisphere'.[7] Behind the stated purpose was a political concern: the Alliance would prevent other Latin American states from following communist Cuba's recent (1959) example of falling under the influence of the Soviet Union.

As part of these initiatives, scholars at leading American universities (Harvard, MIT, Yale, Princeton, Chicago and the University of California at Berkeley, among others) made their reputations as development economists (e.g., Alexander Gerschenkron, Walter Rostow, Everett Hagen and Albert Hirschman), sociologists (led by recognized figures such as Neil Smelser and Seymour Lipset), political scientists (Lucien Pye, Gabriel Almond and Joseph La Palombara) and psychologists (David McClelland). They were concerned with economic growth and development as a new, policy-oriented field of inquiry. These specialists had begun to appear since the end of the 1950s, in economics departments, in recently created multidisciplinary centres studying economic development, as well as in some social sciences departments – e.g., sociology, political science. Those circumstances converged during this eventful decade into the study of the economic factors of growth – capital accumulation, investment and savings; labour and land[8] – culminating in preoccupation with the non-economic aspects of development. Growing interest in these non-economic aspects formed part of the current of thought rooted in the United States known as the 'modernization' current, a variant of the field of development economics. Drawing on an anthropological perspective and a strong kinship with Talcott Parson's structural functionalism, this current conceived economic development as involving fundamental alterations in the social and political structures as societies moved along the 'traditional', 'transitional' and 'modern' society typology.[9]

Besides social mobility – in its sociological, cultural and psychological components – education, technical know-how and the politics of development and entrepreneurship were other central themes for the modernization current in its search for the 'missing component' in the process of economic growth in underdeveloped countries. Among these, entrepreneurship is our focus of attention. At the end of the 1960s it had generated growing interest, reflected in a number of theoretical constructs about entrepreneurial supply, both psychological (McClelland, Hagen, Kunkel) and sociological (Cochran, Lipset, Young) approaches that in various forms were reflecting some Weberian and/or Schumpeterian influence.

Theories about entrepreneurship in economic development were surveyed in a volume published in 1971 by Peter Kilby, an American economist. In an insightful introduction, called 'Hunting the Heffalump', a classic of entrepreneurial literature, he stated, 'The importance given to the entrepreneur' – who in his analogy he compared to the heffalump – as a causal variable in the growth process is strongly influenced by the 'particular scholar's field'.[10] More than thirty years later, in 'Revisiting the Heffalump', he reaffirmed that he was refining his propositions about entrepreneurial tasks, the entrepreneurial personality and the entrepreneurial abilities that he was now seeing as dissimilar depending on the setting in which they take place – underdeveloped countries versus industrialized societies.[11]

It is striking that with few notable exceptions such as Alexander Gerschenkron, who in a 1962 work approached 'economic backwardness [in Europe] in historical perspective',[12] a distinctive characteristic of the 1960s-era modernization literature was its lack of historical perspective. Generally, in these theories there was little concern for the past of societies undergoing economic change, preferring to focus on measuring the causal relationships between the model's variables as the basis for theory testing and generalization. The interest in providing input for policymaking and to make academic work 'applicable' to policymaking promoting economic and social development influenced scholarly work in that decade. It is important to recall the international political context of that 'decade of development' in which comparative research projects came to fruition. Particularly, it was the period of the 'cold war' between the post-war superpowers, which formed the backdrop for the alignment and future of the underdeveloped countries of Latin America which, in the view of the north, was the 'backyard' of the United States.

Latin America as Testing Ground for 'Modernization' Theories

Latin America was an amenable testing ground for some of these theories. One of them was psychological: Everett Hagen's status-withdrawal theory. Interestingly enough, he was an economics professor at MIT. The other two were sociological theories, that of Thomas Cochran – a well-known business historian at the Center for Entrepreneurial History at Harvard Business School – and that of Seymour Lipset – a sociology professor at Berkeley. In his book published in 1962,[13] Hagen provided a mediating psychological explanation (personality formation) for the transition from traditional (authoritarian) into modern (creative) societies that undertake economic growth. His research has recently been portrayed as echoing A. H. Cole's call in the 1950s for combining theory and historical data in a dynamic context.[14]

A Colombian regional group – the *Antioqueños*: the 'Yankees of South America' – 'not simply [for their] greater entry into industry, but also [for] their greater business acumen, entrepreneurial foresight, and organizational skill',[15] was taken as one of the four cases Hagen studied (the remaining three being the Old Believers in Russia, the Nonconformists in England the Samurai in Japan). The provocative ideas he puts forth in support of these choices are attenuated by his decision to cover many centuries in a few pages. His empirical evidence does not measure up to the standards for the collection and analysis of facts and counterfactual evidence. Among the critical reviews of Hagen's book by scholars a noted one was authored by Gerschenkron.[16] The chapter on the *Antioqueños* was severely criticized in 1965 by Frank Safford,[17] the pioneer in Colombian business history. Applying a rigorous historical analysis and summoning a considerable amount of compelling evidence, he dismantled the fragile empirical foundation of Hagen's theses. Ten years later, another American historian, Ann Twinam, concluded her doctoral dissertation on the Antioquian elite at the end of the colonial period by observing that status withdrawal was 'hypothetical', based solely on Hagen's 'own inferences' and drawn from 'his own fertile imagination'.[18] Paradoxically, nascent Colombian business history owes much to Hagen's book. He moved others to delve into and debate his generalizations and to make empirical comparisons. Hagen's determination to discern the factors contributing to economic growth was admirable. He failed, however, because he refused to focus on the questions of who, where, when, how and why, preferring to adopt a kind of determinism that historians abhor.

A second theory applied to Latin America entrepreneurship was sociological role theory through the framework of both Cochran's national value theory and Lipset's entrepreneur as a deviant. Cochran proposed a cultural framework whose key elements are anchored in Talcott Parson's sociology: cultural values, role expectations and entrepreneurial roles, and social sanctions. In this theoretical framework, entrepreneurs represent 'society's modal personality'.[19] In the American culture society's values, according to Cochran, are those of an 'egalitarian atmosphere of an outgoing, pragmatic, democratic society' that from their childhood teaches entrepreneurs that 'co-operation for mutual benefit is good'. According to him, that is not the case in Latin America.[20]

A couple of years before Hagen would publish his well-known work about the theory of social change, Cochran completed his book about the Puerto Rican businessman[21] and three years later co-authored – with an Argentinean anthropologist – another book about entrepreneurship in Argentine culture, which its authors define as a study in cultural change. Both works embrace the idea that the values of these societies in transition determine the role that entrepreneurs play. A constant in Cochran's work is the comparison between the impact of the values or ethos traits prevalent in the United States and Puerto Rico and/or Argentina on entrepreneurial behaviour.

Undoubtedly Cochran made a suitable choice in taking the case of Argentina. In 1930 that country was showing a spectacular start on the road to economic growth and industrialization; but it did not succeed in being sustainable over the long term. In 1960 its economy was not that of the developed country that it seemed to be becoming in 1930. To investigate the cause of this was a very interesting case.

In Argentina he studied a magnate of Italian origin: Torcuato di Tella, a pioneer of the metallurgical and electrical industry in the period 1910–60. His book is more of an entrepreneurial history – focused on di Tella's personality and his role – than a company history. In the eyes of one reviewer from the period, published in an anthropology journal, the volume 'relies rather heavily on conjectural history'; he considered that it 'falls somewhat short of a satisfactory anthropological account' and he saw it as 'one-sided', based almost entirely on the managerial and family point of view.[22] Three decades later an American business historian made the point that Cochran's book was a 'straightforward business biography, with little to suggest the application of anthropological methodology'.[23]

During the 1960s in Latin America there were also repercussions from a theory closely related to Cochran's social roles, likewise based on Parson's pattern variables and associated with a prominent American sociologist – Seymour Lipset – who in 1967 co-edited a well-known book called *Elites in Latin America*.[24] Although Lipset is reiterative in that his theoretical approach is comparative – contrasting the United States with Latin American nations – and his point of departure is that 'No society is equalitarian, ascriptive or universalistic in any total sense', the balance is sufficiently definitive to conclude: 'predominant values which continue to inform the behavior of the elite stem from the continued and combined strength of ascription, particularism, and diffuseness'.[25] These values were portrayed as distinctive of traditional societies.

In this context, and with the same logic as Cochran, Lipset's theory assumes that those who introduce change must be deviants, since they reject the traditional elite's way of doing things.

> '... The restraints upon entrepreneurial activity imposed by the network [of social relations] would be less effective against such a person. Thus, an immigrant may be outside of many of the networks of the nation and freer to engage in entrepreneurial activity', in other words, freer socially to deviate.[26]

It must be said that the available material to which Lipset would refer was relatively scarce and belonged to an embryonic development of social sciences in

Latin America at the beginning of the 1960s. Several of these represented an erudite essay tradition more than rigorous academic research.

As in Cochran's case, Lipset's ideas caused repercussions in the United States academic world, more so than in Latin America, where the 1970s witnessed penetration by other currents of thought – Marxism and dependency theory, addressed in a later section. Nevertheless, it was during these years that Colombia again served as a testing ground. In an exploratory study published in 1966 about industrial entrepreneurs in the Colombian capital of Bogota, United States sociologist Aaron Lipman conducted a cross-sectional study inspired by Lipset's approach and concluded that the entrepreneurial role is 'both unusual and crucial. Colombia is not a nation of commerce.'[27] Without argument and with no empirical proof about predominant values, Lipman stated that 'instead of being an outcome of his cultural stimulation and motivation, Colombian entrepreneurship seems to exist in spite of, and often at odds with, the cultural milieu.'[28] This study approaches the Bogota entrepreneur and defines him as a cultural nonconformist or deviant.

Between 1963 and 1966 and under a broad array of theoretical influences that were not circumscribed by the modernization theory, the Economic Commission for Latin America (ECLA), an agency of the United Nations, put together a four-country project – Argentina, Colombia, Chile and Paraguay – on the industrial entrepreneur in Latin America, that was preceded by a study of industrial entrepreneurs in Brazil conducted by Fernando H. Cardoso.[29] Lipman undertook the project in Colombia, whereas in the other countries Latin scholars coming from other disciplinary and ideological backgrounds did the studies. Cardoso wrote an insightful synthesis of this project that was included in the aforementioned book edited by Lipset. The project was framed in a broader perspective that encompassed 'the structural and historical differences that entrepreneurial activity has taken in Latin America ... and the limitations of the sector as a pressure group and a political force'.[30] It is to be noted that if not framed as entrepreneurial historical typologies, several of the country studies were aimed at sketching features of samples of industrial entrepreneurs amenable to sociological quantitative analysis. The dubious theoretical orientations of some of them notwithstanding, their merit was in gathering data with an ample coverage overcoming the limitations of case studies. Subsequently, ECLA's interest in this endeavour receded. Unfortunately, these pioneer entrepreneurial studies have passed unnoticed for decades to the point that only exceptional reference is made to them in business history and political sociology accounts as well as in recent surveys on Latin American founders of contemporary entrepreneurship and dynamic ventures.[31]

The same fate befell the pioneering works of Cochran and Reina, Lipset and Lipman. During the next two decades there were no followers or research projects and publications ensued on entrepreneurship in the direction of the modernization theory. Yet this decline of interest in culture as an explanatory factor of development took place not only in Latin American but also in the American academic community, as Samuel Huntington has recently noted.[32]

All these conditions notwithstanding, another major intellectual current in the region served to discourage the study of entrepreneurship, for ideological and political reasons. This was dependency theory and Marxism, which enjoyed wide currency in Latin America during the 1960s and '70s.

The Impact of Dependency Theory in the Study of Entrepreneurship

Dependency theory represented the Latin American contribution to the study of economic development. For the purposes of this chapter, there will be only brief mention of its central tenets and its negative effect in discouraging the study of business people, private business and entrepreneurship. There is a vast amount of literature about dependency theory available to the interested reader.[33] A precursor of this theory was the work of the ECLA in the 1950s about 'central-peripheral' relationships, which came to be known as 'ECLA structuralism'. The 1960s and '70s saw fruitful intellectual production on the part of Latin American scholars, for the most part sociologists, centring on ECLA, especially in its headquarters in Santiago de Chile. The classic work is by Cardoso and Faletto,[34] which includes a harsh critique of modernization theory based on its conception of development as an evolutionary, linear process that is part of a passage from a traditional society to a dual one and later a modern one. These concepts were considered excessively general. They also reject the idea that underdeveloped nations exhibit anomalous development and seem to assume that they must repeat the history of developed nations, without taking into account historical phases and various contexts. The central concept is that of the dependency – economic, cultural, technological – that Latin America has experienced with relation to the urban hegemonic centres of various historical stages. In this context, entrepreneurs, together with large landowners, are seen by various dependency authors as internal beneficiaries who are responsible for underdevelopment in their respective countries. They were portrayed as villains and often demonized. In such conditions, it is not surprising that entrepreneurial activity, its actors – entrepreneurs and business people – and entrepreneurship lacked legitimacy as subjects of study. It is not strange that those who sought to promote entrepreneurial studies and business history were called 'apologists of the bourgeoisie' and were viewed with suspicion. In this as in other thematic areas, overarching categories of imperialism and dependency were often applied with at least indifference towards the historical frameworks, even with 'olympian disdain for historical analysis.[35] It should also be added that some of the foreign historians specializing in Latin America

> were concerned primarily with the dominant controversies over imperialism and dependence or with writing company history of a rather traditional kind, rather than with transferring to the study of Latin America some of the major changes which were taking place in business history in the developed world under the influence of historians like Alfred Chandler or Mira Wilkins.[36]

It bears mentioning that despite some ideological affinities, dependency theory was the subject of critiques emanating from some currents of orthodox Marxism. Drawing on the Marxist theory of imperialism, some authors criticized dependency theory for remaining silent on the contemporary character of imperialism and for its careless application of Marxist theory.[37] For others, the theory of economic imperialism was the 'missing link' in dependency theory.[38]

National Culture and Economic Performance Thesis Comeback: Latin America as Part of the World's Losers

In the wake of a revival on culture as an explanatory factor in several realms of life, Lawrence E. Harrison wrote a book that was published by the Harvard Center for International Affairs in 1985. As its title it conveys, its central idea is that 'underdevelopment is a state of mind'. It is based on the author's experiences and reflections from the vantage point of his official mission as a United States Agency for International Development official in several countries of the region between 1965 and 1981. Based in parallel case studies, related basically to his own experiences and observations, he concludes that in most Latin American countries culture has been an obstacle for development.[39] Harrison's book raised protest from several quarters in Latin America as well as from economists and other experts in the region.[40] But at the same time for several years he received favourable reactions from scholars, journalists, politicians and development practitioners active in the renaissance of cultural studies. Several of them reunited in 1999 at a symposium on 'Cultural Values and Human Progress' held at Harvard that led to a book entitled *Cultural Matters: How Values Shape Human Progress*.[41] Nine of the twenty-two chapters dealt with the relationships between culture and economic and political development and were authored by distinguished scholars ranging from David Landes, Francis Fukuyama and Ronald Ingelhart to Seymour Lipset, Jeffrey Sachs and Michael Porter. By 2002 an international research project on 'Culture Matters' was started at Tufts University led by Harrison and is still under way, having published two recent volumes; one of them include case studies from several poor areas of the world, five of them on Latin American countries.[42] Only one of them gives some attention to a historical perspective. Although this project has a broader focus than entrepreneurship – development and poverty being the dependent variables that are determined by culture – it is interesting to note its similarities with the modernization approach of the 1960s.

For the audience of economic and business historians to whom the present chapter is aimed, it should be stressed that the idea of 'national culture' has been at the core of the thought of pre-eminent Harvard historian David Landes for over half a century. In his 1998 book he was definite: 'If we learn anything from the history of economic development it is that culture makes all the difference'. And later on: 'what counts is work, thrift, honesty, patience, tenacity'.[43]

It must be said that the linear model implicit in the approach of a 'national culture' has been the subject of various critiques. As a recent business history handbook chapter on business history and entrepreneurship points out, the underlying premise of its research agenda 'has proven questionable'.[44] As another critic points out, Landes's 'desire to summarize an entire society in one pithy sentence inevitably falls flat'.[45]

Landes dedicated a chapter to 'The South American Way',[46] often taking Argentina as a case study – 'the Latin country with the best chances – a country that like the entire region is in the category of "losers"'. He calls attention to the region's instability and insecurity, which in the nineteenth century was a 'penny-dreadful of conspiracies, cabals, coups and countercoups with all these entailed in insecurity, bad government, corruption, an economic retardation ... At the top, a small group of rascals, well taught by earlier colonial masters, looted freely'. For Landes, Latin America was a 'simulacrum of Iberian society'; Spain exported its weaknesses overseas. Among them 'its spiritual homogeneity and docility, its wealth and pursuit of vanities ... The road to wealth passed, not by work, but by graft and (mis)rule.' In a nutshell, and to no one's surprise, in the eyes of Landes: 'The Latin American countries had no program, then no vision of economic development'.[47] In this grim picture of the vast continent to the south of the United States, there was no place for entrepreneurship nor entrepreneurs. The interesting fact is that these cultural interpretations are prone to be accompanied by a vision where race and geography are also present.[48]

These overriding generalizations are based on debatable empirical evidence and do not leave space to counter factual evidence, at least regarding the causes for South America remaining among the poorest parts of the world. This does not deny that Landes's book

> is just beautifully written, filled with bon mots and witty observations, speckled with devastating and at times irreverent dismissals of opposing views. Landes commands a seemingly endless arsenal of interesting and neat anecdotes and historical miniatures that are used in virtuoso fashion to illustrate a point. The width and depth of the

historical knowledge at his disposal is simply so vast that even his most determined opponents will have to admit their respect for this work.[49]

With Landes's vision, justifiably called 'Eurocentrically triumphant' by one reviewer, 'few business historians will agree with everything it says – but everyone will be awed by its erudition and verve'.[50] Without denying Landes's characteristic insight and caustic wit,[51] business historians who have studied this part of the world would certainly agree with few things he wrote on Latin America.

Business History and Local/Regional Culture: An Alternative to Modernization Theory, Value Analysis and National Culture Perspective and Dependency Theory

Landes's stance is reminiscent both of the 'westernization' bias and lack of empirical evidence of the modernization school of thought examined above. Interestingly enough, during the same decade in which Landes's book was published, a growing business historiography was already in existence that in a variety of ways addressed the topics under contest. That is, the relationship between culture and entrepreneurship.[52] That historiography was the product of both Latin American and foreign researchers.

In fact, it was not until the turn of the 1970s that the study of entrepreneurship in economic development resurged in Latin America, now viewed from a different angle rooted in socio-economic historical perspectives, devoid of both the ideological overtones proper to the 'theology of dependency' and the methodological and ethnocentric drawbacks that permeated modernization theories.

In the first case, research advanced in both regional settings pointed out the distinction between foreign capital and foreign last names for the case of Spanish immigrants who came from northern Spain and became prominent businessmen, especially in the period between 1870 and 1910.[53] In Argentina, a counterpoint to Cochran's study came out with research focused on the regional and local setting as a locus of economic development and of entrepreneurial activity, pioneered by a carefully crafted piece on entrepreneurship in an Argentine province – Mendoza – in the period 1861–1914 written by an American historian in 1979.[54] In the decades after this study, Argentine economic and business historians were contributing numerous works about entrepreneurs and family businesses in the wine, sugar and cattle ranching sectors of the inland Argentine provinces – Mendoza, Patagonia and Cuyo, principally. At the same time, studies on British, Italian and French immigrants engaged in a variety of businesses and entrepreneurial ventures since the last decades of the nineteenth century became one of the outputs of growing Argentinean business history, as attested by a recent survey of the literature.[55]

These works belonged to a category of business history, which has also appeared in Mexico and Colombia, where studies about the origins and formation of regional entrepreneurship saw particular development. In the case of Colombia, as a counterpoint to Hagen's debatable method and conclusions researchers from several disciplines contributed to grace the following decades with valuable historic works based on detailed primary (and secondary) source research. These included works on Antioqueño mining, commerce, socio-cultural values, coffee, industrialization, ethnic origins, politics, colonization, technical education, and transportation.[56] In the same vein, studies about the origins of entrepreneurship in other regions of this Andean country gradually came out.[57] In the north-east region of Mexico, neighbouring the United States, Monterrey, the centre of Mexican industrialization, had at the end of the 1990s a broad and rich bibliography.[58]

In various countries there were also advances in the study of immigrants as groups with outstanding entrepreneurial activity who were not dissenters but partners and/or competitors of local entrepreneurs and who, in many cases, became part of local elites. Mexico and Argentina are leaders in this type of study.[59] Those works were examining, for example, the articulation of entrepreneurs within the society and the local culture and their business practices in the local economy.[60] In Argentina, research about foreign capital companies, for example the railroads, banks and British meat processors, represented the modal category of Argentine business history.[61] These studies, without explicitly attempting to, raised many questions about the alleged ideas of rejection of foreigners, or of foreigners as exemplars of entrepreneurial values that supposedly only they possess, in contrast to local businessmen.

In closing this section, it should be stressed that modernization theory made a modest contribution to the study of entrepreneurship and its cultural determinants in Latin America; the reader will be perplexed to realize that four decades later, and at a time in which entrepreneurship is at centre stage for its role in 'value creation', the national values perspective, with its rampant 'culture matters' determinism, seems to be more inclined to develop practical guidelines and input development policy than to advance knowledge.

Latin American Backwardness and Substitutes for Economic Prerequisites: Another Fruitful Perspective for Research

It is a good idea to recall that another writer of the 1960s, also a Harvard professor, the economic historian Alexander Gerschenkron, has in the past few years attracted new interest in his ideas about economic backwardness in historical perspective.[62] This interest has as much to do with the vicissitudes of Latin American economic development in the years of globalization, as opposed to the rapid pace of development in East Asia. Gerschenkron's central notion 'is the positive role of relative economic backwardness in inducing systematic substitution for supposed prerequisites for industrial growth'.[63] For the case of business historians in Latin America it would be very useful to take into account that, according to this prominent economic historian, aside from the substitutes, there is something very important in the effect on entrepreneurs of passing through the professional training of industrialization.

Studies have been carried out about industrialization and entrepreneurship in industrial centres of Argentina (Buenos Aires), Brazil (Sao Paulo, Minas Gerais), Colombia (Medellin), Chile (Santiago de Chile) and Mexico (Monterrey and Mexico City/Puebla) from various perspectives. They have supported the idea of the importance of entrepreneurial experience and learning.

Complementing Gershenkron's thesis, in the case of gold mining in Antioquia, various works converge on what constituted from the mid-nineteenth century a 'practical entrepreneurial school',[64] prior to the industrialization of the regional capital – Medellin – that started in the first decade of the twentieth century. It also preceded the pioneer formal training in business education in same country at the beginning of the twentieth century, not by accident located in a school of mining and engineering.[65]

Elements towards a Synthesis of Latin American Entrepreneurship

The present state of business history in Latin America does not allow reliance on works of synthesis, either at the sub-continent level or for countries where this field of study shows major advances. This is a major shortcoming that makes it difficult for the international reader interested in comparative perspectives fully to understand the present chapter, which is focused on a specific stream of business history – the links between culture, entrepreneurship and economic growth. This limitation notwithstanding, a tentative outline for a synthesis of Latin American entrepreneurship in the 1850–2000 period is attempted, based on regional and country surveys of the business history literature utilized throughout this paper.[66] They permit identification in a nutshell of the following as the most important features and patterns in Latin American entrepreneurship and entrepreneurial behaviour: wealthy urban elites have been key entrepreneurial actors in early economic development; entrepreneurs have shown high diversification of investment and entrepreneurial activity; family capitalism with business and entrepreneurial families as key actors has played centre stage; business has been closely intertwined with politics and the state, the accumulation of political capital being a critical entrepreneurial capability; foreign capital has played an important role and evolved through varied organizational forms; European immigration has been noticeable; and state-owned enterprise was important throughout the twentieth century.

Concluding Remarks: Towards an Analytical Scheme for Entrepreneurial History

In closing this paper it should be recalled that the interplay between cultural values and entrepreneurship is a promising field of research in business history in Latin America. The experiences derived from the eventful evolution of theory and research on this topic in this part of the world over the last fifty years impart several lessons. One is the drawback of trying to test grand theoretical schemes of the type of 'modernization' theory or national culture through static, cross-sectional research strategies, devoid of any historical perspective. The orientation of the recent revival of current research on national culture demonstrates that the pitfalls of the large research projects carried out in the 1960s are prone to be repeated; the lessons from them seem to have been obliterated. A second lesson is that the emphasis on culture at the expense of institutions, resource endowment and other environmental factors is a drawback in understanding economic growth. A third lesson is positive: the criticism of those approaches by nascent business history in Latin America was furthered by research that became a counterpoint to many of the preconceptions and generalizations of the modernization theory. More to the point, five areas of business history research have proved to be promising in the region: origins of local and regional entrepreneurship; origins of industrialization; business elites; entrepreneurial and family business history; and immigrant networks. The revival of interest in Weberian, Schumpeterian, Sombartian, Veblerian and Gerschenkronian theories related to entrepreneurship and values has led to recent theoretical and methodological advances in the international community of business historians.[67] These advances in topics such as entrepreneurship and family firms, entrepreneurial networks and diasporas, and more generally entrepreneurship, culture and historical explanation, offer an opportunity for the strengthening of Latin American business history. The challenge is to incorporate them critically in the research agenda for the next decades.

A step in that direction has to do with entrepreneurial history, of which there are valuable contributions within Latin American business historiography. The purpose would be to explore ways to articulate it into ongoing comparative research projects on entrepreneurial typologies as reported in several of the chapters of this volume. A limitation is that for no countries of the region are there scholarly business/entrepreneurial history dictionaries similar to those available in the United Kingdom and Italy,[68] nor are there collections of brief entrepreneurial biographies such as those that appeared in the last decade in Spain.[69] With this in mind, what follows refers to a project to develop an analytical framework for doing research on histories of individual entrepreneurs and/or entrepreneurial families. This framework has two applications: first, it serves to orient scholarly historical biographies of entrepreneurs and, second, it can be used to analyse existing biographies. The framework is composed of a set of five elements, each of which has a series of variables to study that could prove operational. Thus, there is a base of developing and analysing entrepreneurial typologies, permitting aggregate analysis that makes comparative research possible. This could open doors for specific Latin American countries to be articulated within ongoing projects, as exists in the Global Entrepreneurship Monitor (GEM) which now includes eight Latin American countries – Argentina, Brazil, Chile, Colombia, Peru, Dominican Republic, Uruguay and Venezuela – or the developing entrepreneurship project in Latin America sponsored by the Inter-American Development Bank.[70]

The framework in question[71] has been developed in Colombia in the management school of a private university: University of the Andes, an institution pioneering business history in Latin America, where teaching and research in this field has been ongoing since 1974. During the past ten years the conceptual framework has been developing and maturing and realizing its application potential. An initial output concerns senior undergraduate honour and MBA theses – around twenty-five of them – that have contributed short biographical profiles of contemporary entrepreneurs from very diverse sectors; documents of about fifty pages in length, based on oral history and primary and secondary sources. The framework has been adjusted over the years and has proven its viability and its potential for advancing beyond the entrepreneur case-study by attempting to standardize the facts in their stories and provide a basis for quantitative research on entrepreneurs and their lifetime ventures.

The second strand of work is an analysis of existing entrepreneurial biographies and autobiographies with the assistance of the framework. Both outputs contribute to the formation of a data set of entrepreneurs – Colombian, in this case. An outline of the framework appears below. It is composed of six elements: 1. socio-economic, political and institutional context in which the entrepreneur developed; 2. economic behaviour; 3. socio-economic and demographic background variables; 4. relationships with politics and the state; 5. lifestyle; and 6. mentality.

1. *Socio-economic, political and institutional context*: The entrepreneur is an economic agent in the market articulated into a given social and political structure. Without denying his agency, it is clear that market and environmental conditions are ever present and interplay with the rest of the categories of the framework under consideration. Attention to the various environmental

conditions in which the entrepreneur has lived and deployed his action is at the core of historical entrepreneurial biographies. Important as they are, institutional conditions regarding property rights, contractual conditions and rule of law do not completely cover this category. Social structure considerations, especially with regard to inequality and social mobility, are also to be considered. All in all for the influence of environmental conditions on the entrepreneur, as Jones and Wadhwani have recently recalled, 'Schumpeter's basic premise that entrepreneurs often acted as agents of change rather than as captives of their environment'[72] should not be forgotten.

2. *Economic behaviour*: This refers basically to the entrepreneur's functions in the economic development of his country/region/locality. It includes alertness to opportunities, creation of new ventures, innovation – including adaptation of technology to local conditions – risk-taking, information-seeking and synthesis, markets in which he operates, creation of new markets, managerial functions, credit and financing, diversification/specialization of investments, and long- and short-term vision. It addresses productive, non-productive or destructive functions in the economy played by the entrepreneur as a response to the structure of incentives.

3. *Socio-economic and demographic background variables*: This encompasses age, foreign/regional origin, social origin of parents, origin of initial accumulation, social mobility, educational level, formation as entrepreneur, time of entry into entrepreneurial activity, socialization in entrepreneurship, role of family in business, place within family structure, social networking – family, regional, ethnic, professional – regional/international mobility, religious affiliation, motives for engaging in entrepreneurship, managerial style and distinctive personality traits.

4. *Relationships with politics and the state*: This deals with voting/abstention in elections, assuming public office – through election or appointment – political campaign financing, use of state concessions, state contracting, lobbying, rent-seeking mechanisms, promotion/leadership in business associations and engagement in networking to promote/resolve political crises, promotion/leadership in third-sector organizations and belonging to families linked to politics.

5. *Lifestyle*: This concerns the role of business in personal/family life, cosmopolitanism, use of free time, membership in and the role of social clubs, frugality/wastefulness (consumption patterns) and the role of networking – friendship, social, professional, ethnic, regional, religious – in everyday life.

6. *Mentality*: Ideas and personally held positions both in discourse and as reflected in practices related to the state's role in economic development, market as the supreme allocator, role of religion in business, business competition, monopoly and profit-seeking. Also in matters related to rational calculus, trust within business relations, value of time, hard work, thrift, honesty, patience,

tenacity, detachment of business from personal/emotional considerations, globalization, social exclusion and inequality, business ethics and social responsibility, adherence to the law and rules of the game – both formal and informal – and success and failure in entrepreneurial activity.

8 EDUCATION AND ENTREPRENEURSHIP IN TWENTIETH-CENTURY SPAIN: AN OVERVIEW

José L. García-Ruiz

Introduction

Since Joseph A. Schumpeter published his *Theorie der wirtschaftlichen Entwicklung* in 1911,[1] an important role has been assigned to 'entrepreneurship' in economic growth, but until recently in too imprecise a way. In recent years, thanks to three large initiatives – the Observatory of European Small and Medium Enterprises (SMEs), belonging to the European Union; the Centre for Entrepreneurship, SMEs and Local Development, belonging to the Organisation for Economic Co-Operation and Development (OECD); and the Global Entrepreneurship Monitor (GEM) – and the work of some scholars it has been possible to make progress in dealing scientifically with entrepreneurship, that is, elaborating theories that can be empirically tested.[2] These researches have been of interest to governments, particularly those from European countries in which entrepreneurship has been in difficulties for many years. Thus, in 2003, the European Commission brought out the well-known *Green Paper on Entrepreneurship in Europe*, which is based mainly on research done by David B. Audretsch, who proposed a debate on several initiatives to stimulate entrepreneurship in Europe.[3]

Reflecting this concern, the Spanish Consejo Económico y Social (CES) published in 2005 a report entitled *El proceso de creación de empresas y el dinamismo empresarial*, which to a great extent was based on GEM reports.[4] These reports have always paid attention to factors involved in creating businesses where public policies can take action (Table 8.1).

Table 8.1: GEM Evaluation of Factors Involved in Creating Businesses in Spain, 2003–5 (points out of a maximum of five).[5]

Factor	2003	2004	2005
Access to Physical Infrastructure	3.38	3.73	3.64
Trade Infrastructure	2.93	3.20	3.26
Support for Growth and Development of Firms	–	–	3.05
Government Programmes: Presence, Aid	3.04	3.12	3.01
Protection of Intellectual Rights	2.87	2.97	2.89
Government Policy: Bureaucracy, Procedure	2.81	2.87	2.81
Post-Secondary Education	2.68	2.74	2.75
Social and Cultural Norms	2.56	2.78	2.74
Opening up of Domestic Market: Barriers	2.78	2.76	2.70
Government Policy: Support, Emphasis on Measures	3.01	2.95	2.69
Financial Backing	2.49	2.44	2.54
Technology and Research & Development Transfer	2.61	2.48	2.52
Opening up of Domestic Market: Reaction Capacity	2.13	2.18	2.16
Primary and Secondary Education	1.82	1.86	1.87

The CES analysts attached great importance to the relationship between education and entrepreneurship and were highly concerned by the low score obtained by educational factors, as considered in the *Informe Ejecutivo GEM España 2003*, which was the one used. It was clear that government policies offering support to entrepreneurial initiative were not delivering in this area. So, the CES analysts proposed 'making people aware of the importance of entrepreneurial qualities as a basic new skill from primary school level' and 'developing links between schools and the private sector'. This involved setting up structures, plans and measures to support this objective. In the university field, these initiatives must be more ambitious, including 'among the university functions that of promoting the entrepreneurial spirit' and seeking 'to exploit knowledge acquired in the university and to transfer it to society by means of firms created by the university community'.[6]

The data in Table 8.1 show that some improvement could be observed between 2003 and 2005, the time when the CES made their report public, but there was still some way to go. Both the *Green Paper* and the CES report have provided a basis for the Spanish government and the autonomous communities to make every effort in recent years in initiatives completely unheard of in the field of education. Thus, for example, the Community of Madrid has organized since 2005 an annual competition entitled 'Dream today to manage tomorrow', involving students and teachers of primary, secondary and professional schools in preparing stories, comics and video game scripts on the subject matter. What is more, in December 2006, the governing board of the Complutense University of Madrid approved the regulations for the creation of 'technology-based firms', started up by teachers and researchers wishing to market their laboratory work.

That and other similar initiatives in the Madrid area are being coordinated by a specialized institution of the Community of Madrid (the Oficina del Emprendedor de Base Tecnológica de la Comunidad de Madrid).

Given the interest shown recently by public policies in the relationship between education and the entrepreneurial spirit, we shall devote this paper to investigating the evolution of the training of entrepreneurs and managers between 1964 and the present time through the available bibliography on the subject and the data provided by the official survey on the working population (the Encuesta de Población Activa, EPA, provided by the Instituto Nacional de Estadística). This latter has never before been exploited for the full period (the EPA started in 1964).

Education and Entrepreneurship

As Santos explained in 1997, Schumpeter's approach to entrepreneurship has been widely diffused inside and outside the academic world, and has been the starting point for several studies attempting to characterize the entrepreneur. The psychologist David C. McClelland, the sociologist Everett E. Hagen and the economist Harvey Liebenstein have been the most notable in the attempts to develop the Schumpterian paradigm. For McClelland, humanity has three basic needs: achievement, belonging and power. Each individual will feel these needs in a different way. In the case of the entrepreneur, the need for achievement through work will be stronger than the other ones. For Hagen and Liebenstein, the process which gives birth to entrepreneurs can be best explained by social factors rather than individual ones. Hagen finds that entrepreneurs tend to appear among cultural minorities which are outcasts in society. In the heart of these minorities are the conditions that induce individuals to be inclined to the Schumpeterian 'creative destruction'. Liebenstein considers that the market, which is never in a state of perfect competition, is unable by itself to make firms work in a completely efficient manner. There will always be an 'inefficiency X' which can only be solved by the entrepreneur. For Liebenstein, the entrepreneur's main contribution will be to motivate workers to put the firm as near as possible to the production frontier defined by technology.[7]

The role of education in training the entrepreneurial spirit is very hazy in those lines of Schumpterian research, obsessed as they were with the 'traits approach', which looks for innate characteristics in people. A long time passed before Alfred Marshall's warnings were heeded. The great Cambridge economist was very concerned to see that his country was lagging behind the new industrial leaders, Germany and the United States, and among the reasons for this phenomenon he mentioned the education factor.[8] An added problem was that the British educational system did not appear to be the most suitable for stimulating business initiative. Not only was it the case that the British population received scant formal education, it was also a fact that those who did have access to education were not trained with knowledge enabling them to be better entrepreneurs and managers. Years later, the sociologist Martin J. Wiener expressed his agreement with these observations when linking the training received by the British elite to the loss of entrepreneurial values in a highly successful book.[9] The national culture approach of Wiener's book has been widely criticized, but the persistent patterns of wealth and poverty in the world have in recent years led to a renewed interest in identifying variations in entrepreneurial performance caused by culture.[10]

The provision of primary education by the British state began in 1879, and this was followed with some delay by secondary education.[11] Research carried out to measure the impact produced by the formal education system in creating firms came up with pessimistic findings, a fact highlighted by James Foreman-Peck. Education did not serve to raise people up the social business ladder, though it did have effects of this type on professional and civil service ladders.[12] It can even be stated that panel studies tend to support the idea that the individual who had received education in contemporary history had fewer chances of developing an entrepreneurial spirit.[13] The situation improved after the Second World War, with the introduction, for example, of business schools, which were faithful models of American management, but by the end of the twentieth century the British education system as a whole was still an obstacle for the country's competitive advantage.

In a recent doctoral thesis defended in Oxford University by Mike Hicks[14] it is shown that, at the beginning of the twentieth century, British business managers had little university training, rather less than Americans, and a great deal less than the Germans. If one looks at the leading industrial countries in the twentieth century it is clear that British managers were only better educated than the Japanese, though the latter were soon to show enormous interest in training and before the Second World War were on a par with Germany. The British made very slow progress and the business leaders of the country throughout the whole of the twentieth century remained below the level of Germans and Americans (very similar in the post-war period) and a long way behind the impressive levels of Japan (with over 90 per cent of its managers boasting university training in recent years).

Hicks's thesis is consistent with what Marshall could see around 1900 and with the extensive literature which has highlighted British neglect of formal education as a cause of the country's industrial decline. In a recent splendid synthesis of the history of British management, John F. Wilson and Andrew W. Thomson have shown how it took a long time to convince British people that entrepreneurs and managers are not 'born', but 'made'; the backwardness can be seen in the fact that, nowadays, firms' expenditure per head on the training of each manager is 4,438 euros in Germany and only 1,625 euros in Great Britain.[15] The country's entrepreneurs and managers are still far worse trained than other professions. In the years before the 2008 crisis, the United Kingdom experienced phenomenal economic growth, which made its citizens highly confident, but the authors of the above-mentioned book and international experts in competitiveness such as Michael E. Porter do not think that this kind of progress could be sustainable without the education system being taken more seriously.[16] Nowadays many scholars are convinced that Edith T. Penrose was right when she postulated that firms succeed or fail in competitive worlds on the basis of their resources and the skill of their managers, in the training of which education plays a vital role.[17]

The European model for good business education is Germany. According to Carlsson et al. (2007), the first school of agriculture was created in Germany around 1770 and the first school of mining in 1776; one century afterwards, the first organized industrial laboratories appeared in Germany in the 1870s, in firms that sought to commercialize inventions based on new breakthroughs in organic chemistry.[18] It is well known that the Prussian state put into practice a compulsory education system after the defeat in Jena in 1806. Soon afterwards, in 1809, the Humboldt University was born in Berlin. This university was described by Peter Drucker, the expert in business management, as the first modern university.[19] In 1825 Karlsruhe Polytechnic was added to the system, following the French model, and it was reorganized in 1833 by Karl F. Nebenius, becoming a model of its kind. The number of students in technical universities (Technische Hochschulen) grew quickly at the turn of the century and those centres played a crucial role in the education of the business elite.[20] Business-related specialized studies began in 1913, when the first Kaufmann diploma was awarded. This is not a late date if we think that similarly in the United States business studies did not become widespread until the beginning of the twentieth century.

In Germany not only are business managers well trained (particularly in engineering), but workers also reached a relatively high educational level quite early on. As the nineteenth century merged into the twentieth, it began to become clear that British leadership was in jeopardy in the face of the industrial force of Germany and the United States, and for an astute observer like Werner Sombart it was a 'very significant fact that the poor German countries had only preceded their more fortunate Western rivals in one area: the organization of public instruction'.[21] Years later, the American historian David S. Landes showed himself to be in agreement with these theories when he pointed out that Germany's success in the 'Second Industrial Revolution' had been greatly to do with the existence of a good education system, ranging from professional training to university level.[22] The complex industrialization which was characteristic in the twentieth century soon showed up the limitations of the 'practical man' and established the need for an increasingly larger extension of scientific-technical knowledge, as Robert T. Locke explained.[23]

About the current situation the study of Van der Sluis et al. (2003) is interesting,[24] providing a review of empirical studies about the impact of schooling on entrepreneurship selection and performance. Five main conclusions result from the paper. First, the impact of education on selection into entrepreneurship is ambiguous, neither positive nor negative. Second, the effect of education on performance is positive and significant. Third, the return on a marginal year of schooling in terms of the income it generates is 6.1 per cent in the United States. Fourth, the effect of education on earnings is smaller for entrepreneurs than for employees in Europe, but equal or larger in the United States. Fifth, all results obtained so far are potentially biased. A warning: the authors say that estimation and identification strategies used to identify the effect of education on performance have merely measured the (conditional) correlation between education and performance rather than the causal effect, which is the estimate of interest. To summarize, the available empirical evidence seems to establish that education has returns for American entrepreneurs but this is not clear for European ones.

Two recent contributions to the debate in Spain differ in their theoretical base. For Velasco-Barroetabeña and Saiz-Santos (2007),

> the economic literature on entrepreneurship has clearly shown that, even when some famous entrepreneurs have emerged from social and personal strata with low education levels, the entrepreneurs with a good education level (at least in developed countries) are more likely to be successful than their less educated colleagues ... It's better to forget 'If you don't know where you are going, any road will take you there' [as was said by the Cheshire cat to Alice in the Lewis Carrol's well-known book]. In a less metaphorical way: to be a genius in business, first you must know the work.[25]

On the contrary, Congregado et al. (2008) adopt the sceptical view of Van der Sluis et al.[26] In a following section we will review that book in detail because it uses data from the EPA as we have done and it could be interesting to make some comparative analysis.

Education of Entrepreneurs in Spain According to the EPA, 1964–2004

The Starting Point: A Study from the Bancaja Foundation

Following the line of research on human capital initiated by Mas et al. (1995) and Palafox et al. (1995), the Bancaja Foundation (a foundation supported by the Valencia savings bank Bancaja) published in 2003 a work entitled *Actividad y ocupación por niveles de estudios*.[27] This work was widely distributed in the media and its main conclusions were three: 1. the educational level of the Spanish working population showed an impressive rise in the last thirty years of the twentieth century; 2. the greater the educational level, the higher the chances of finding a good job; and 3. Spanish entrepreneurs are not characterized on the whole by having a high educational level, falling some way behind firms' managers.

To give support to the first conclusion, data were provided in the work showing that in 1970, 88.6 per cent of those working only had primary studies, whereas in 2000, 26.7 of those working were in this situation. At the top, university graduates accounted for 4.3 per cent of those in work in 1970 and 19 per cent in 2000. The second conclusion was supported by the fact that those with higher education had maintained activity rates above 70 per cent throughout the whole period, with a rising trend from 1982 and reaching in 2000 scores very close to 80 per cent. The activity rate in the population with middle studies had grown in the early 1980s, remained unchanged between 1986 and 1996 with values around 60 per cent and, subsequently, had risen once more to nearly 65 per cent. Finally, the population with primary studies had shown a fall in activity, ranging from 50 to 30 per cent, in rounded-up figures.

It was perhaps the third conclusion that caused most surprise: Spanish entrepreneurs had less training than the Spanish average, and certainly they were worse trained than their managers. In 2000, scarcely 11 per cent of entrepreneurs were university educated, when, as we have seen, this figure rose to 19 per cent for the population as a whole. For this reason, even when the percentage regarding non-compulsory secondary studies was very similar (27.8 per cent in the case of entrepreneurs and 27.4 per cent in the general case), Spanish entrepreneurs seemed to be characterized as illiterates or with nothing more than compulsory studies to a very great extent: specifically, 61.5 per cent.

The education level of managers was quite different: 54.2 per cent had university studies (compared to 10.7 per cent of entrepreneurs) and only 13.7 per cent had no training or just compulsory education (compared to 61.5 per cent of entrepreneurs). In view of this information, the Bancaja researchers suggested that entrepreneurial activity is quite unlike management. Entrepreneurial activity seems not to need formal education, whereas management activity demands specific knowledge only acquired after long years devoted to study and research in one's field.

The Bancaja work was the first to use data from the EPA to measure the influence of education in training entrepreneurial skills (entrepreneurship and management). The work refers to the 1990s and it is our aim to extend the research from the period starting in 1964 up to the present time. This is because during these more than forty years there has been a great structural transformation in the Spanish economy and we may find significant variations compared to the situation described for the most recent period.

The Level of Studies of Entrepreneurs and Managers in 1964

Juan J. Linz gave a course in 1960 in the Escuela de Organización Industrial (EOI) on introduction to the sociology of the industrial society. It was well received and served for the distinguished sociologist to launch the school on research activities. Thus the project 'The Spanish entrepreneur as a human factor in economic development' got under way. The project made it possible to find out, for the first time, the level of training of Spanish managers and entrepreneurs. In this project, Linz had the admirable help of his disciple Amando de Miguel, to the extent that the latter's was the first signature on the article published by both on the topic in the journal *Arbor*.[28]

In Table 8.2 there is a summary of the main findings of the study by Linz and De Miguel regarding educational level. It must be pointed out that the research centred on entrepreneurs and managers (without distinction) of industrial firms, located in thirteen particularly industrialized provinces and with more than fifty workers; that is, the idea was to discover the educational level of the Spanish business elite in a broad sense.

Table 8.2: Level of Studies of Entrepreneurs and Managers in Firms with more than Fifty Workers around 1960, by Provinces Studied and Size of Firm (% in each province or size).[29]

Region	Primary	Secondary	Technician	Engineer	Lawyer	Business	Economist	Other	No Reply
Alicante	31	12	–	12	25	6	–	–	12
Asturias	–	–	7	93	–	–	–	–	–
Barcelona	10	10	19	22	9	19	1	4	4
Biscay	11	7	6	28	13	15	7	10	3
Cadiz	14	64	–	7	–	–	14	–	–
Cordoba-Seville	25	10	–	25	15	5	5	15	–
Corunna-Pontevedra	5	30	–	20	5	25	–	15	–
Guipuzkoa	20	8	12	20	8	28	–	–	4
Madrid	4	14	9	38	12	8	5	8	3
Saragossa	31	12	6	12	6	6	–	12	6
Valencia	32	16	3	6	19	13	–	3	6
Total	13	13	10	26	11	14	3	6	4
Small	29	17	6	13	5	17	–	10	3
Normal	23	14	14	15	7	14	3	7	5
Average	11	16	11	24	9	17	4	4	5
Large	3	8	11	33	17	17	3	5	3
Giant	1	6	7	48	17	6	4	9	1
Total	13	13	10	26	11	14	3	6	4

The information in the table clearly shows that the engineering profession dominated the Spanish business elite, with 26 per cent of Spanish managers holding
that qualification and another 10 per cent being industrial technicians (*peritos*).
Some way behind came those who had studied business (14 per cent) or law
(11 per cent). The predominance of engineers was absolute in Asturias, a region
strong in the mining and metallurgical trades. There was also a strong presence of
engineering in the large industrialized provinces (Barcelona, Madrid and Biscay)
and of particular note was the fact that in Barcelona the number of industrial
technicians was almost the same as that for engineers. The business structure
impinged on the higher or lower recruiting of firms' engineers: nearly half of the
business managers in very large and a third in the large firms were engineers. This
proportion fell sharply in the small firms.

Lawyers were the second most important professional group in top management in large and very large firms, followed closely by those with qualifications
in business (*comercio*), special studies, which were widely popular before the profession of economist became established.[30] In the big firms it was difficult to find
managers with no specific form of training, but this, on the contrary, was normal
in smaller firms (49 per cent) or reduced size ones (42 per cent). Managers with
very little training were common in the Spanish Levant (Valencia, Alicante), a
business world dominated by small firms, and in Cadiz (Andalusia), where as
many as 64 per cent of managers had only basic education.

In the 1950s, the Spanish state was aware that engineers needed complementary training to be able to carry out their management functions adequately.
Thus, the Ministries of National Education and Industry jointly published the
Ministerial Order of 12 July 1955, setting up the first Spanish business school:
the Escuela de Organización Industrial (EOI). The EOI was born in the heart
of the Comisión Nacional de Productividad Industrial (CNPI), created by
the government in 1952 to complement the work of the Instituto Nacional de
Racionalización del Trabajo (INRT), set up in 1946. The aim of all these public
bodies was the same, improving the productivity of Spanish industry, but the
INRT was part of the autarkic policies initiated by the Instituto Nacional de
Industria (INI) in 1941, whereas the CNPI and the EOI were financed by the
'American aid' which had begun to arrive in Spain in 1950.

The EOI was to play a fundamental role in the 'Americanization' of Spanish
firms, a process that was taking place simultaneously throughout Europe in the
wake of the resources provided by the Marshall Plan.[31] The EOI provided middle
and higher studies. To follow a middle course it was necessary to have an official
diploma accrediting a high enough technical or scientific level in the opinion
of the school. In order to study the higher grade, an engineering diploma or
a university degree in related areas was required. What is more, proof had to
be supplied of experience in the civil service or in business. Therefore, the EOI

sprang into life to teach production and business organization to professionals with higher studies.

The reorganization of the university studies of political, economic and business administration sciences, which took place in July 1953, served to make the business studies more solid. As is shown in Table 8.3, registration for these had begun ten years previously, but the first graduates did not emerge until 1948: just 37 against the 1,223 registered at the beginning of the degree course. Around 1970, the year in which the Education Act separated studies in economic and business administration from those in political sciences and sociology, the number of graduates came to over a thousand (though the exact figure is not shown in the table). This clearly explains the low number of economists found by De Miguel and Linz among the Spanish entrepreneurial elite around 1960.

Table 8.3: Students Registered and Graduates in Political, Economic and Business Sciences, 1943–70.[32]

Year	Registered	Graduates	Year	Registered	Graduates
1943	1,223	–	1957	4,082	96
1944	1,021	–	1958	5,104	99
1945	1,024	–	1959	5,742	138
1946	1,524	–	1960	6,365	188
1947	1,890	–	1961	7,034	189
1948	1,613	37	1962	8,200	176
1949	2,095	85	1963	10,356	334
1950	2,140	92	1964	11,087	345
1951	1,720	75	1965	11,950	502
1952	1,882	56	1966	16,850	378
1953	1,534	94	1967	18,657	827
1954	1,816	90	1968	20,000	782
1955	2,291	74	1969	20,347	964
1956	3,290	46	1970	23,373	–

By the time of the 50th anniversary of the EOI, two research projects had been carried out on its history, and these enable us to make progress in improving our knowledge of what this business school has really meant.[33] The source of inspiration for the EOI was the Istituto Postuniversitario per lo Studio dell'Organizzazione Aziendale (IPSOA), which had been recently created in Turin (Italy) under American influence. The industrial engineer Fermín de la Sierra, head of the department of scientific organization of the INRT, was given the task of making direct contact with specialists in the United States to implement a curriculum in the EOI, and he opted to use as a model the work done by Ralph M. Barnes, lecturer in the University of California in Los Angeles (UCLA), who he had met when he was teaching in the University of Iowa. De la Sierra was responsible for the publication in Spanish in 1950 of the *Manual de métodos de trabajo* (original title: *Work Methods Manual*) by Barnes, a work which was highly successful and went through various editions. Barnes and De la Sierra were strong supporters of the American methods which sought the 'one best time' (F. W. Taylor) and the 'one best motion' (F. B. and E. L. M. Gilbreth). These management ideas had already been in existence for four decades and were being replaced by others which stressed the importance of the human factor (the so-called 'Human Relations School'), but they were certainly propounded by the team of engineers recruited by De la Sierra to teach in the branch of production. In the other branch, business organization, the teaching staff took on graduates in law and business.

Among the students in the first two academic years of the EOI, there was a predominance of engineers (54), technicians and quantity surveyors (35) but there was also a large number of doctors and graduates in law and arts (30) and insurance actuaries and those with diplomas in business (35). The impression is given that the two branches of the EOI (production and business organization) tended to be sealed compartments, with highly different views of the business world; on the one hand were the engineers, highly concerned with production, and, on the other, those who thought that accounting, administrative and commercial organization were as important as production. The chairman of the EOI, De la Sierra, who was an engineer increasingly interested in business and economic matters, did as much as possible to act as a bridge between both worlds. One effective way was to invite national and international experts who were showing the advantages of engineers and economists collaborating in their work. The course on quality control which was given in 1962 by the American engineer Joseph J. Juran was a real event.

Following along the path of the EOI, other business schools (apart from the EOI branch in Barcelona) soon sprang up; against everyone's predictions, they were set up by religious institutions. The Jesuits added to their long-established Universidad de Deusto (1916) – which had made such a strong contribution to the training of the Basque entrepreneurial elite – business schools such as the Instituto Católico de Administración y Dirección de Empresas (Madrid, 1956), the Escuela Superior de Técnica Empresarial (Bilbao, 1956) and the Escuela Superior de Administración y Dirección de Empresas (Barcelona, 1958). Meanwhile Opus Dei went ahead with the Instituto de Estudios Superiores de la Empresa (Barcelona, 1956) and the Padres Reparadores weighed in with the Escuela Superior de Gestión Comercial y Marketing (ESIC), founded in Madrid in 1965.[34]

The heavy presence of the Catholic Church in the field of business training appears to be due to the lack of confidence inspired by the Taylorist paradigm of the scientific work organization and its dehumanized nature. Books by Jesuits such as Martín Brugarola, Pedro Uriarte or Mariano Sánchez-Gil left no doubt as to the preference of the Church for the human relations model against that of the scientific work organization. Brugarola went so far as to say that the expression 'human relations' was the same as 'Christian relations'.[35] Accepting these criticisms, but from a lay viewpoint, the Instituto de Empresa was founded in Madrid in 1973. It is generally agreed that the schools promoted by the Church, the EOI (despite its frequent institutional crises) and the Instituto de Empresa have played a very positive role in training Spanish managers to tackle the challenges of globalization which have characterized the world economy in recent times.

A Source to be Tapped: The Survey of the Working Population

The EPA survey appeared in 1964 as a means of completing the available information in the general population censuses. The long gaps between each census (ten years) and the highly general character of its information made it essential to have specialized statistical research devoted to registering very specific aspects of the workforce. Spain was thus following the recommendations of the International Labour Organization (ILO) and the pioneering efforts in this field which the large European countries (Germany, France, United Kingdom) were starting to make immediately after the end of the Second World War.

Between 1964 and the present day, the EPA methodology has evolved. The 1964 schedule contained 25 items, including one on 'Active population according to its socio-economic condition and cultural level' (by sexes), which accurately distinguished between different classes of entrepreneurs and managers. The 1972 schedule provided information on our topic in the item 'Active population by socio-economic category, months worked and studies completed', introducing some changes in the definitions of entrepreneurs and managers. In 1976 changes were introduced in the names of the studies, in order to adapt them to international uses, even though up to the year 2000 no official classification of education existed in Spain

Between the third quarter of 1976 and the first of 1987 the process was started of collecting more detailed information on studies, according to a one-digit coding: 1. primary education; 2. basic secondary education; 3. higher certificate; 4. professional training; 5. pre-higher studies; 6. higher studies; 7. no formal studies; and 8. illiterate. In 1987 an item was added to this coding, that of 'three school or faculty courses passed'. In 1992 a much more detailed two-digit coding was introduced. Finally, in 2000 a Spanish version of the International Standard Classification of Education (UNESCO, 1997) was introduced. Just as there have been changes in the information available on education, similar changes have been seen in the concept of entrepreneur and manager. All in all, we believe that the series presented is sufficiently homogeneous (we stopped at 2004 to prevent us being affected by the change in the methodology of the EPA introduced in 2005).

Education of Entrepreneurs in the Franco Era (1964–75)

In Table 8.4 there is a summary of the series-making work we have carried out with the EPA data for the period 1964–75.

The main conclusions to draw from the table are:

1. Entrepreneurs were a category in relative decline. During the *desarrollista* (high but unbalanced growth) stage of the Francoist economy, the proportion of entrepreneurs in the whole of the working population showed a marked fall, from 37.2 per cent in 1964 to 34.2 in 1970 and 27.8 per cent in 1975. These data are consistent with the increasing number of wage earners in societies emerging from underdevelopment.

2. Men predominated in the whole group. The last known item of data (1971) tells us that 70.6 per cent of entrepreneurs were men.

3. Most were not employers, that is, the only job they created was their own. Employers always accounted for a small fraction of entrepreneurs, around 9–10 per cent. These employers were overwhelmingly male: in 1971, the percentage of males was 85.3 per cent, very much higher than was the case in entrepreneurs as a whole.

4. Entrepreneurs had a lower level of education than the working population as a whole but employers, particularly those in the most sophisticated sectors, were people who stood out as a result of their education. The advance of education beyond primary levels was to be seen in the working population on the whole, but even in 1975 more than 82 per cent of those working were illiterate or had only primary studies. That percentage rose to 93.8 per cent in the case of entrepreneurs, but dropped to 76.7 when only employers were counted (76.4 per cent if it was in industrial sectors and commerce). For 1970 we have information on employers in large firms, contrasting the fact that in this group only 65.7 were scarcely educated, compared to 95.2 per cent for entrepreneurs and 89 per cent for all the working population. Obviously the quality of entrepreneurial initiatives improved with education.

5. Higher studies also made progress between 1964 and 1975, but at the end of the dictatorship little more than 2 per cent of those working had this level of training. Data inform us that between 1964 and 1975, employers maintained an educational level which was very much higher than the average of the working population and the whole of the entrepreneurs (who had a wretchedly low level). In 1970, about 5–6 per 100 employers had completed higher studies, whereas this was true for only 2 per cent of those in work and less than 1 per cent of entrepreneurs. EPA data for 1971–5 on the level of higher education of entrepreneurs and employers are simply not credible. These data do not match at all those presented for 1970 and 1976. It is hard to accept that the level of higher education of employers was lower than that for the working population.

Table 8.4: Indicators of the Educational Level of Spanish Entrepreneurs, 1964–75 (%).[36]

	1964	1965	1966	1967	1968	1969	1970	1971	1972	1973	1974	1975
Entrepreneurs/Working Population	37.2	37.6	38.0	37.4	37.0	35.9	34.2	30.4	28.6	29.2	28.7	27.8
Male Entrepreneurs/Entrepreneurs	72.8	71.6	72.4	72.5	72.8	72.8	71.6	70.6	–	–	–	–
Employers/Entrepreneurs	9.1	8.8	8.9	9.7	9.0	8.9	9.0	7.4	9.7	9.9	9.7	10.5
Male Employers/Employers	88.0	85.3	85.9	85.2	85.0	84.3	84.6	85.3	–	–	–	–
Low Education Level/Working Population	93.3	92.6	91.4	92.1	91.2	90.8	89.0	87.4	87.0	84.6	83.5	82.4
Low Education Level/Entrepreneurs	96.7	96.4	96.1	96.0	95.8	95.2	95.2	95.9	99.2	93.9	94.0	93.8
Low Education Level/Employers	83.8	82.1	81.2	82.5	81.4	80.2	75.7	80.6	79.8	76.0	74.2	76.7
Low Education Level/Employers in Industry & Commerce	82.5	80.9	79.7	81.7	80.6	79.3	75.1	80.8	80.1	76.6	74.0	76.4
Low Education Level/Employers in Big Industry & Commerce	75.7	72.5	67.6	71.7	71.7	72.5	65.7	–	–	–	–	–
Higher Studies/Working Population	1.5	1.5	1.5	1.5	1.5	1.5	2.0	2.0	2.1	2.2	2.2	2.3
Higher Studies/Entrepreneurs	0.8	0.7	0.7	0.7	0.8	0.8	0.9	0.2*	0.3*	0.3*	0.3*	0.2*
Higher Studies/Employers	3.8	4.1	3.8	3.8	4.0	4.2	5.2	2.2*	2.0*	2.2*	2.1*	1.6*
Higher Studies/Employers in Industry & Commerce	4.0	4.4	4.2	4.1	4.1	4.3	5.6	1.8*	1.8*	1.8*	1.7*	1.4*
Higher Studies/Employers in Big Industry & Commerce	4.4	5.2	4.2	4.5	5.6	3.8	6.0	–	–	–	–	–

* = possible error in the source, since the data do not fit at all between the information for 1970 and that for 1976.

Education of Entrepreneurs Awaiting Entry to the European Economic Community (1976–86)

Continuing with our elaboration of the EPA data, we now present Table 8.5, referring to the education of Spanish businessmen when their greatest challenge was the Spanish entrance into the European Economic Community (EEC; achieved in 1986).

From analysing the table we derive the following:

1. In times of economic turmoil set off by successive oil crises, the proportion of entrepreneurs as a percentage of those in work fell and remained at figures of around 22 per cent. It has to be borne in mind that the figure of those in employment fell sharply because of the general increase in unemployment. Consequently, the absolute number of entrepreneurs fell.

2. Though it may appear surprising, the EPA data tell us that males in this period were predominant in the entrepreneurial class to a greater extent than in the Francoist period. Nearly 80 per cent of entrepreneurs and more than 90 per cent of the employers replying to the EPA said they were men. It may be that in such a difficult period women entrepreneurs gave up the struggle before men, and settled for other roles in society.

3. Employers seem to have acquired greater weight within the group of entrepreneurs, but there may be some methodological problem between the figures for the Francoist period and those for this period, since the leap from 10.5 per cent in 1975 to 15.8 per cent in 1976 is too much. In any case, employers tended to fall in number in that period, from 15.8 to 14.5 per cent. In this way, during the crisis years, both quality and quantity were lost among entrepreneurs.

4. As has already been mentioned, progress in education was astonishing during these years in which a return to democracy took place. The EPA points out that figures for those working with no or only minimal training, which in 1976 were around 80 per cent, fell to about 60 per cent ten years later. Entrepreneurs, and particularly employers, followed the same trend, although this did not prevent a situation near the time of Spain's entry into the EEC of nearly 80 per cent of the entrepreneurs being practically untrained. In the case of employers, this problem only concerned 55–6 per cent.

5. The effort in education also reached the university, which began to take in large numbers of students. Up to 5 per cent of those working had a university education in 1986, a figure which was double in the case of employers and reached 3.5 per cent in the case of entrepreneurs.

Table 8.5: Indicators of the Educational Level of Spanish Entrepreneurs, 1976–86 (%).[37]

	1976	1977	1978	1979	1980	1981	1982	1983	1984	1985	1986
Entrepreneurs/Working Population	21.2	20.9	20.9	22.2	21.8	21.8	21.7	22.2	23.1	22.9	22.3
Male Entrepreneurs/Entrepreneurs	78.2	78.4	79.7	79.8	78.9	78.9	79.1	78.1	78.5	78.1	77.3
Employers/Entrepreneurs	15.8	15.4	16.2	15.7	15.9	15.5	15.2	14.5	14.6	14.1	14.5
Male Employers /Employers	91.1	91.7	91.8	91.5	90.8	91.0	90.6	90.7	90.6	90.0	88.5
Low Education Level/Working Population	80.5	80.0	77.9	80.4	75.3	62.6	71.4	67.9	66.3	63.6	60.8
Low Education Level/Entrepreneurs	90.1	89.4	88.6	88.0	86.3	86.5	85.3	84.0	82.6	80.8	78.4
Low Education Level/Employers	70.1	68.2	66.4	66.6	64.3	64.7	63.9	62.2	57.6	56.4	55.4
Higher Studies/Working Population	2.6	2.7	2.9	3.2	3.3	3.4	3.6	4.2	4.5	4.8	5.0
Higher Studies/Entrepreneurs	2.1	2.3	2.4	2.4	2.7	2.6	2.7	3.1	3.1	3.2	3.5
Higher Studies/Employers	7.1	7.8	7.3	7.9	8.2	9.0	8.6	10.0	9.5	9.9	9.9

The Education of Entrepreneurs in a Spain Involved in Globalization (1987–2004)

The sources help us to extend the analysis for the years in which the Spanish entrepreneurial class has dealt with the challenge of globalization, following the entry of Spain into the EEC (1986). It has been a period of growth and convergence towards the living standards of the most developed countries, but also of profound changes in the economic structure (e.g. tertiarization, an enormous increase in building) and in business (e.g. intensifying of the presence of foreign capital, Spanish multinationals in Latin America, continual mergers and takeovers) in Spain. Indicators on educational levels of Spanish entrepreneurs between 1987 and 2004 are shown in Table 8.6.

The conclusions are easy to obtain:

1. The entrepreneur has continued his relative decline, since his weighting in the working population has gone from 22 per cent in 1987 to little more than 16 per cent in 2004. Even so, these were entrepreneurs who have actively boosted the creation of firms – albeit with modest amounts of capital – and who continue to play an important role, especially if we compare their situation to that of other large developed countries.[38]

2. The presence of women among entrepreneurs has tended to rise, but still by 2004, 72 per cent were male. A greater advance was shown among employers, since there was a fall from 87 per cent of male presence in this section in 1987 to 77 per cent in 2004. Women have managed to make significant progress in this most complicated field, but also one which makes the greatest contribution to economic development.

3. The good news is that the proportion of employers has not ceased to grow within the entrepreneurial group as a whole. In going from 16 per cent in 1987 to 33.5 per cent in 2004, the proportion has more than doubled. Employers account for the cream of the Spanish entrepreneurial class. There has been a clear qualitative gain.

4. The poor level of education of the Spanish working population is something which clearly belongs to the past. In contradiction to what is sometimes stated in the world of journalism, there is no better proof of the progress made recently in the Spanish education system than the fact that in 2004 fewer than 20 per cent of those in employment had no more than a basic level of training (thus inverting the situation existing at the end of the Franco era, when that percentage was 80 per cent). In the 1990s, the educational level of employers, as measured, was below the one corresponding to the whole of the working population, something unheard of before. In any case, we are talking, for 2004, of 21.5 per cent for employers and 19.4 per cent for those in work, that is, figures which

Table 8.6: Indicators of the Educational Level of Spanish Entrepreneurs, 1987–2004 (%).[39]

	1987	1988	1989	1990	1991	1992	1993	1994	1995
Entrepreneurs/Working Population	21.9	21.2	22.5	19.6	19.2	20.0	20.3	20.6	20.4
Male Entrepreneurs/Entrepreneurs	75.9	75.9	78.8	76.3	75.7	75.2	75.3	74.9	73.3
Employers/Entrepreneurs	15.7	15.8	25.3	19.3	21.0	22.0	21.8	22.5	23.7
Male Employers /Employers	87.2	86.8	92.2	86.5	86.0	84.3	84.2	83.5	82.4
Low Education Level/Working Population	57.3	55.3	51.7	49.3	47.3	45.0	42.3	39.7	37.3
Low Education Level/Entrepreneurs	74.9	73.2	63.5	68.3	66.2	63.0	60.3	57.3	53.8
Low Education Level/Employers	56.4	53.8	32.1*	52.1	49.6	48.0	46.8	44.8	39.9
Higher Studies/Working Population	11.0	11.2	11.9	12.3	12.8	13.2	14.0	14.8	15.5
Higher Studies/Entrepreneurs	6.2	6.3	6.2	7.3	7.8	7.7	7.9	8.7	9.9
Higher Studies/Employers	14.1	14.9	9.5	15.3	16.4	14.2	14.4	15.2	17.0

	1996	1997	1998	1999	2000	2001	2002	2003	2004
Entrepreneurs/Working Population	20.3	19.8	19.2	18.2	17.4	17.2	16.6	16.1	16.1
Male Entrepreneurs/Entrepreneurs	73.7	74.3	74.0	74.2	73.8	73.3	73.5	72.8	72.0
Employers/Entrepreneurs	25.2	26.4	27.3	29.8	29.7	30.5	31.7	33.3	33.5
Male Employers /Employers	82.4	82.0	79.7	79.8	79.5	78.0	77.8	78.6	77.2
Low Education Level/Working Population	34.3	32.2	30.2	28.1	25.7	24.0	22.6	20.8	19.4
Low Education Level/Entrepreneurs	49.4	46.3	44.5	41.3	38.1	35.8	33.8	31.2	28.1
Low Education Level/Employers	36.9	36.3	34.8	32.4	30.2	27.7	26.7	24.0	21.5
Higher Studies/Working Population	16.9	17.3	17.9	18.4	27.8	28.7	29.3	29.7	30.8
Higher Studies/Entrepreneurs	11.5	11.7	12.0	13.1	19.8	20.5	20.7	21.9	23.7
Higher Studies/Employers	18.6	17.2	17.8	19.2	25.2	25.7	26.1	26.4	28.1

* = possible error in the source.

are low and totally acceptable in both cases. For entrepreneurs as a whole, the figure rises to 28.1 per cent, a figure which is not at all alarming.

5. In the vertex of the educational pyramid it is amazing – knowing where we started from – that in 2004 almost 31 per cent of those in work had completed some form of university studies. Employers, who had always been distinguished by their high level of training, had to yield top place in the early years of the twenty-first century, but in 2004 they recorded the highest figure in their history: 28.1 per 100 employers were graduates. Some way behind, with 23.7 per cent, was the majority of the business class.

The EPA in a New Study from Bancaja

In the last years, Bancaja has supported a research programme to promote entrepreneurship among young people. In this context, Bancaja published in 2008 a study entitled *El capital humano y los emprendedores en España*, written by Congregado et al., where the authors begin by warning that in Spain 'many people believe that higher education helps to create civil servants but not entrepreneurs'.[40] In addition, some scholars have proposed that the diplomas are only 'signals' to be recruited in the labour market, but they are not necessarily related to higher productivity. Those who become self-employed do not need to show a diploma and their education level would very likely be below the average, but this does not mean less productivity.[41] The Bancaja study used a broad definition of entrepreneur, including self-employed, employers and salaried managers, because for the authors the role of the entrepreneur is to create new firms but also to manage them. In fact, the entrepreneur spends much more time managing firms than creating them:

> The contribution of the entrepreneur to economic growth will not be correctly assessed until his double function of creating and managing firms is recognized. In this work the entrepreneur is called 'businessman'. The businessman is an entrepreneur when his time and capabilities are devoted to creating new firms; the businessman is a manager when his time and capabilities are devoted to managing them.[42]

According to Congregado et al., the literature on entrepreneurship has evolved from the entrepreneur as the man of the 'knowledge spillover' to the entrepreneur as the man of the 'knowledge filter', that is, from seeing the entrepreneur as responsible for the diffusion of knowledge to seeing him as the person who determines the relationship between the whole existing knowledge and the useful knowledge for commercial purposes.[43] The contribution of the businessmen to economic growth has to be related to some qualitative element of their work that is impossible to be replicated by the workers. The quality of the entrepreneurial factor is not easily observable, but in Congregado et al. it is approximated by the average formal education. The authors of the book support a Coasian view of entrepreneurship rather than a Schumpeterian view. The main managerial functions are coordination and motivation of the workforce and it is very difficult to carry out these tasks without the proper education. They also put the stress on quality when they admit that a low number of entrepreneurs would not be a problem if this meant a higher quality of entrepreneurship: more workers per entrepreneur. Increases in size are usually associated with increases in average productivity.[44]

In the following lines we will try to summarize the main quantitative results of Congregado et al. In 1977, about 84.4 per cent of the businessmen had basic or primary studies. There were also 4.7 per cent of illiterates. Then, 9 of each 10 businessmen were below the compulsory level of education for young people at that moment. Only 2 per cent boasted a university degree and less than 0.6 per cent had a diploma of higher professional education. For the rest, 4.6 per cent had completed the compulsory secondary level and 3.5 per cent had received classes in post-compulsory studies. In 2006, the improvement in the level of education of businessmen had been substantial, but as a collective they remained below the average of the working population. The share of workers with advanced studies was above that registered for businessmen: 13.1 per cent against 9.8 per cent in graduates or doctors; 9.6 per cent against 5.9 per cent in intermediate university degrees; 9.8 per cent against 7.4 per cent in higher professional studies; and 23.7 per cent against 21.9 per cent in post-compulsory studies. Differences were prominent in university studies, but moderate in the rest. Between 1977 and 2006, all the groups of businessmen had improved their education levels. The differences among them had been reduced but they were still very important. Certainly, salaried managers were the most educated, well ahead of the employers who, in their turn, showed a clear advantage over the self-employed.[45]

The average per capita human capital of the Spanish businessmen in 2006 was similar to the corresponding level for the EU-15 in 1996. The lag was more important for the businessmen than for the whole working population. The relative lack of human capital in Spain in the business world is a feature to keep in mind.[46] The current average Spanish businessman had a stock of human capital (10.2 years of education attendance) around 10 per cent below the stock of the working population (11.3 years). However, in the last decades, that of businessmen has improved constantly, with a cumulative increase of 138.8 per cent. This increase was greater than that of the working population and has reduced by a half the distance between the two categories in 1977 (in the mid-1980s the gap was 25 per cent). It is noticeable that salaried managers had a high human capital (14.9 years), whereas employers (10.5) and self-employed (9.1) were well behind. People with the responsibility for launching and coordinating the work of others had a human capital above the average, in contrast with the self-employed who were located below the average, even when these differences were narrowing in recent years.[47]

Despite the improvement in education, the human capital of Spanish businessmen in 2006 was less than that of their colleagues in neighbouring countries: around 12 per cent less (1.4 years of learning) in comparison with the EU-15 average. In fact, Spain was only above Greece, Italy and Portugal. The improvement had been spread into the whole country. Nevertheless, the disparities of the education levels among provinces and regional communities were dominant. Madrid and north-east entrepreneurs had always enjoyed a higher stock of human capital per capita. It is remarkable that the total number of self-employees, employers and salaried managers was about the same in the period 1977–2006. However there was an important fall in the number of self-employees that was compensated by the vigorous growth of the other two categories. This is proof of the growing complexity of the business structure, with increases in the size of firms and a growing professionalization of managers. The analysis of the personal features of the businessmen reveals a certain degree of rejuvenation, but on average the entrepreneurs continue to be older than the workers. Males were predominant in the business class, but the presence of women was growing very fast among the employers and the salaried managers. We can add that businessmen were readier than workers to be involved in migrations inside the country and also that many immigrants were becoming Spanish businessmen, but their relevance at the moment was small.[48]

Concluding Remarks

The first information about the education of Spanish entrepreneurs came from a report commissioned in 1960 by the EOI, the first business school set up in Spain. This report was focused in the entrepreneurs and managers of firms with more than fifty workers and located in the most industrialized provinces. Its conclusions were very optimistic (70 per cent of the businessmen enjoyed an education level above the compulsory stage) but the sample was clearly biased towards the business elite. In Madrid nearly 80 per cent had received a specific education, inverting the situation at the end of the nineteenth century when only 11 per cent of the 209 outstanding businessmen of the city claimed to be in possession of a diploma.[49] A first analysis of the biographical dictionaries published by LID with detailed information on the Spanish business elite reached conclusions less optimistic than the EOI's survey: for more than 55 per cent of 288 business leaders in contemporary history we do not know their education level (presumably it was very low).[50]

The first official data, coming from the EPA, related to 1964 and showed a reality much less brilliant in relation with the whole class of the entrepreneurs: 96.7 per cent of them had a low educational level (83.8 per cent in the case of the employers). Between 1964 and 2004, the EPA data show an important improvement in the education of the Spanish entrepreneurs, in a trend that resembles that for the whole Spanish population. The structural transformation of the Spanish economy was accompanied by a clear improvement in education levels. But contrary to some popular beliefs we have found that the more ambitious entrepreneurs, those that create jobs and are not merely self-employed, have always enjoyed an educational level well above the average for the whole working population. In the deficient training of the Spanish entrepreneurs as a whole one of the influences had been the late implementation of business studies. Our conclusion is clear: education improves the quality of entrepreneurship.

Some surveys on the characteristics of Spanish entrepreneurs in recent times show a polarization: about 40 per cent with primary studies and about 40 per cent with university studies.[51] The methodology of these surveys has been unable to separate entrepreneurs from managers and this can explain the divergence with our results. On the contrary, Congregado et al. based their research on the EPA data (since 1977) and their figures and conclusions are similar to ours: education adds quality to entrepreneurship. This study is also interesting because it sheds light on regional variations[52] and on the backwardness in education of Spanish businessmen: the average per capita human capital of Spanish businessmen in 2006 was similar to the corresponding level for the EU-15 in 1996.

NOTES

García-Ruiz and Toninelli, 'Introduction'

1. See, for example, D. B. Audretsch and A. R. Thurik, 'What's New about the New Economy? Sources of Growth in the Managerial and Entrepreneurial Economies', *Industrial and Corporate Change*, 1 (2001), pp. 267–315; D. B. Audretsch (ed.), *Entrepreneurship: Determinants and Policy in a European–US Comparison* (Boston, MA, Dordrecht and London: Kluwer Academic Publisher, 2003); W. J. Baumol, E. Litan and C. J. Schramm, *Good Capitalism, Bad Capitalism and the Economics of Growth and Prosperity* (New Haven, CT: Yale University Press: 2007); Monitor Group, *Paths to Prosperity: Promoting Entrepreneurship in the Twenty-First Century* (Cambridge, MA: Monitor, 2009).

2. We regret to say that paradoxically the recent outbreak of suicides by entrepreneurs hit by the recession which occurred, for instance, in northern Italy in the last two years turns out as a tragic confirmation of the previous entrepreneurial boom. In just one industrial region (Veneto) in one year 22 entrepreneurs committed suicide. Information available at http://icrl.wordpress.com/2010/03/09/imprenditori-suicidi/ (last accessed 7 April 2010).

3. Global Entrepreneurship Monitor, *National Entrepreneurship Assessment: Italy* (Babson Park, MA: GEM, 1999). For several different historical case studies, see D. S. Landes, J. Mokyr and W. J. Baumol (eds), *The Invention of Enterprise* (Princeton, NJ: Princeton University Press, 2010).

4. W. J. Baumol, 'Entrepreneurship in Economic Theory', *American Economic Review*, 2 (1968), pp. 64–71, on p. 64.

5. N. H. Leff, 'Entrepreneurship and Economic Development: The Problem Revisited', *Journal of Economic Literature*, 1 (1979), pp. 46–64.

6. P. A. Toninelli, *Storia d'impresa* (Bologna: Il Mulino, 2006), ch. 1.

7. See, for instance, P. J. Olivi, *Tractatus de emptionibus and venditionibus, de usuris, de restituionibus*, which is included in G. Todeschini, *Un trattato di economia politica francescana* (Roma: Istituto Storico Italiano per il Medioevo, 1980). Later, in the mid-fifteenth century, Benedetto Cotrugli, born in Ragusa and trained in Bologna, wrote in his *Della mercatura e del mercante perfetto* that the business undertaker could be compared to a commanding officer, as he knew how to 'devise plans ... and foresee' and like 'an able captain in matters of wars, has a good eye, and can tell the best place to put his camp, and from which points it can be penetrated' so he 'can tell if and where he is likely to run into difficulties, suffer damage and so on'. O. Nuccio and F. Spinelli, 'The Historical

Primacy of the Italian Entrepreneur', *Review of Economic Conditions of Italy*, 1 (2000), pp. 189–98, on p. 189.

8.   Quoted in M. Blaug, 'Entrepreneurship Before and After Schumpeter', in R. Swedberg, *Entrepreneurship: The Social Science View* (Oxford: Oxford University Press, 2000), pp. 76–88, on p. 78.

9.   Ibid., p. 80.

10. A. Marshall, *Principles of Economics*, 8th edn (London: Macmillan, 1977), p. 115.

11. M. Casson and A. Godley, 'Entrepreneurship and Historical Explanation', in Y. Cassis and I. Pepelasis Minoglou (eds), *Entrepreneurship in Theory and History* (Basingstoke: Palgrave Macmillan, 2005), pp. 25–59, on p. 28.

12. J. A. Schumpeter, *The Theory of Economic Development: An Enquiry into Profits, Capital, Credit and Interest in the Business Cycle* (Cambridge, MA: Harvard University Press, 1934); J. A. Schumpeter, *Business Cycles. A Theoretical, Historical, and Statistical Analysis of the Capitalist Process* (New York: McGraw-Hill, 1939).

13. 'The most plausible answer to the question why some human societies progress so much faster than others is to be sought, in my view, not so much in fortuitous accidents ... or in favorable natural environment ... but in human attitudes to risk-taking and money-making. It is the economy in which businessmen are reckless and speculative, where expectations are highly volatile, but with an underlying bias towards optimism, where high and growing profits are projected into the future and lead to the hasty adoption of "unsound" projects involving overexpansion, which is likely to show a higher rate of progress over long periods; while it is an economy of sound and cautious businessmen who are slow at reacting to current events, which is likely to grow at a slow rate' (N. Kaldor, 'The Relation of Economic Growth and Cyclical Fluctuations', *Economic Journal*, 253 (1954), pp. 53–71, on pp. 67–8).

14. E. F. Denison, *The Sources of Economic Growth of the United States and the Alternative Before Us*, Supplementary Paper 13 (New York: Committee for Economic Development, 1962), esp. ch. 15.

15. T. Veblen, *The Theory of Business Enterprise* (New York: Scribner's, 1904); A. Berle and G. Means, *The Modern Corporation and Private Property* (New York: Macmillan, 1932); R. Coase, 'The Nature of the Firm', *Economica*, 4 (1932), pp. 386–405; E. T. Penrose, *The Theory of the Growth of the Firm* (Oxford: Basil Blackwell, 1959).

16. G. Jones and R. D. Wadhwani, 'Entrepreneurship', in G. Jones and J. Zeitlin (eds), *The Oxford Handbook of Business History* (Oxford: Oxford University Press, 2008), pp. 501–28, on p. 502.

17. L. Galambos, 'The Emerging Organizational Synthesis in Modern American History', *Business History Review*, 3 (1970), pp. 279–90.

18. J. A. Schumpeter, *Capitalism, Socialism and Democracy* (New York: Harper & Row, 1942); J. A. Schumpeter, *L'imprenditore e la storia dell'impresa: Scritti 1927–1949*, ed. A. Salsano (Torino: Bollati Boringhieri, 1993).

19. As recently suggested in T. Knudsen and R. Swedberg, 'Capitalist Entrepreneurship: Making Profit through the Unmaking of Economic Orders', *Capitalism and Society*, 4:2 (2009), pp. 1–26.

20. P. Romer, 'Economic Growth', in *The Concise Encyclopaedia of Economics* (2007), available at: http://www.econlib.org/library/Enc1/EconomicGrowth.html.

21. W. J. Baumol and R. Strom, 'Useful Knowledge of Entrepreneurship: Some Implications of the History', in Landes et al. (eds), *The Invention of Enterprise*, pp. 527–42, on p. 527.

22. F. Amatori, 'Entrepreneurial Typologies in the History of Industrial Italy (1880–1960): A Review Article', *Business History Review*, 3 (1980), pp. 359–86.
23. This finding is in line with G. Tortella, J. L. García-Ruiz, J. M. Ortiz-Villajos and G. Quiroga, *Educación, instituciones y empresa: Los determinantes del espíritu empresarial* (Madrid: Academia Europea de Ciencias y Artes, 2008).

1 Amatori, 'Determinants and Typologies of Entrepreneurship'

1. F. Amatori, 'Entrepreneurship', *Imprese e storia*, 34 (2006), pp. 233–67.
2. C. Cipolla, *Before the Industrial Revolution* (London: Metheun, 1976), pp. 98–9.
3. P. Wilken, *Entrepreneurship: A Comparative and Historical Study* (Norwood, NJ, Ablex Publishing Corporation, 1979).
4. This chronological sketch was discussed in greater depth in my essay 'Big and Small Business in Italy's Industrial History', *Rivista di Storia economica*, 2 (2008), pp. 207–24.
5. F. Bonelli, 'Il capitalismo italiano: Linee generali d'interpretazione', in *Storia d'Italia. Annali 1: Dal feudalesimo al capitalismo* (Turin: Einaudi, 1978), pp. 1195–255; L. Cafagna, *Dualismo e sviluppo nella storia d'Italia* (Venice: Marsilio, 1989).
6. Bonelli, 'Il capitalismo italiano', p. 1204.
7. G. Mori, 'L'economia italiana dagli anni Ottanta fino alla Prima guerra mondiale', in G. Mori (ed.), *Storia dell'industria elettrica in Italia 1 Le origini: 1882–1914* (Rome-Bari: Laterza, 1992), pp. 3–106.
8. V. Castronovo, *Giovanni Agnelli* (Turin: UTET, 1971); see also the entry by Franco Amatori and Giuseppe Berta in the *Biographical Dictionary of Italian Entrepreneurs* (*BDIE*) (unpublished; see appendix in the main text).
9. AA.VV., *Il Politecnico di Milano 1863–1944* (Milan: Electa, 1981); C. G. Lacaita, 'Ingegneri e scuole politecniche nell'Italia liberale', in S. Soldani and G. Turi (eds), *Fare gli italiani: Scuola e cultura nell'Italia contemporanea*, 2 vols (Bologna: Il Mulino, 1993), vol. 1, pp. 213–53; A. Guagnini, 'The Formation of Italian Electrical Engineers: The Teaching Laboratories of the Politecnici of Turin and Milan, 1887–1914', in F. Cardot (ed.), *Histoire de l'électricité dans le monde 1880–1980* (Paris: PUF, 1987), pp. 283–99.
10. E. Decleva, 'Conti, Ettore', in *Dizionario Biografico degli Italiani*, 73 vols to date (Roma: Istituto Della Enciclopedia Italiana, 1960–), vol. 28, pp. 389–99; *BDIE*; L. Segreto, *Giacinto Motta: Un ingegnere alla testa del capitalismo industriale italiano* (Rome-Bari: Laterza, 2005).
11. F. Polese, *Alla ricerca di un'industria nuova: Il viaggio all'estero del giovane Pirelli e le origini di una grande impresa (1870–1877)* (Venice: Marsilio, 2004).
12. M. Gobbini, 'Breda, Ernesto', in *BDIE*.
13. G. Toniolo, 'Oscar Sinigaglia (1877–1953)', in A. Mortara, *I protagonisti dell'intervento pubblico in Italia* (Milan: CIRIEC and Franco Angeli, 1984), pp. 405–30.
14. F. Amatori, 'Donegani, Guido', in *BDIE*.
15. P. Rugafiori, 'Agostino Rocca (1895–1978)', in Mortara, *I protagonisti*, pp. 383–403.
16. G. Berta, *Le idee al potere: Adriano Olivetti tra la fabbrica e la comunità* (Milan: Edizioni di Comunità, 1980).
17. M. Moroni, 'Guzzini', in *BDIE*.
18. F. Amatori, 'Per un dizionario biografico degli imprenditori marchigiani', in S. Anselmi (ed.), *Le Marche* (Turin: Einaudi, 1987), pp. 592–4.
19. E. Sori, 'Merloni, Aristide', in *BDIE*.
20. M. Pacini, 'Benelli, Giuseppe', in *BDIE*.

21. P. Maranesi, 'Cecchetti, Adriano Francesco', in *BDIE*.
22. M. Lungonelli, 'Giorgini, Giovanni Battista', in *BDIE*.
23. S. Schipani, 'Fontana, Zoe', in *BDIE*.
24. M. Boneschi, 'Leonardi, Elvira', in *BDIE*.
25. E. Merlo, 'Albini, Walter', in *BDIE*.
26. E. Merlo, 'Coveri, Enrico', in *BDIE*.
27. D. Montanari, 'Beretta, Pietro', in *BDIE*.
28. A. Mantegazza, 'Agusta, Giovanni and Domenico', in *BDIE*.
29. F. Amatori, 'Ferrari, Enzo', in *BDIE*.
30. A. Colli, 'Barilla, Pietro', in *BDIE*.
31. B. Buitoni and G. P. Gallo, *Pasta e cioccolato: Una storia imprenditoriale* (Perugia: Prota-gon, 1992).
32. G. Subbrero, 'La Ferrero di Alba: Appunti per un profilo storico', in F. Chiapparino and R. Romano, *Il cioccolato: Industria, mercato e società in Italia e Svizzera (XVIII–XX sec.)* (Milan: Franco Angeli, 2007), pp. 151–68.
33. R. Coriasso, 'Lavazza, Famiglia', in *BDIE*.
34. M. Pirani, 'Tre appuntamenti mancati dell'industria italiana', *Il Mulino*, 6 (1991), pp. 1045–51.
35. M. Comei, 'Divella, Francesco', in *BDIE*.
36. P. Pierucci, 'De Cecco, Filippo', in *BDIE*.
37. A. Dell'Orefice, 'D'Amato, Salvatore', in *BDIE*.
38. S. Candela, 'Florio, Ignazio senior', in *BDIE*.
39. N. De Ianni, 'Canzio, Bruno Canto', in *BDIE*.
40. G. Bruno, 'Capuano, Maurizio', in *BDIE*.
41. M. Fatica, 'Cenzato, Giuseppe', in *BDIE*.
42. P. R. Coppini, 'Bastogi, Pietro', in *BDIE*.
43. F. Bonelli, *Lo sviluppo di una grande impresa in Italia: La Terni dal 1884 al 1962* (Turin: Einaudi, 1975); E. Novello, 'Breda, Vincezo Stefano', in *BDIE*.
44. P. Rugafiori, *Ferdinando Maria Perrone: Da Casa Savoia all'Ansaldo* (Turin: UTET, 1992); F. Conti, 'I Perrone fra impresa e politica', in P. Hertner (ed.), *Storia dell'Ansaldo Vol. 3: Dai Bombrini ai Perrone 1903–1914* (Bari: Laterza, 1996), pp. 225–56.
45. M. Doria, *Ansaldo* (Milan: Franco Angeli, 1989).
46. F. Bonelli, 'Bocciardo, Arturo', in *BDIE*.
47. G. Mori, 'L'industria dell'acciaio in Italia', in Hertner (ed.), *Storia dell'Ansaldo Vol. 3*, pp. 31–66.
48. G. F. Lepore and C. Sonzogno, *L'impero della chimica* (Rome: Newton Compton, 1990).
49. Amatori, 'Donegani, Guido', in *BDIE*.
50. Toniolo, 'Oscar Sinigaglia'; L. Villari, *Le avventure di un capitano d'industria* (Turin: Einaudi, 2008); G. L. Osti and R. Ranieri, *L'industria di Stato dall'ascesa al potere: Trent'anni nel gruppo Finsider* (Bolgona: Il Mulino, 1993).
51. F. Bonelli, 'Alberto Beneduce, il credito industriale e le origini dell'IRI', in IRI, *Alberto Beneduce e i problemi dell'economia italiana del suo tempo* (Rome: Atti della giornata di studio per la celebrazione del 50° anniversario dell'istituzione dell'Iri, Edindustria, 1985); M. Franzinelli and M. Magnani, *Beneduce: Il finanziere di Mussolini* (Milan: Mondadori, 2009).
52. M. Colitti, *Energia e sviluppo in Italia: La vicenda di Enrico Mattei* (Bari: De Donato, 1979).

53. I. Mandolesi, 'Capanna, Alberto', in *BDIE*.

54. G. L. Fontana (ed.), *Schio e Alessandro Rossi: Imprenditorialità, politica, cultura e paesaggi sociali del secondo Ottocento* (Rome: Edizioni di Storia e Letteratura, 1985).

55. D. Bigazzi, 'Grandi imprese e concentrazione finanziaria: La Pirelli e la Fiat nel mercato mondiale', in *Storia della società italiana, vol. XX: L'Italia di Giolitti* (Milan: Teti editore, 1981), pp. 87–143; Polese, *Alla ricerca di un'industria nuova.*

56. M. Fumagalli, 'Falck, Giorgio Enrico', in *BDIE*; H. James, *Family Capitalism: Wendels, Haniels, Falcks, and the Continental European Model* (Cambridge, MA: Harvard University Press, 2006).

57. M. Balconi, *La siderurgia italiana (1945–1990): Tra controllo pubblico e incentivi di mercato* (Bologna: Il Mulino, 1991), p. 103.

58. P. Bairati, *Vittorio Valletta* (Turin: UTET, 1983).

59. P. Bricco, *Olivetti, prima e dopo Adriano: Industria, cultura, estetica* (Naples: L'Ancora del Mediterraneo, 2005).

60. See Colitti, *Energia e sviluppo in Italia*, as well as the more recent D. Pozzi, *Dai gatti selvatici al cane a sei zampe: Tecnologia, conoscenza e organizzazione nell'AGIP e nell'ENI di Enrico Mattei* (Venice: Marsilio, 2009).

61. R. Romano, 'Borghi, Giovanni', in *Dizionario Biografico degli Italiani*, vol. 34, pp. 498–500.

62. A. Colli, 'Fumagalli, Eden', in *Dizionario Biografico degli Italiani*, vol. 50, pp. 720–2.

63. C. Castellano, *L'industria degli elettrodomestici in Italia: Fattori e caratteri* (Turin: Giappichelli, 1965).

64. G. Fuà and C. Zacchia (eds), *Industrializzazione senza fratture* (Bologna: Il Mulino, 1983). See also G. Becattini, *Dal distretto industriale allo sviluppo locale: Svolgimento e difesa di un'idea* (Turin: Bollati Boringhieri, 2000); and A. Colli, *I volti di Proteo: Storia della piccola impresa in Italia nel Novecento* (Turin: Bollati Boringhieri, 2002).

65. A. Colli, *Il quarto capitalism: Un profilo italiano* (Venice: Marsilio, 2002). Colli utilizes the concept of 'Fourth Capitalism' based on an idea first expressed by Giuseppe Turani in *I sogni del grande Nord* (Bologna: Il Mulino, 1996).

2 Sapfo Pepelasis, 'Entrepreneurial Typologies in a Young Nation State'

I wish to dedicate this essay to Franco Amatori, who over the years has been a source of inspiration to me. Research for this paper was funded by the Centre for Economic Research at AUEB; the European Union Program on Entrepreneurship; and PEVE 1 at AUEB. It has benefited from the research assistance of Elisavet Lagou of the Vovolinis Archive, Olga Kouklaki, the AUEB students Maria Amapatzidou and Apostolis Rigas and the PhD candidate Mihalis Papadakis. Thanks are also due to Evi Antonatos, Eleni Calligas and Kristy Davis for their editorial assistance.

1. For the significance of 1909 and the so called 'Goudi' revolution of that year, see Γ. Β. Δερτιλής [Dertilis], *Τὸ 1909 και η διαδικασία κοινωνικών και θεσμικών μεταβολών στην Ελλάδα* (Αθήνα: Εξάντας, 1977); Γ. Β. Δερτιλής [Dertilis], *Ιστορία του Ελληνικού Κράτους 1830–1920*, 2 vols (Αθήνα: Εστία, 2005).

2. See *Εφημερίς της Κυβερνήσεως* [*Greek Government Gazette*] (1830–1909).

3. J. Foreman-Peck, 'Measuring Historical Entrepreneurship', in Cassis and Pepelasis Minoglou (eds), *Entrepreneurship in Theory and History*, pp. 77–108.

4. A first effort in this direction is J. Foreman-Peck and I. Pepelasis Minoglou, 'Entrepreneurship and Convergence: Greek Businessmen in the Nineteenth Century', *Rivista di Storia Economica*, 3 (2000), pp. 279–303; and I. Πεπελάση Μίνογλου [Pepelasis Minoglou], 'Επιχειρηματικότητα', in *Η Ανάπτυξη της Ελληνικής Οικονομίας τον 19ο Αιώνα (1830–1914) επιμ Κ. Κωστής και Σ. Πετμεζάς* (Αθήνα: ALPHA BANK, 2006), pp. 463–96. It is the case that Greek scholarship has neither shown a lively interest in business (as an entrepreneurial phenomenon *per se*) nor in studying entrepreneurship at an aggregate level. It has largely adopted the micro perspective of the study of individual businesspersons, families, firms, sectors, cities or regions. For a survey of the historiography of Greek enterprise, see M. Dritsas, 'Business History in Greece: The State of the Art and Future Prospects', in F. Amatori and G. Jones (eds), *Business History Around the World* (Cambridge: Cambridge University Press, 2003), pp. 255–70. There are, however, a few exceptions to this general pattern. Aliki Vaxevanoglou examines Greek capitalists as an entity and hence touches upon general features of entrepreneurship. See Α. Βαξεβάνογλου [Vaxevanoglou], *Οι Έλληνες Κεφαλαιούχοι 1900–1940: Κοινωνική και Οικονομική Προσέγγιση* (Αθήνα: Θεμέλιο, 1994). In addition, Dertilis in his seminal opus *Ιστορία του Ελληνικού Κράτους* makes many valuable observations regarding entrepreneurial supply and culture.

5. It should be noted right at the start that the corporate sector lacked an internal articulation and cohesiveness and was small in terms of the number of enterprises it contained. See I. Pepelasis Minoglou, 'The Greek Joint-Stock Company and Institutional Change, 1830–1909' (unpublished draft, December 2009).

6. The impact of Ottoman rule was not the same everywhere and in certain areas of Greece, Western rule and presence – Venetian/Genoan or even British – left a deep imprint.

7. R. Clogg, *A Concise History of Modern Greece* (Cambridge: Cambridge University Press, 1992).

8. Real per capita income had increased by almost one-third and the share of the non-agricultural sectors in Gross Domestic Product had risen from about 15 per cent to about 45 per cent. Dertilis, *Ιστορία του Ελληνικού Κράτους*; Γ. Κωστελένος et al. [Kostelenos et al.], *Ακαθάριστο Εγχώριο Προϊόν: 1830–1939* (Αθήνα: ΚΕΠΕ, 2007).

9. Χ. Αγριαντώνη [Agriantonis], *Οι Απαρχές της Εκβιομηχάνισης στην Ελλάδα τον 19ο Αιώνα* (Αθήνα: Εμπορική Τράπεζα της Ελλάδος, 1986); Dertilis, *Ιστορία του Ελληνικού Κράτους*; K. Kostis, 'The Formation of the Greek State', in F. Birtek and T. Dragonas (eds), *Citizenship and the Nation-State in Greece and Turkey* (New York: Routledge, 2005), pp. 18–36; Kostelenos et al., *Ακαθάριστο Εγχώριο Προϊόν*; Α. Φραγκιάδης [Franghiadis], *Ελληνική Οικονομία 19ος 20ός Αιώνας* (Αθήνα: Νεφέλη, 2007).

10. For nineteenth-century modernization in Greece, see Dertilis, *Ιστορία του Ελληνικού Κράτους*; N. Mouzelis, 'The Concept of Modernization: Its Relevance for Greece', *Journal of Modern Greek Studies*, 2 (1996), pp. 215–27.

11. Formal partnerships could take the shape of either general (i.e. unlimited liability) or limited (liability) partnerships. Although this latter form was provided for in the implanted Napoleonic Code in 1835, a preliminary investigation at the State Archive of Ermoupolis for the years 1865, 1875, 1882, 1886, 1887, 1888, 1890, 1893, 1894, 1895 suggests that it was not very popular among the population of partnership-based firms.

12. C. Agriantonis and M. C. Chadziioannou (eds), *The Athens Silkmill* (Athens: Institute of Neohellenic Research, 1997); Μ. Χ. Χατζηϊωάννου [Chadziioannou], *Οικογενειακή Στρατηγική και Εμπορικός Ανταγωνισμός Ο Οίκος Γερούση τον 19ο Αιώνα* (Αθήνα: ΜΙΕΤ, 2003).

13. Δ. Πολέμης [Polemis], *Τα Ιστιοφόρα της Άνδρου* (Άνδρος: Καΐρειος Βιβλιοθήκη, 1991).
14. Στ. Παπαγεωργίου and I. Πεπελάση Μίνογλου [Papageorgiou and Pepelasis Minoglou], *Τιμές και Αγαθά στην Αθήνα (1834): Κοινωνική Συμπεριφορά και Οικονομικός Ορθολογισμός της Οικογένειας Βάσσου Μαυροβουνιώτη* (Αθήνα: ΜΙΕΤ, 1988); Σ. Ασδραχάς [Asdrachas], *Βίωση και Καταγραφή του Οικονομικού* (Αθήνα: Εθνικό Ίδρυμα Ερευνών, 2007).
15. The words 'at least' used because data on registered capital are known for only 218 SA start-ups (Pepelasis Minoglou, 'The Greek Joint-Stock Company').
16. The identities of founding shareholders are known for more than two-thirds of SA start-ups. The total registered number of company founders was around 7,500 but as some natural personae or institutions and companies were registered in more than one company there is some double counting involved and thus the 'net' number was something under 7,000. Let it be underlined here that in this paper we do not take into consideration the company founders of the 19 self-help associations and hence the phenomenon of social entrepreneurship as the latter did not involve 'pure entrepreneurs' but rather other segments of society.
17. Asdrachas, *Βίωση και Καταγραφή*.
18. Λ. Παπαγιαννάκης [Papayiannakis], *Οι Ελληνικοί Σιδηρόδρομοι (1882–1910) Γεωπολιτικές, οικονομικές και κοινωνικές διαστάσεις* (Αθήνα: ΜΙΕΤ, 1982), p. 132.
19. I. Pepelasis Minoglou, 'Women and Greek Family Capitalism, 1780–1940', *Business History Review*, 3 (2007), pp. 517–38.
20. Further research may possibly reveal the existence of a primitive form of pyramid structures.
21. The state was a cofounder in the National Bank of Greece Ethniki Trapeza tis Ellados (est. 1841); the national steamship company Elliniki Atmoploia (est. 1856); and the horse-drawn railway firm Ipposididirodromoi Athinon kai Perihoron (est. 1884). Moreover, it was the sole shareholder in the minor railway company Etaireia ton Mesimvrinon Sidirodromon tis Ellados (est. 1890).
22. Pepelasis Minoglou, 'The Greek Joint-Stock Company'.
23. F. Amatori, 'Entrepreneurship', Working Paper (Baltimore, MD: IAESBE, Johns Hopkins University, 2007); Casson and Godley, 'Entrepreneurship and Historical Explanation'.
24. S. Gekas and M. C. (C)Hadziioannou, 'The Trade-Minded Greek Entrepreneurs, 1780s–1900s' (Haifa: Papers from the Workshop on Entrepreneurship and Culture: Near and Middle Eastern Perspectives, organized by the Onassis Foundation and Haifa University, 2008); [Pepelasis Minoglou], 'Επιχειρηματικότητα'.
25. This general attitude exists although the existing business history literature contains some anecdotal apospasmatic accounts of such processes/attempts. See Agriantonis, *Οι Απαρχές της Εκβιομηχάνισης*; and Agriantonis and Chadziioannou (eds), *The Athens Silk-mill*.
26. Pepelasis Minoglou, 'The Greek Joint-Stock Company'.
27. Leff, 'Entrepreneurship and Economic Development', p. 49.
28. There was also an element of political agency. Namely, the capacity of a segment of entrepreneurial actors in the nascent corporate sector to influence political decision-making so as to protect their and their companies' vested or incipient property rights. Political agency contained both elements of positive and negative influences on economic development and it will be the subject of part of a separate paper. Here I would like to focus only on one such episode of political agency. In 1877 a 2 per cent flat taxation rate was imposed on the net profits of all SA companies, including SA banks. Initially, the intention of the government was to impose a higher rate on the net profits of the main banks

– the National Bank of Greece (NBG) was to be taxed 12 per cent on its profits – and of high income bankers. This proposal never materialized due to the strong opposition of the governor of the NBG. When, in 1880, the 2 per cent rate tax on the net profits of SA conmpanies was increased to 3 per cent, the governor of the NBG agreed to this rise and in exchange he obliged the government to agree not to increase this rate for the next 25 years. Indeed, this bank received political protection as it was exempted both when the state increased the rate of the tax on SA profits to 5 per cent in 1885 and when it imposed a 2 per cent stamp tax on the certificates of dividends in 1887. The most likely group of actors outside bankers to have had political agency would be engineers –contractors and industrialists – but we should be reminded here that these actors were also part of the wider sphere of banking-affiliated entrepreneurial initiatives. Δ. Συρμαλόγλου [Syrmaloglou], *Φορολογία η Χρεοκοπία, Η φορολογική πολιτική στη Βουλή των Ελλήνων 1862–1910* (Αθήνα: Μεταμεσονύκτιες Εκδόσεις, 2007).

29. Leff, 'Entrepreneurship and Economic Development'; S. Thomadakis, 'Coordinated Industrialization Institutional Agendas for Less Favoured Countries', in M. Storper, S. Thomadakis and L. Tsipouri (eds), *Latecomers in the Global Economy* (London: Routledge, 1998), pp. 107–28.

30. Γ. Αναστασόπουλος [Anastasopoulos], *Ιστορία της Ελληνικής Βιομηχανίας 1840–1940, Τόμος Α (1840–1884)* (Αθήνα: Ελληνική Εκδοτική Εταιρεία, 1946/7).

31. S. Thomadakis, 'Monetary Arrangements and Economic Power in Nineteenth-Century Greece: The National Bank in the Period of Convertibility (1841–77)', *Journal of the Hellenic Diaspora*, 4 (1985), pp. 55–90.

32. Kostis, 'The Formation of the Greek State'.

33. The latter story is described in detail in I. Pepelasis Minoglou, 'Non-Bank Financial Corporates, 1832–1909: A Note in Greek Banking History' (Malta: Papers from the European Association for Banking and Financial History Conference, 2007).

34. Papayiannakis, *Οι Ελληνικοί Σιδηρόδρομοι*.

35. The diaspora bank was the Bank of Constantinople, the other Greek bank was the Bank of Epiro Thesally and the two foreign banks were Hambros & Sons and the Banque d'Escompte de Paris.

36. The shift in the interest of the mercantile diaspora was the outcome of a number of complex factors. In a very few words: diaspora Greeks were, on the one hand, facing increasing competition in their host countries for a large number of reasons and, on the other hand, they were attracted to the quickening in the path of modernization of the state system in Greece circa the mid-1870s (Dertilis, *Ιστορία του Ελληνικού Κράτους*; Kostis, 'The Formation of the Greek State').

37. I. Pepelasis Minoglou, 'Between Informal Networks and Formal Contracts, International Investment in Greece during the 1920s', *Business History*, 2 (2002), pp. 40–64. Dertilis, *Ιστορία του Ελληνικού Κράτους*.

38. The legal framework for the operation of SA companies throughout the period under study (and up to the passing of the Company Act in 1920) was the Napoleonic Commercial Code of 1807, which was introduced formally into post-independence Greece in 1835. For details on the *ad hoc* improvements and changes made by company founders in governance and architectural design of SA start-ups, see K. Aivalis and I. Pepelasis Minoglou,, 'A Preliminary Analysis of Early Corporate Governance in Greece: 1850–1909' (Bergen: Papers from the EBHA Annual Conference, 2008).

39. See also K. Κωστής and B. Τσοκόπουλος [Kostis and Tsokopoulos], *Οι Τράπεζες στην Ελλάδα 1898–1928* (Αθήνα: Παπαζήσης, 1988).

40. Leff, 'Entrepreneurship and Economic Development'.

41. The Bank of Constantinople itself founded in Greece the Bank of EpiroThessaly and cofounded the General Commercial and Credit Bank.

42. Pepelasis Minoglou, 'The Greek Joint-Stock Company'.

43. Χ. Χατζηισωσήφ [Hadziiosif], *Η Γηραιά Σελήνη Η Βιομηχανία στην Ελληνική Οικονομία 1830–1940* (Αθήνα: Θεμέλιο, 1993).

44. M. Granovetter, 'Business Groups and Social Organization', in N. Smelser and R. Swedberg (eds), *Handbook of Economic Sociology* (Princeton, NJ: Princeton University Press, 2005), pp. 429–50; Pepelasis Minoglou, 'Between Informal Networks and Formal Contracts'.

45. For a survey of the modernization debate in Greece, see Mouzelis, 'The Concept of Modernization'.

46. Information is shown in approximate chronological order of date of birth of entrepreneurs.

47. Β. Θεοδόρου, and Χ. Λούκος [Theodorou and Loukos], *Το Αρχείον της Βιομηχανίας 'Κλωστήριον και Υφαντήριον Ε. Λαδόπουλου και Υιοι εν Σύρω* (Αθήνα: Εταιρεία Μελέτης Νεοελληνισμού-Μνήμων, 1996); Vovolinis Archive, Athens, File 1269: E. Ladopoulos, Skokos Diary, 1892.

48. Chadziioannou, *Οικογενειακή Στρατηγική*.

49. Χ. Μούλιας [Moulias], *Το Λιμάνι της Σταφίδας, Πάτρα, 1828–1900* (Πάτρα: Περί Τεχνών, 2000); Ν. Μπακουνάκης [Bakounakis], *Πάτρα 1828–1860, Μία Ελληνική Πρωτεύουσα στον 19ο αιώνα* (Αθήνα: Καστανιώτης, 1995).

50. Vovolonis *Lexicon*; Κ. Παπαθανασόπουλος [Papathanassopoulos], *Εταιρεία Ελληνικής Ατμοπλοίας (1855–1872), Τα αδιέξοδα του προστατευτισμού* (Αθήνα: ΜΙΕΤ, 1988); *Νεώτερον Εγκυκλοπαιδικόν Λεξικόν 'Ηλίου'* [Encyclopedia Lexicon 'Elios'] (Αθήνα, 1948–54), vol. 10.

51. Vovolinis Archive, File 1269; [*Encyclopedia Lexicon 'Elios'*], vol. 17.

52. Vovolinis Archive, File 1269; *Βιομηχανική Επιθεώρησις* [*Industrial Review*] (1955); [Kostis and Tsokopoulos], *Οι Τράπεζες στην Ελλάδα*.

53. Vovolinis Archive, File 600, handwritten notes, Matsas Z. Antonios and 'oikogeneia Matsa'.

54. Κ. Βοβολίνης [Vovolinis], *Μέγα Ελληνικόν Βιογραφικόν Λεξικόν* (Αθήνα, 1958); and [*Encyclopedia Lexicon 'Elios'*], vol. 15.

55. [Vovolinis], *Μέγα Ελληνικόν Βιογραφικόν Λεξικόν*.

3 Toninelli and Vasta, 'Italian Entrepreneurship'

Previous versions of this chapter have been presented at The Historical Determinants of Entrepreneurship – a pre-conference of session 110 of the XV World Economic History Congress, Utrecht 2009 – held in Madrid (Instituto Rocasolano, CSIC, 30–1 October 2008), at the Workshop on Italian Entrepreneurship organized by CISEPS at the University of Milano-Bicocca on 20 March 2009 and at the ASSI Incontri di storia dell'impresa at the Bocconi University on 22 May 2009. The authors wish to thank the organizers and the participants to those meetings, and particularly Franco Amatori, Youssef Cassis, Giovanni Dosi, José L. García-Ruiz, Roberta Garruccio, Raoul Nacamulli, Carlo Salvato, Gabriel Tortella and Emma Zavarrone, for useful comments and insights. A further special thanks is due to Franco Amatori, coordinator of the project on the *Dizionario biografico degli imprenditori italiani*, who has allowed us to use a preprint version of the first two volumes which is the base of the dataset we have built. Financial support from CISEPS is acknowledged.

1. Baumol et al., *Good Capitalism, Bad Capitalism*, p. ix.

2. These can be summarized as follows: 1. entrepreneurial cluster (Silicon Valley is the classic case); 2. anchor firm model (spin-off of technology and human capital from existing companies); 3. event-driven entrepreneurship (economic crises which foster self-employment); 4. local-hero entrepreneur (although not frequent, two significant cases can be mentioned: Boeing in Seattle at the time of the First World War and, recently, Medtronic in Minneapolis). Monitor Group, *Paths to Prosperity*.

3. For instance, S. A. Shane, 'Explaining Variation in Rates of Entrepreneurship in the United States: 1899–1988', *Journal of Management*, 5 (1996), pp. 747–81; P. Temin, 'The American Business Elite in Historical Perspective' in E. Brezis and P. Temin (eds), *Elites, Minorities and Economic Growth* (Amsterdam: Elsevier, 1999), pp. 19–39; Foreman-Peck, 'Measuring Historical Entrepreneurship'.

4. J. Mokyr, 'Entrepreneurship and the Industrial Revolution in Britain', in Landes et al. (eds) *The Invention of Enterprise*, pp. 183–210.

5. Schumpeter, *Business Cycles*; Schumpeter, *L'imprenditore e la storia dell'impresa*; M. Casson, *The Entrepreneur: An Economic Theory* (Oxford: Martin Robertson, 1982); Casson and Godley, 'Entrepreneurship and Historical Explanation'.

6. For a survey, see R. Giannetti and M. Vasta (eds), *Evolution of Italian Enterprises in the Twentieth Century* (Heidelberg and New York: Phisica-Verlag, 2006).

7. Amatori, 'Entrepreneurial Typologies in the History of Industrial Italy'.

8. D. Bigazzi, *La storia d'impresa in Italia: Saggio bibliografico: 1980–1987* (Milano: Franco Angeli, 1990).

9. F. Amatori and F. Brioschi, 'Le grandi imprese private: famiglie e coalizioni', in F. Barca (ed.), *Storia del capitalismo italiano dal dopoguerra ad oggi* (Roma: Donzelli, 1987), pp. 118–53; M. Doria, *L'imprenditoria industriale in Italia dall'unità al 'miracolo economico': Capitani d'industria, padroni, innovatori* (Torino: Giappichelli, 1998); M. Doria, 'Gli imprenditori tra vincoli strutturali e nuove opportunità', in F. Amatori et al., *Storia d'Italia. Annali 15: L'industria* (Torino: Einaudi, 1999), pp. 619–87; F. Amatori and A. Colli, *Impresa e industria in Italia dall'Unità a oggi* (Venezia: Marsilio 1999).

10. Colli, *Il quarto capitalismo*; A. Colli, *The History of Family Business, 1850–2000* (Cambridge: Cambridge University Press, 2003); P. A. Toninelli, *Industria, impresa e stato: Tre saggi sullo sviluppo economico italiano* (Trieste: Edizioni dell'Università di Trieste, 2003); G. Federico and P. A. Toninelli, 'Business Strategies from Unification up to the 1970s', in Giannetti and Vasta (eds), *Evolution of Italian Enterprises*, pp. 191–238.

11. See A. Gramsci, *Note sul Machiavelli, sulla politica e sullo stato moderno* (Torino: Einaudi 1966); A. Gramsci, *Il Risorgimento* (Torino: Einaudi 1966); A. Gerschenkron, *Economic Backwardness in Historical Perspective: A Book of Essays* (Cambridge, MA: Belknap Press of Harvard University, 1962).

12. R. Garruccio, 'Genealogia di una riflessione su imprenditorialità, innovazione e potere' (Milano, 2008), p. 13.

13. About 1,200 were the entries initially scheduled for the dictionary, conceived and edited by Franco Amatori, who supervised a number of researchers throughout Italy, in order to cover all the national territory. The entries were to be filled on the basis of a set of precise and detailed questions. This scheme has enabled us to collect the information contained

in the database. For more information, see the appendix to Amatori's chapter in this volume, above, pp. 29–31.

14. Yet it has to be considered that this distribution is not representative of the real geographical allocation of entrepreneurs, as the initial choice of the names to be inserted in the list was purposely biased in order to cover all the national territory.

15. The problem – as known – is if and how attributing positions of responsibility to members of the family to the detriment of managers might hinder the success of the firm. On this, see G. Jones and M. B. Rose, *Family Capitalism*, Special Issue of *Business History*, 4 (1993); M. B. Rose (ed.), *Family Business* (Aldershot: Edward Elgar, 1995); Colli, *The History of Family Business*.

16. The SPAD version 5 is the software used in the analysis. For these elaborations, the procedures CORMU (Analyse de Correspondances Multiples), RECIP (Classification hierarchique sur facteurs) and PARTI-DECLA (Coupre de l'Arbre et Description des Classes) were used. The related outputs are available from the authors upon request. Concerning cluster analysis, see B. S. Everitt, *Cluster Analysis* (London: Edward Arnold, 1993).

17. The formula used for the correction of inertia is the following (considering lambda as the proportion of inertia each eigenvalue accounts for and *s* equal to the number of variables involved), according to S. Bolasco, *Analisi multidimensionale dei dati: Metodi, strategie e criteri d'interprestazione* (Roma: Carocci Editore, 1999), p. 139:

$$p(\lambda) = \left(\frac{s}{s-1}\right)^2 * \left(\lambda - \frac{1}{s}\right)^2$$

The computing involves only eigenvalues with a proportion of inertia higher than the average inertia.

18. A value test higher than 2 means that the categories place themselves with statistical significance around the dimension, that is in a non-casual way. See Bolasco, *Analisi multidimensionale*, pp. 152–3.

19. To visualize the categories in this table consistently with those of dimensions 1 and 2, for each category the coordinate's sign has been inverted.

20. To visualize the categories in this table consistently with those of dimensions 1 and 2, for each category the coordinate's sign has been inverted.

21. L. Lebart, 'Complementary Use of Correspondence Analysis and Cluster Analysis', in M. Greenacre and J. Blasius (eds), *Correspondence Analysis in the Social Sciences* (London: Academic Press, 1994), pp. 162–78.

22. Schumpeter, *L'imprenditore e la storia dell'impresa*.

4 Tortella et al., 'Entrepreneurship'

The authors wish to thank members of the Economic History Seminar at the Universidad Complutense, of the Centro de Estudios Monetarios y Financieros (CEMFI), of the Banca d'Italia, of the Latin American Center at Columbia University and the Economics Workshop of Stanford University, in particular José María Ortiz-Villajos, Rafael Repullo, Samuel Bentolilla, Juan Carlos Martínez-Oliva, Stefano Fenoaltea, Federico Barbiellini-Amidei, John Coatsworth, Alan Dye, Alfonso Quiroz, Herbert Klein, Gavin Wright and Paul David for their comments and suggestions. This research is being sponsored by the Consejería de Educación, Comunidad de Madrid, Research Project DETESEMP (S2007/HUM-0433).

1. K. Boulding, *The Meaning of the Twentieth Century: The Great Transition* (New York: Harper & Row, 1965), p. 153.

2. Schumpeter, *The Theory of Economic Development*; J. H. von Thünen, *Isolated State: An English Edition of Der Isolierte Staat* (1826; Oxford: Pergamon Press, 1966).
3. R. Cantillon, *Essai sur la nature du commerce en général* (1755; Paris, Institut national d'etudes démographiques, 1952); A. Smith, *An Inquiry Into the Nature and Causes of the Wealth of Nations* (1776; New York: Modern Library, 1937).
4. G. Tortella, *The Development of Modern Spain: An Economic History of the Nineteenth and Twentieth Centuries* (Cambridge, MA: Harvard University Press, 2000), p. 207.
5. A. García-Sanz, 'Empresarios en la España del antiguo régimen: Ganaderos trashumantes, exportadores de lana y fabricantes de paños' in F. Comín and P. Martín Aceña (eds), *La empresa en la historia de España* (Madrid: Editorial Civitas, 1996), pp. 93–113, on pp. 111–13.
6. A. Carreras and X. Tafunell, 'Spain: Big Manufacturing Firms between State and Market, 1917–1990', in A. D. Chandler, F. Amatori and T. Hikino (eds), *Big Business and the Wealth of Nations* (Cambridge: Cambridge University Press, 1999), pp. 277–304, on p. 301.
7. A. Carreras and X. Tafunell, 'La gran empresa en la España contemporánea: Entre el Mercado y el Estado', in F. Comín and P. Martín Aceña (eds), *La empresa en la historia de España* (Madrid: Civitas, 1996), pp. 73–90, on p. 90; and Carreras and Tafunell, 'Spain', pp. 299, 302.
8. A. Carreras, X. Tafunell and E. Torres Villanueva, 'La historia empresarial en España', in Erro (ed.), *Historia empresarial*, pp. 319–437, on p. 334.
9. In the prologue to E. Torres Villanueva (ed.), *Los 100 empresarios españoles del siglo XX* (Madrid: LID, 2000), p. 15.
10. M. F. Guillén, *The Rise of Spanish Multinationals: European Business in the Global Economy* (New York: Cambridge University Press, 2005), p. 8.
11. See D. H. Aldcroft, 'Education and Britain's Growth Failure, 1950–1980', in G. Tortella (ed.), *Education and Economic Development since the Industrial Revolution* (Valencia: Generalitat Valenciana, 1990), pp. 223–45; D. C. Coleman, 'Gentlemen and Players', *Economic History Review*, 1 (1973), pp. 252–75; and the articles collected in Tortella (ed.), *Education and Economic Development*, and C. E. Núñez and G. Tortella (eds), *La maldición divina: Ignorancia y atraso económico en perspectiva histórica* (Madrid: Alianza Editorial, 1993).
12. Aldcroft, 'Education and Britain's Growth Failure'.
13. R. Giannetti, 'L'istruzione e la formazione del capital umano', in P. Toninelli (ed.), *Lo sviluppo economico moderno dalla rivoluzione industriale alla crisi energetica (1750–1973)* (Venezia: Marsilio, 1997), pp. 511–31.
14. T. W. Schultz 'The Value of the Ability to Deal with Disequilibria', *Journal of Economic Literature*, 3 (1975), pp. 827–46.
15. N. Barnia, R. W. Ebers and M. S. Fogarty, 'Universities and the Startup of New Companies: Can We Generalize from Route 128 and Silicon Valley?', *Review of Economics and Statistics*, 4 (1993), pp. 761–6; T. Bates, 'Entrepreneur Human Capital Inputs and Small Business Longevity', *Review of Economics and Statistics*, 4 (1990), pp. 333–58; D. S. Evans and L. C. Leighton, 'Some Empirical Aspects of Entrepreneurship', *American Economic Review*, 3 (1989), pp. 519–35; A. M. Van Praag and J. S. Cramer, 'Roots of Entrepreneurship and Labour Demand: Individual Ability and Low Risk Aversion', *Economica*, 269 (2001), pp. 45–62; Y. Wong, 'Entrepreneurship, Marriage and Earnings', *Review of Economics and Statistics*, 4 (1986), pp. 693–9.
16. Núñez and Tortella (eds), *La maldición divina*.

17. Torres Villanueva (ed.), *Los 100 empresarios españoles*; J. Vidal Olivares (ed.), *Cien empresarios valencianos* (Madrid: LID, 2005); F. Cabana (ed.), *Cien empresarios catalanes* (Madrid: LID, 2006); D. J. Jeremy (ed.), *Dictionary of Business Biography: A Biographical Dictionary of Business Leaders Active in Britain in the Period 1860–1980*, 5 vols (London: Butterworths, 1984–6); D. J. Jeremy and G. Tweedale (eds), *Dictionary of Twentieth-Century Business Leaders* (London: Bowker: 1994).

18. Cantillon, *Essai sur la nature du commerce en général*, pp. 22–31.

19. Schultz, 'The Value of the Ability to Deal with Disequilibria'; I. M. Kirzner, 'Entrepreneurial Discovery and the Competitive Market Process: An Austrian Approach', *Journal of Economic Literature*, 1 (1997), pp. 60–85; Casson and Godley, 'Entrepreneurship and Historical Explanation'.

20. A. de Miguel and J. J. Linz, 'Nivel de estudios del empresariado español', *Arbor*, 219 (1964), pp. 33–63.

21. Y. Cassis, *Big Business: The European Experience in the Twentieth Century* (Oxford: Oxford University Press, 1999), pp. 132–42.

22. Cited in M. Sanderson, *The Universities and British Industry, 1850–1970* (London: Routledge & Kegan Paul, 1972), p. 5.

23. A. Marshall, *Industry and Trade: A Study of Industrial Technique and Business Organization; and of their Influences on the Conditions of Various Classes and Nations* (1919), 3rd edn (London: Macmillan, 1927), p. 351.

24. H. Berghoff, 'Public Schools and the Decline of the British Economy, 1870–1914', *Past and Present*, 129 (1990), pp. 148–67, on p. 166.

5 Fernández-Pérez and Puig, 'Dynasties and Associations in Entrepreneurship'

Paloma Fernández Pérez acknowledges financial support from Spanish public research project ECO2008-00398/ECON and from ICREA Academia 2008 research award. Núria Puig aknowledges financial support from Spanish public research project SEJ-2006 15151. Preliminary versions of this study have been presented at the Residencia de Estudiantes in Madrid (30 October 2008), the EBHA/BHC Conference of Milan (13 June 2009) and the XVth IEHA Conference of Utrecht (7 August 2009).

1. Cassis and Minoglou (eds), *Entrepreneurship in Theory and History*; P. Fernández Pérez and M.B. Rose (eds), *Innovation and Entrepreneurial Networks in Europe* (Oxford: Routledge, 2010). About the Spanish case, see P. Fernández-Pérez, 'Small Firms and Networks in Capital Intensive Industries: The Case of Spanish Steel Wire Manufacturing', *Business History*, 49:5 (2007), pp. 647–67.

2. Colli, *The History of Family Business*; A. Colli, P. Fernández-Pérez and M. B. Rose, 'National Determinants of Family Firm Development? Family Firms in Britain, Spain and Italy in the Nineteenth and Twentieth Centuries', *Enterprise and Society*, 4:1 (2003), pp. 28–64; J. Tàpies and J. L. Ward (eds), *Family Values and Value Creation: The Fostering of Enduring Values within Family-Owned Businesses* (London: Palgrave Macmillan, 2008); K. E. Gersick, J. A. Davis, M. McCollom and I. Lansberg, *Generation to Generation: Life Cycles of the Family Business* (Cambridge, MA: Harvard Business School Press, 1997); P. Z. Poutziouris, C. X. Smyrnios and S. B. Klein (eds), *Handbook of Research on Family Business* (Aldershot: Edward Elgar, 2006); Rose (ed.), *Family Business*. On the Spanish case, see also C. Galve and V. Salas, *La empresa familiar en España: Fundamen-*

tos económicos y resultados (Bilbao: Fundación BBVA, 2003); F. Sanuy, *Informe Sanuy: Defensa del petit comerç i crítica de La Caixa* (Barcelona: La Campana, 2005); J. M. Valdaliso, *La familia Aznar y sus negocios* (Madrid: Marcial Pons, 2006).

3. D. Landes, *Dynasties: Fortunes and Misfortunes of the World's Great Family Businesses* (New York: Viking, 2006), pp. ix–xii.

4. Ibid.

5. See ibid.; H. James, *Family Capitalism: Wendels, Haniels, Falcks, and the Continental European Model* (Cambridge, MA: Harvard University Press, 2006).

6. J. Nadal, 'Los Bonaplata: Tres generaciones de industriales en la España del siglo XIX', *Revista de Historia Económica*, 1 (1983), pp. 79–95; J. Nadal, 'Los Planas, constructores de turbinas y material eléctrico (1858–1949)', *Revista de Historia Industrial*, 1 (1992), pp. 63–94; F. Cabana, *Fabricants i empresaris* (Barcelona: Enciclopédia Catalana, 1992–4); F. Cabana, *SA Damm: Mestres cervesers des de 1876* (Barcelona: SA Damm, 2001); F. Cabana, *La saga dels cotoners* (Barcelona: Proa, 2006); Cabana (ed.), *Cien empresarios catalanes*; A. Solà-Parera, 'Actituds i comportaments de la gran burgesia barcelonina a mitjan s. XIX', *Quaderns de l'Institut Català d'Antropologia*, 3:4 (1981), pp. 101–27; A. Solà-Parera, 'Una família burgesa de la Plana de Vic: Els Moret, de Roda', in A. Solà-Parera et al., *Osona i Catalunya al segle XIX: Estudis d'història* (Vic: Eumo Editorial, 1990), pp. 201–20; A. Solà-Parera, *Aigua, indústria i fabricants a Manresa, 1759–1860* (Sant Vicenç de Castellet: Centre Estudis Bages, 2004); G. W. McDonogh, *Good Families of Barcelona: A Social History of Power in the Industrial Era* (Princeton, NJ: Princeton University Press, 1986).

7. P. Pascual and J. Nadal, *El coure II La Farga Lacambra: Un estudi socioeconòmic* (Vic: Eumo/La Farga Group, 2008); J. Planas, 'El Instituto Agrícola Catalán de San Isidro y la organización de los intereses agrarios (1880–1936)', *Revista Española de Estudios Agrosociales y Pesqueros*, 217 (2008), pp. 13–48; M. Gutiérrez, *Full a full: La indústria paperera de l'Anoia (1700–1998): Continuitat I modernitat* (Igualada: Publicacions Abadia Montserrat, 1999); F. Valls, *La Catalunya atlàntica: Aiguardents i texitis a l'arrencada industrial catalana* (Vic: Eumo, 2004); J. M. Benaul, 'Els empresaris de la industrialització: Una aproximació des de la indústria textil llanera catalana, 1815–1870', *Recerques*, 31 (1995), pp. 93–113; E. Deu, 'La construcción de telares mecánicos en Sabadell (1863–1960): Francesc Duran Cañameras y sus sucesores', *Revista de Historia Industrial*, 2 (1992), pp. 183–190.

8. R. Boix and V. Galletto, 'El mapa de los distritos industriales de España', *Economía Industrial*, 359 (2006), pp. 165–84; R. Boix and V. Galletto, 'The New Map of the Industrial Districts in Spain and the Comparison with Italy and the United Kingdom: Improving International Comparison of Industrial Districts with Common Methodologies' (Regions in Focus? Regional Studies Association International Conference, Lisbon, 2–5 April 2007).

9. M. Guinjoan, C. Murillo and J. Pons, *L'empresa familiar a Catalunya: Quantificació i característiques* (Barcelona: CIDEM/Fundació Joaquim Molins, 2004).

10. M. A. Gallo, 'Family Businesses in Spain: Tracks Followed and Outcomes Reached by Those among the Largest Thousand', *Family Business Review*, 4 (1995), pp. 245–54.

11. Instituto de la Empresa Familiar website, www.iefamiliar.com, accessed June 2009.

12. Guinjoan et al., *L'empresa familiar a Catalunya*, table 9 and graph 21.

13. P. Fernández-Pérez and N. Puig, 'Knowledge and Training in Family Firms of the European Periphery: Spain in the Eighteenth to Twentieth Centuries'. *Business History*, 1 (2004), pp. 79–100; P. Fernández-Pérez and N. Puig, 'Bonsais in a Wild Forest? A

Historical Interpretation of the Longevity of Large Spanish Family Firms', *Revista de Historia Económica: Journal of Iberian and Latin American Economic History*, 3 (2007), pp. 459–97; P. Fernández-Pérez and N. Puig, 'Global Lobbies for a Global Economy: The Creation of the Spanish Institute of Family Firms in International Perspective', *Business History*, 5 (2009), pp. 712–33; N. Puig and P. Fernández-Pérez, 'The Education of Spanish Entrepreneurs and Managers: Madrid and Barcelona Business Schools, 1950–1975', *Paedagogica Historica*, 5 (2003), pp. 651–72; N. Puig and P. Fernández-Pérez, 'La gran empresa familiar española en el siglo XX: Claves de su profesionalización', *Revista de Historia de la Economía y de la Empresa*, 2 (2008), pp. 93–122; N. Puig and P. Fernández-Pérez, 'A Silent Revolution: The Internationalization of Large Spanish Family Firms', *Business History*, 3 (2009), pp. 462–83.

14. This generational approach is developed in N. Puig 'La empresa en Cataluña: Identidad, supervivencia y competitividad en la primera región industrial de España', in J. L García Ruiz and C. Manera (eds), *Historia empresarial de España: Un enfoque regional en profundidad* (Madrid: LID, 2006), pp. 27–56.

15. J. Nadal, *Moler, tejer y fundir: Estudios de historia industrial* (Barcelona: Ariel, 1992), pp. 84, 154.

16. These are defined as family owned and/or managed firms that by the end of 2005 had a turnover in excess of 40 million euros and had experienced at least one successful succession process. The 84 firms that fit into this definition are listed in the Appendix. It should be reminded that family capitalism is primarily a Catalan phenomenon in the Spanish context, as these 84 firms amount to one-third of the largest historical family firms in Spain.

17. On Antoni Miquel i Costas, see the work of M. Gutiérrez in Cabana (ed.), *Cien empresarios catalanes*, p. 198. On Damià Mateu, Joan Jorba Rius, Pau Salvat i Espasa, Isaac Carasso, Joseph Vilà i Marqués, Joan Miquel i Avellí, and Esteve Monegal Prat, see respectively studies by López Carrillo, Oliveras Samitier, Cabana, Aymerich, Moreno Castaño, Sala and Puig Raposo in Cabana (ed.), *Cien empresarios catalanes*, pp. 264, 308, 331, 343–4, 349, 353, 451.

18. Cabana (ed.), *Cien empresarios catalanes*. See also Puig, 'La empresa en Cataluña'.

19. N. Luján, *La lucha contra el frío y el calor, y en favor de la hygiene: Contribución de una familia de industriales catalanes a lo largo de 75 años* (Barcelona: Compañía Roca Radiadores, 1992); P. Fernández in Cabana (ed.), *Cien empresarios catalanes*, pp. 407–13.

20. A. Solé, 'Reshaping Entrepreneurship after a Civil War: The Case of the Industrial Districts in Catalonia during the 1930s' (EBHA Conference, Bergen, 21–3 August 2008).

21. J. Moreno, 'Estrategias de expansión de una empresa familiar catalana: Agrolimen, 1937–2007', *Revista de Historia Industrial*, 3 (2009), pp. 49–89.

22. Cabana (ed.), *Cien empresarios catalanes*, pp. 515–16.

23. The Brand Council, *Top Brands: El libro de las grandes marcas en España*, I (Madrid: TopBrands and The Brand Council, 2002), p. 38.

24. Cabana (ed.), *Cien empresarios catalanes*, pp. 589–90.

25. For a short overview of the first generations of these family firms in Catalonia, see ibid.

26. J. S. Coleman, 'Social Capital in the Creation of Human Capital', *American Journal of Sociology*, (Supplement) 94 (1988), pp. 95–120; R. Putnam, 'Bowling Alone: America's Declining Social Capital', *Journal of Democracy*, 6:1 (1995), pp. 65–78.

27. P. W. Laird, *Pull: Networking and Success since Benjamin Franklin* (Cambridge, MA: Harvard University Press, 2006).

28. The leading role of Barcelona, and Catalonia as a whole, in the creation of associations of all kinds, has been recently demonstrated in C. Marcuello (ed.), *Capital social y organizaciones no lucrativas en España* (Bilbao: FBBVA, 2007).

29. According to P. Saiz and P. Fernández-Pérez, 'Intangible Assets and Competitiveness in Spain: An Approach through Trademark Registration Data in Catalonia, 1850–1946' (EBHA-BHC Conference, Milan, 11–13 June 2009).

30. Fernández-Pérez and Puig, 'Global Lobbies for a Global Economy'.

31. Source: personal elaboration from the catalogue of associations in the city of Barcelona published in P. Solà-Gussinyer, *Història de l'associacionisme català contemporani: Barcelona i comarques de la seva demarcación* (Barcelona: Generalitat de Catalunya, Departament de Justícia, 1993). Research assistance from Paola Bozzo is gratefully acknowledged.

32. The firms of the table have family members of at least the second generation with management responsibilities and 40 million euros of turnover. In the second column the cases in which the generation is in full control are indicated between brackets. Members of the Instituto de la Empresa Familiar (IEF) are: Celsa, Catalana Occidente, Puig, Almirall, Planeta, Esteve, Molins, Uniland, Freixenet, Nutrexpa and Agrolimen. Sources: personal elaboration with research assistance of Rafael Castro and María Fernández-Moya.

33. Personal elaboration with research assistance of Rafael Castro and María Fernández-Moya.

34. Personal elaboration with research assistance of Rafael Castro and María Fernández-Moya.

35. Personal elaboration with research assistance of Rafael Castro and María Fernández-Moya.

6 Foreman-Peck and Zhou, 'Entrepreneurial Culture or Institutions?'

1. M. Weber, *The Protestant Ethic and the Spirit of Capitalism* (1905; New York: Dover, 2003), p. 39.

2. M. J. Wiener, *English Culture and the Decline of the Industrial Spirit, 1850–1980* (Cambridge: Cambridge University Press, 1981), p. 111.

3. W. D. Rubinstein, *Capitalism, Culture, and Decline in Britain 1750–1990* (London and New York: Routledge, 1993), p. 3.

4. D. S. Landes, *The Wealth and Poverty of Nations: Why Some are so Rich and Some are so Poor* (London: Abacus; New York: W. W. Norton, 1998), pp. 516–17.

5. Ibid., p. 517.

6. W. J. Baumol, 'Entrepreneurship: Productive, Unproductive and Destructive', *Journal of Political Economy*, 5:1 (1990), pp. 893–921.

7. L. Guiso, P. Sapienza and L. Zingales, 'Does Culture Affect Economic Outcomes?', *Journal of Economic Perspectives*, 2 (2006), pp. 23–48, on p. 23.

8. L. Klapper, L. Laeven and R. Rajan, 'Entry Regulation as a Barrier to Entrepreneurship', *Journal of Financial Economics*, 3 (2006), pp. 591–629; A. Ciccone and E. Papaioannou, 'Red Tape and Delayed Entry', *Journal of the European Economic Association*, 2:3 (2007), pp. 444–58.

9. R. J. Barro and R. M. McCleary, 'Religion and Economic Growth across Countries', *American Sociological Review*, 5 (2003), pp. 760–81.

10. H. Feldmann, 'Protestantism, Labor Force Participation, and Employment across Countries', *American Journal of Economics and Sociology*, 4 (2007), pp. 795–816.

11. Guiso et al., 'Does Culture Affect Economic Outcomes?', p. 35.

12. Foreman-Peck, 'Measuring Historical Entrepreneurship'.

13. W. D. Rubinstein, *Men of Property: The Very Wealthy in Britain since the Industrial Revolution* (London: Croom Helm, 1981).

14. We have excluded agricultural employment from the sample because migrants are likely to have greater difficulty entering agriculture as entrepreneurs and most agricultural self-employment could not be classified as entrepreneurial. Agriculture provides little experience for urban industrial entrepreneurship.

15. 5 per cent samples from IPUMS (http://usa.ipums.org/usa/); 1910 is the first year that the employer/employee question is asked.

16. A. Godley, 'Migration of Entrepreneurs', in M. Casson et al. (eds), *The Oxford Handbook of Entrepreneurship* (Oxford: Oxford University Press, 2006), pp. 601–10. F. Cetin, *My Grandmother: A Memoir* (London: Verso, 2008), p. 107, reconstructs a traumatic Armenian family history and tracks their migrant entrepreneurs from Turkey to the United States before the First World War.

17. T. Saloutos, *The Greeks in the United States* (Cambridge, MA: Harvard University Press, 1964), pp. 16, 23, 33. In the poem *The Waste Land* (1922), T. S. Eliot introduces a Smyrna currant exporter by the name of Eugenides.

18. O. Pamuk, *Istanbul, Memories of a City* (London: Faber & Faber, 2005), pp. 157–9.

19. A. Constant, Y. Shachmurove and K. F. Zimmermann, 'What Makes an Entrepreneur and Does it Pay? Native Men, Turks and Other Migrants in Germany', CEPR Discussion Paper, 4207 (Washington, DC, 2004).

20. T. Bates, 'Financing Small Business Creation: The Case of Chinese and Korean Immigrant Entrepreneurs', US Census Bureau, Working Papers, 96–9 (Washington, DC: Center for Economic Studies, 1996).

21. J. Levie, 'Immigration, In-Migration, Ethnicity and Entrepreneurship in the United Kingdom', *Small Business Economics*, 2:3 (2007), pp. 143–69.

22. M. Lofstrom, 'Labour Market Assimilation and the Self Employment Decision of Immigrant Entrepreneurs', *Journal of Population Economics*, 15 (2002), pp. 83–114.

23. For instance Koreans were not included because although sufficiently numerous in 2000, in 1910 there were too few working as employers outside agriculture.

24. The base case in the analysis is 'other North America'.

25. T. J. Hatton, 'How Much Did Immigrant "Quality" Decline in Late Nineteenth Century America?', *Journal of Population Economics*, 13 (2000), pp. 509–25.

26. A. Godley, *Jewish Immigrant Entrepreneurship in New York and London 1880–1914: Enterprise and Culture* (London: Palgrave, 2001).

27. S. W. Kung, *Chinese in American Life: Some Aspects of Their History, Status, Problems and Contributions* (Seattle, WA: University of Washington Press, 1962), pp. 180–1.

28. T. J. Hatton and A. Leigh, 'Immigrants Assimilate as Communities, Not Just as Individuals' (The Economics of Migration, Diversity and Culture Conference, Bologna, September 2006; paper revised in 2007).

29. Suggested to us by Tim Hatton.

30. J. Foreman-Peck, 'A Political Economy of International Migration 1815–1914', *Manchester School*, 4 (1992), pp. 359–76.

31. R. H. Lee, *The Chinese in the United States of America* (Hong Kong: Hong Kong University Press, 1960), p. 79.

32. X. Clark, T. J. Hatton and J. G. Williamson, 'Explaining US Immigration 1971–1998', *Review of Economics and Statistics*, 2 (2007), pp. 359–73.
33. For example, D. S. Evans and B. Jovanovic, 'An Estimated Model of Entrepreneurial Choice under Liquidity Constraints', *Journal of Political Economy*, 97 (1989), pp. 808–27; B. Xu, 'A Re-Estimation of the Evans-Jovanovic Entrepreneurial Choice Model', *Economic Letters*, 58 (1998), pp. 91–5.
34. S. C. Parker, *Economics of Self-Employment and Entrepreneurship* (Cambridge: Cambridge University Press, 2004).
35. Siqueria's analysis of the United States 2000 census finds that being married increases the chances of Brazilian immigrants owning their own business. A. C. O. Siqueira, 'Entrepreneurship and Ethnicity: The Role of Human Capital and Family Social Capital', *Journal of Developmental Entrepreneurship*, 1 (2007), pp. 31–46.
36. J. Collins, 'Cultural Diversity and Entrepreneurship: Policy Responses to Immigrant Entrepreneurs in Australia', *Entrepreneurship and Regional Development*, 15 (2003), pp. 137–49.
37. According to t-tests.
38. Calculated from IPUMSusa 5 per cent sample.
39. Calculated from IPUMSusa 5 per cent sample.
40. Adam Smith's implication that the 'First Industrial Nation' was also 'a nation of shop-keepers', therefore was perhaps no chance association.
41. Calculated from IPUMSusa 5 per cent sample.
42. Wiener, *English Culture*.
43. J. Foreman-Peck and J. Smith, 'Business and Social Mobility into the British Elite, 1870–1914', *Journal of European Economic History*, 3 (2004), pp. 485–518.
44. Compare 'One can only speculate about the reasons why so relatively few Mexican-Americans have moved into business occupations' (L. Grebler, J. W. Moore and R. C. Guzman, *The Mexican-American People: The Nation's Second Largest Minority* (New York: Free Press, 1970), p. 216.
45. T. Boswell and J. R. Curtis, *The Cuban-American Experience: Culture, Images and Perspectives* (Totowa, NJ: Rowman & Allanheld, 1984), pp. 3, 87.
46. C. Jones, *The Chinese in America* (Minneapolis, MN: Lerner Publication, 1972), p. 86.
47. Y. Ichihashi, *Japanese in the United States: A Critical Study of the Problems of the Japanese Immigrants and Their Children* (1932; New York: Arno Press, 1969), ch. 16.
48. E. Bonacich and J. Modell, *The Economic Basis of Ethnic Solidarity: Small Business in the Japanese-American Community* (Berkeley, CA: University of California Press, 1980), pp. 37–45.
49. The two samples are 'stacked' and the variables for each year multiplied by the appropriate year dummy in a single equation estimate to allow the significance of difference between pairs of coefficients to be tested.
50. The relevant percentages in Table 6.1 are not significantly different according to a two-sample t test with equal variances.
51. M. P. Corcoran, 'Emigrants, Eirepreneurs and Opportunities', in R. H. Bayof and T. J. Meagher (eds), *The New York Irish* (Baltimore, MD: Johns Hopkins University Press, 1996), p. 466.
52. A. Moskos, *Greek Americans: Struggle and Success*, 2nd edn (New Brunswick, NJ: Transaction, 1989), p. 111.

53. M. Bucheli, *Bananas and Business: The United Fruit Company in Colombia, 1899–2000* (New York: New York University Press, 2005), p. 48.

7 Dávila, 'Entrepreneurship and Cultural Values in Latin America, 1850–2000'

The ample support received from the School of Management, Universidad de los Andes (Bogota, Colombia) for the research and writing of this chapter is acknowledged.

1. Cassis and Pepelasis Minoglou, *Entrepreneurship in Theory and History*, p. 11. See also Jones and Wadhwani, 'Entrepreneurship'.
2. It should be noted that the latter only exceptionally have enjoyed the size and scale of the large business enterprise distinctive of Chandlerian managerial capitalism.
3. M. Cerutti, 'Estudio introductorio', in M. Cerutti, *Empresas y grupos empresariales en América Latina, España y Portugal* (Monterrey: Universidad Autónoma de Nuevo León, Universidad de Alicante, 2006), pp. 9–40, on p. 26.
4. See C. Dávila, 'Introduction', *Business History Review*, 3 (2008), pp. 439–44; M. I. Barbero and C. Dávila, 'Introduction: A View from Latin America', *Entreprises et Histoire*, 54 (2009), pp. 6–15.
5. See M. I. Barbero, 'Business History in Latin America: Issues and Debates', in Amatori and Jones, *Business History around the World*, pp. 317–37; M. I. Barbero, 'Business History in Latin America: A Historiographical Perspective', *Business History Review*, 3 (2008), pp. 555–75. See also C. Dávila, 'La historia empresarial en América Latina', in Erro (ed.), *Historia empresarial*, pp. 349–81; and Dávila, 'Introduction'.
6. United Nations Development Decade; A Programme for International Economic Co-operation (i), G.A. Res. 1710 (XVI), 19 December 1961.
7. John F. Kennedy Presidential Library and Museum, at http://www.jfklibrary.org/ JFK+Library+and+Museum/News+and+Press/New+JFK+Exhibit+Celebrates+US +Latin+American+Friendship.htm [accessed 13 March 2010].
8. A pioneering work on economic growth was that of R. M. Solow, 'A Contribution to the Theory of Economic Growth', *Quarterly Journal of Economics*, 70 (1956), pp. 65–94.
9. See N. J. Smelser and S. M. Lipset (eds), *Social Structure and Mobility in Economic Development* (Chicago, IL: Aldine, 1966), p. v.
10. P. Kilby, 'Hunting the Heffalump', in P. Kilby (ed.), *Entrepreneurship and Economic Development* (New York: Free Press, 1971), pp. 1–40, on p. 3.
11. P. Kilby, 'The Heffalump Revisited', *Journal of International Entrepreneurship*, 1 (2003), pp. 13–29.
12. Gerschenkron has been called the 'doyen' of economic history in the United States. A. Fishlow, 'Alexander Gerschenkron: A Latecomer who Emerged Victorious. Review Essay of A. Gerschenkron, *Economic Backwardness in Historical Perspective: A Book of Essays* (1962)' (EH.net Project 2001, Significant Works in Economic History, posted in 2003), p. 2.
13. E. Hagen, *On the Theory of Social Change* (Homewood, IL: Dorsey Press, 1962).
14. T. A. B. Corley, 'Historical Biographies of Entrepreneurs', in Casson et al. (eds), *The Oxford Handbook of Entrepreneurship*, pp. 138–57.
15. Hagen, *On The Theory of Social Change*, p. 376.
16. A. Gerschenkron, 'Reviewed Work: On the Theory of Social Change: How Economic Growth Begins by Everett E. Hagen', *Economica*, 32 (1965), pp. 90–4.

17. F. Safford, 'Significación de los antioqueños en el desarrollo económico colombiano: Un examen crítico de la tesis de Everett Hagen', *Anuario Colombiano de Historia Social y de la Cultura*, 3 (1965), pp. 18–27.
18. A. Twinam, 'Miners, Merchants and Farmers: The Roots of Entrepreneurship in Antioquia, 1763–1810' (PhD dissertation, Yale University, 1976), p. 313. See also C. Dávila, 'Books that Made a Difference: *On the Theory of Social Change: How Economic Growth Begins*, by Everett Hagen', *Business History Review*, 1 (2006), pp. 131–4.
19. Kilby, 'Hunting the Heffalump', p. 13.
20. T. Cochran, 'The Entrepreneur in Economic Change', *Explorations in Entrepreneurial History* (Summer 1965), pp. 25–37.
21. T. Cochran, *The Puerto Rican Businessman: A Study in Cultural Change* (Philadelphia, PA: University of Pennsylvania Press, 1959).
22. R. A. Adams, 'Book Review of Entrepreneurship in Argentine Culture: Torcuato Di Tella and S.I.A.M. Thomas C. Cochran and Ruben Reina. Research Assistant, Sue Nutall. Philadelphia: University of Pennsylvania Press, 1962', *American Anthropologist*, 1 (1964), pp. 176–7, on p. 177.
23. D. Sicilia, 'Cochran's Legacy: A Cultural Path Not Taken', *Business and Economic History*, 1 (1995), p. 34.
24. S. Lipset and A. Solari (eds), *Elites in Latin America* (New York: Oxford University Press, 1967). This book came out of a seminar held in Montevideo (Uruguay) in 1965, as part of a research project on Comparative National Development led by Lipset, initially in Berkeley and afterward in Harvard.
25. S. Lipset, 'Values, Education and Entrepreneurship', in Lipset and Solari (eds), *Elites in Latin America*, pp. 3–60, on pp. 6, 12.
26. Ibid., p. 23.
27. A. Lipman, *The Colombian Entrepreneur in Bogota* (Coral Gables, FL: University of Miami Press, 1969), p. 21. To confirm this statement Lipman cross-referenced Hagen, *On the Theory of Social Change*, p. 30. Lipman's book was originally published in Spanish in 1966: A. Lipman, *El empresario bogotano* (Bogota: Tercer Mundo, 1966).
28. Lipman, *The Colombian Entrepreneur*, p. 37.
29. Fernando H. Cardoso became one of the pioneers of the theory of dependence: F. H. Cardoso and E. Faletto, *Dependencia y desarrollo en América Latina* (Mexico: Siglo XXI, 1969). He was perhaps the best-known Latin American scholar in North America and Europe during the seventies. In the nineties he became president of Brazil during two periods (1995–9; 1999–2003).
30. F. H. Cardoso, 'The Industrial Elite', in Lipset and Solari (eds), *Elites in Latin America*, pp. 94–114, on p. 94.
31. H. Kantis, P. Angelelli and V. Moori Koenig, *Developing Entrepreneurship* (Washington, DC: Interamerican Development Bank, 2007); and Global Entrepreneurship Monitor, *GEM Colombia 2006: Reporte de resultados* (Bogota: Universidad de los Andes, Universidad Icesi, Universidad del Norte, Pontificia Universidad Javeriana, 2007).
32. S. Huntington, 'Foreword: Cultures Count', in L. E. Harrison and S. Huntington (eds), *Culture Matters: How Values Shape Human Progress* (New York: Basic Books, 2000), pp. xiii–xvi, on p. xiv.
33. A sample of good reference works on dependency theory include R. Chilcote, 'Dependency: A Critical Synthesis of the Literature', *Latin American Perspectives*, 1 (1974), pp. 4–29; T. Halperin, '"Dependency Theory" and Latin American Historiography', *Latin*

American Research Review, 1 (1982), pp. 115–30; C. Kay, *Latin American Theories of Development and Underdevelopment* (London: Routledge, 1989).

34. Cardoso and Faletto, *Dependencia y desarrollo en América Latina*.

35. R. Miller, *Britain and Latin America in the Nineteenth and Twentieth Centuries* (London: Longman, 1993), p. 22. See also H. Pérez-Brignoli, 'The Economic Cycle in Latin America Agricultural Export Economies, 1880–1930: A Hypothesis for Investigation', *Latin American Research Review*, 2 (1980), pp. 3–33.

36. R. Miller, 'Business History in Latin America: An Introduction', in C. Dávila and R. Miller (eds), *Business History in Latin America: The Experience of Seven Countries* (Liverpool: Liverpool University Press, 1999), pp. 1–16, on p. 7.

37. R. Fernández and J. F. Ocampo, 'The Latin American Revolution: A Theory of Imperialism, Not Dependence', *Latin American Perspectives*, 1 (1974), pp. 30–61.

38. S. Bodenheimer, 'The Ideology of Developmentalism: American Political Science's Paradigm – Surrogate for Latin American Studies', *Berkeley Journal of Sociology*, 15 (1970), pp. 95–173.

39. L. E. Harrison, *Underdevelopment is a State of Mind: The Latin American Case* (Cambridge, MA: Harvard University Center for International Affairs, 1985).

40. For an overview of recent developments and debates in cultural interpretations, see Huntington, 'Foreword', p. xiv.

41. Harrison and Huntington (eds), *Culture Matters*.

42. L. E. Harrison and J. Kagan (eds), *Developing Cultures: Essays on Culture Change* (New York: Routledge, 2006); L. E. Harrison and P. L. Berger (eds), *Developing Cultures: Case Studies* (New York: Routledge, 2006).

43. Landes, *The Wealth and Poverty of Nations*, pp. 516, 523.

44. Jones and Wadhwani, 'Entrepreneurship', p. 506.

45. J. Mokyr, 'Eurocentricity Triumphant', *American Historical Review*, 4 (1999), pp. 1241–6, on p. 1241.

46. Landes, *The Wealth and Poverty of Nations*, ch. 20.

47. Ibid., pp. 315, 313, 312, 314.

48. Mokyr, 'Eurocentricity Triumphant', p. 1242.

49. Ibid., p. 1241.

50. Ibid., p. 1242.

51. C. Morris, 'Review of David Landes, The Wealth and Poverty of Nations', *New York Times, Sunday Book Review* (29 October 2006).

52. C. Dávila (ed.), *Empresa e historia en América Latina: Un balance historiográfico* (Bogota: Conciencias, Tercer Mundo Editores, 1996); Dávila, 'La historia empresarial en América Latina'; Barbero, 'Business History in Latin America: Issues and Debates'.

53. M. Cerutti, 'Regional Studies and Business History in Mexico since 1975', in Dávila and Miller (eds), *Business History in Latin America*, pp. 116–27.

54. W. J. Fleming, 'The Cultural Determinants of Entrepreneurship and Economic Development: A Case Study of Mendoza Province, Argentina, 1861–1914', *Journal of Economic History*, 1 (1979), pp. 211–24.

55. R. García, *Historia empresarial e historia económica en Argentina: Un balance a comienzos del siglo XXI*, Monografía 95 (Bogota: Facultad de Administración, Universidad de los Andes, 2007).

56. For recent surveys of business history in Antioquia, see C. Dávila and B. Rodríguez, 'Naturaleza y perspectivas de la historia empresarial en Colombia', in M. I. Barbero and R. Jacob (eds), *La nueva historia de empresas en América Latina y España* (Buenos Aires:

Temas Grupo Editorial, 2008), pp. 109–39; V. Alvarez, 'Empresas y empresarios de Antioquia: Un intento de balance historiográfico', in Universidad Eafit, *Las regiones y la historia empresarial* (Medellin: Universidad Eafit, 2004), pp. 77–104.

57. See C. Dávila, 'Business History in Colombia', in Dávila and Miller (eds), *Business History in Latin America*, pp. 83–115.

58. Cerutti, 'Regional Studies and Business History in Mexico', p. 120.

59. On northern Mexico, see ibid.; on Argentina, see R. García, 'Business History in Argentina', in Dávila and Miller (eds), *Business History in Latin America*, pp. 17–42; García, *Historia empresarial e historia económica en Argentina*.

60. Such is the case of the Barcelonetttes, immigrants from a locality in France who settled in Puebla, Mexico. See L. Gamboa, *Les barcelonettes a Puebla, 1845–1928* (Puebla: Instituto de Ciencias Sociales y Humanidades, Benemérita Universidad Autónoma de Puebla, 2004).

61. García, 'Business History in Argentina'.

62. A. Gerschenkron, 'La modernización empresarial', in M. Weiner, *Modernización* (Mexico: Roble, 1969), pp. 311–24.

63. Fishlow, 'Alexander Gerschenkron', p. 2.

64. R. Brew, *El desarrollo económico de Antioquia desde la Independencia hasta 1920* (Bogota: Ediciones Banco de la República, 1977).

65. A. Mayor, *Ética, trabajo y productividad en Antioquia* (Bogota: Tercer Mundo, 1984).

66. See note 5 above.

67. See, for example, A. Godley and O. Westall (eds), *Business History and Business Culture* (Manchester: Manchester University Press, 1996); R. Cuff, 'Notes for a Panel on Entrepreneurship in Business History', *Business History Review*, 1 (2002), pp. 123–32; Cassis and Pepelasis Minoglou, *Entrepreneurship in Theory and History*; and G. Jones and R. D. Wadhwani (eds), *Entrepreneurship and Global Capitalism* (Cheltenham: Edward Elgar Publishing, 2007).

68. See other chapters in the present volume.

69. Torres Villanueva (ed.), *Los 100 empresarios españoles*; Vidal Olivares (ed.), *Cien empresarios valencianos*.

70. Global Entrepreneurship Monitor, *GEM Colombia 2006*; Kantis et al., *Developing Entrepreneurship*.

71. C. Dávila, 'Perfil biográfico de empresarios: Orientación conceptual y esquema de análisis', in C. Dávila, L. F. Molina, G. Pérez and J. M. Ospina, *Una mirada a la historia del mercadeo en Colombia: Testimonio de Enrique Luque Carulla, 1903–2006* (Bogota: Universidad de los Andes, Facultad de Administración, 2008), pp. 21–50.

72. Jones and Wadhwani (eds), *Entrepreneurship and Global Capitalism*, p. 507.

8 García-Ruiz, 'Education and Entrepreneurship in Twentieth-Century Spain'

I am very grateful for the support of my colleagues of the research programme DETESEMP-CM S2007/HUM-0433 (Community of Madrid) in the elaboration of this paper.

1. Translated as Schumpeter, *The Theory of Economic Development*.

2. Z. J. Acs and D. B. Audretsch (eds), *Handbook of Entrepreneurship Research* (Boston, MA: Kluwer, 2003); S. A. Shane, *A General Theory of Entrepreneurship: The Individual-Opportunity Nexus* (Aldershot: Edward Elgar, 2003); W. B. Gartner, K. G. Shaver, N.

M. Carter and P. D. Reynolds (eds), *Handbook of Entrepreneurial Dynamics: The Process of Business Creation* (Thousand Oaks, CA: Sage, 2004); Cassis and Pepelasis Minoglou (eds), *Entrepreneurship in Theory and History*; Y. Cassis and I. Pepelasis Minoglou (eds), *Country Studies in Entrepreneurship: A Historical Perspective* (Basingstoke: Palgrave Macmillan, 2006); D. B. Audretsch, *The Entrepreneurial Society* (Oxford: Oxford University Press, 2007); A. Cuervo (ed.), *Entrepreneurship: Concepts, Theory and Perspective* (Berlin: Springer, 2007); E. Sheshinski, R. J. Strom and W. J. Baumol, *Entrepreneurship, Innovation and the Growth Mechanism of the Free-Enterprise Economies* (Princeton, NJ: Princeton University Press, 2007).

3. European Commission, *Green Paper on Entrepreneurship in Europe* (Brussels: European Commission, 2003).

4. Consejo Económico y Social, *El proceso de creación de empresas y el dinamismo empresarial*, Report 5/2005 (Madrid: CES, 2005). In the same year was published the first overall historical survey on Spanish entrepreneurship: J. M. Valdaliso, *El espíritu emprendedor en España: un análisis histórico* (Madrid: Instituto Superior de Formación del Profesorado/Ministerio de Educación y Ciencia, 2005).

5. Global Entrepreneurship Monitor, *Informe Ejecutivo GEM España 2005* (Madrid: Instituto de Empresa, 2006), table 57.

6. Consejo Económico y Social, *El proceso de creación de empresas*, pp. 112–13.

7. See M. Santos, *Los economistas y la empresa: Empresa y empresario en la historia del pensamiento económico* (Madrid: Alianza, 1997). See also D. C. McClelland, *The Achieving Society* (Princeton, NJ: Van Nostrand, 1961); E. E. Hagen, *The Economics of Development* (Homewood, IL: Richard D. Irwin, 1980); H. Leibenstein, *General X-Efficiency Theory and Economic Development* (Oxford: Oxford University Press, 1978).

8. Marshall, *Industry and Trade*.

9. Wiener, *English Culture*.

10. G. Jones and R. D. Wadhwani, *Entrepreneurship and Business History: Renewing the Research Agenda*, Working Paper 07–007 (Harvard Business School, 2006).

11. For an overview, see D. H. Aldcroft, *Education, Training and Economic Performance 1944 to 1990* (Manchester: Manchester University Press, 1992).

12. Foreman-Peck and Smith, 'Business and Social Mobility into the British Elite'.

13. Foreman-Peck, 'Measuring Historical Entrepreneurship'.

14. M. Hicks, 'The Recruitment and Selection of Young Managers by British Business, 1930–2000' (PhD dissertation, Oxford University, 2004).

15. J. F. Wilson and A. Thomson, *The Making of Modern Management: British Management in Historical Perspective* (Oxford: Oxford University Press, 2006), pp. 173–5.

16. M. E. Porter, *The Competitive Advantage of Nations* (New York: Free Press, 1990).

17. Penrose, *The Theory of the Growth of the Firm*.

18. B. Carlsson, Z. J. Acs, D. B. Audretsch and P. Braunerhjelm, *The Knowledge Filter, Entrepreneurship and Economic Growth*, Paper 2007–057 (Jena: Jena Economic Research Papers, 2007).

19. P. Drucker, 'From Capitalism to Knowledge Society', in D. Neef (ed.), *The Knowledge Economy* (Boston, MA: Butterworth-Heinemann, 1998), pp. 15–34.

20. H. Hartmann, *Education for Business Leadership: The Role of the German Hochschulen* (Paris: OEEC, 1955), pp. 47, 53.

21. W. Sombart, *El apogeo del capitalism*, 2 vols (1902; Mexico: Fondo de Cultura Económica, 1946), vol. 1, p. 72.

22. D. S. Landes, *The Unbound Prometheus: Technological Change and Industrial Developement in Western Europe from 1750 to the Present* (Cambridge: Cambridge University Press, 1969).

23. R. R. Locke, *The End of Practical Man: Entrepreneurship and Higher Education in Germany, France and Great Britain, 1880–1940* (Greenwich, CT: JAI Press, 1984).

24. J. Van der Sluis, C. M. Van Praag and W. Vijverg, *Education and Entrepreneurship in Industrialized Countries*, Discussion Paper TI 2003-046/3 (Amsterdam: Tinbergen Institute, 2003).

25. R. Velasco-Barroetabeña and M. Saiz-Santos, *Políticas de creación de empresas y su evaluación*, Working Paper 118 (Madrid: Fundación Alternativas, 2007), p. 39.

26. E. Congregado, L. Hernández, J. M. Millán, J. L. Raymond, J. L. Roig, V. Salas, J. L. Sánchez-Asín and L. Serrano, *El capital humano y los emprendedores en España* (Valencia: IVIE / Bancaja, 2008).

27. M. Mas, F. Pérez, E. Uriel and L. Serrano, *Capital humano: Series históricas (1964–1992)* (Valencia: Fundación Bancaja, 1995); J. Palafox, J. G. Mora and F. Pérez, *Capital humano, educación y empleo* (Valencia: Fundación Bancaja, 1995); Bancaja, *Actividad y ocupación por niveles de studios*, Working Paper 33, Human Capital Series (Valencia: Fundación Bancaja, 2003).

28. De Miguel and Linz, 'Nivel de estudios'.

29. There are rows which do not add up exactly to 100 because of rounding, but there is some mistake in the Saragossa row, which only adds up to 91. Source: de Miguel and Linz, 'Nivel de estudios', pp. 47, 53.

30. J. Fernández-Aguado, *Historia de la Escuela de Comercio de Madrid y su influencia en la formación gerencial española, 1850–1970* (Madrid: AECA & ICOTME, 1997).

31. N. Puig, 'Educating Spanish Managers: The United States, Modernizing Networks and Business Schools in Spain, 1950–1975', in R. P. Amdam, R. Kvalshaugen and E. Larsen (eds), *Inside the Business Schools: The Content of European Management Education* (Oslo: Abstrakt Press, 2003), pp. 58–86.

32. CECA, *Estadísticas básicas de España, 1900–1970* (Madrid: CECA, 1975), pp. 426–9.

33. E. De Diego-García, 'Historia de la Escuela de Organización Industrial' (unpublished manuscript, 2000); P. A. Muñoz, *EOI, 1955–2005: 50 años en vanguardia* (Madrid: EOI, 2005).

34. For the ESIC, see J. L. García-Ruiz, 'Cultural Resistance and the Gradual Emergence of Modern Marketing and Retailing Practices in Spain, 1950–1975', *Business History*, 3 (2007), pp. 367–84.

35. M. F. Guillén, *Guía bibliográfica sobre organización de la empresa española hasta 1975*, Working Paper 9502 (Madrid: Fundación Empresa Pública, 1995); J. L. García-Ruiz, *Grandes creadores en la historia del management* (Barcelona: Ariel, 2003), ch. 3.

36. Data from EPA. The expression 'low education level' in Tables 8.4–6 means not having completed secondary studies.

37. Data from EPA.

38. According to Tortella et al., *Educación, instituciones y empresa*, p. 74, the situation of Spain around 2005 was similar to that in the United Kingdom and much above that in France or the United States.

39. Data from EPA.

40. Congregado et al., *El capital humano*, p. 15.

41. Ibid., p. 44.

42. Ibid., p. 169.

43. Ibid., p. 172; concept drawn from Carlsson et al., *The Knowledge Filter*.

44. Congregado et al., *El capital humano*, pp. 205, 206, 207.

45. Ibid., pp. 46, 48, 55.

46. Ibid., p. 61.

47. Ibid., p. 99.

48. Ibid., p. 210.

49. Fernández-Aguado, *Historia de la Escuela de Comercio de Madrid*, p. 417.

50. Tortella et al., *Educación, instituciones y empresa*, p. 51.

51. C. García-Tabuenca, J. De Jorge-Moreno and F. Pablo-Martí, *Emprendedores y espíritu empresarial en España en los albores del siglo XXI* (Madrid: Fundación Rafael del Pino, 2004); C. García-Tabuenca, J. L. Crespo-Espert, F. Pablo-Martí and F. J. Crecente-Romero, *La actividad emprendedora: Empresas y empresarios en España, 1997–2006* (Madrid: Fundación Rafael del Pino, 2008).

52. In line with J. Monreal (ed.), *Formación y cultura empresarial en la empresa española* (Madrid: Civitas, 2004).

WORKS CITED

AA.VV., *Il Politecnico di Milano 1863–1944* (Milan: Electa, 1981).

Acs, Z. J., and D. B. Audretsch (eds), *Handbook of Entrepreneurship Research* (Boston, MA: Kluwer, 2003).

Adams, R. A. 'Book Review of Entrepreneurship in Argentine Culture: Torcuato Di Tella and S.I.A.M. Thomas C. Cochran and Ruben Reina. Research Assistant, Sue Nutall. Philadelphia: University of Pennsylvania Press, 1962', *American Anthropologist*, 1 (1964), pp. 176–7.

[Agriantonis] Αγριαντώνη, Χ., *Οι Απαρχές της Εκβιομηχάνισης στην Ελλάδα τον 19ο Αιώνα* (Αθήνα: Εμπορική Τράπεζα της Ελλάδος, 1986).

Agriantonis, C., and M. C. Chadziioannou (eds), *The Athens Silkmill* (Athens: Institute of Neohellenic Research, 1997).

Aivalis, K., and I. Pepelasis Minoglou, 'A Preliminary Analysis of Early Corporate Governance in Greece: 1850–1909' (Bergen: Papers from the EBHA Annual Conference, 2008).

Aldcroft, D. H., 'Education and Britain's Growth Failure, 1950–1980', in Tortella (ed.), *Education and Economic Development*, pp. 223–45.

—, *Education, Training and Economic Performance 1944 to 1990* (Manchester: Manchester University Press, 1992).

Alvarez, V. 'Empresas y empresarios de Antioquia: Un intento de balance historiográfico', in Universidad Eafit, *Las regiones y la historia empresarial* (Medellin: Universidad Eafit, 2004), pp. 77–104.

Amatori, F. 'Entrepreneurial Typologies in the History of Industrial Italy (1880–1960): A Review Article', *Business History Review*, 3 (1980), pp. 359–86.

—, 'Per un dizionario biografico degli imprenditori marchigiani', in S. Anselmi (ed.), *Le Marche* (Turín: Einaudi, 1987), pp. 592–4.

—, 'Entrepreneurship', *Imprese e storia*, 34 (2006), pp. 233–67.

—, 'Entrepreneurship', Working Paper (Baltimore, MD: IAESBE, Johns Hopkins University, 2007).

—, 'Big and Small Business in Italy's Industrial History', *Rivista di Storia economica*, 2 (2008), pp. 207–24.

Amatori, F., and F. Brioschi, 'Le grandi imprese private: famiglie e coalizioni', in F. Barca (ed.), *Storia del capitalismo italiano dal dopoguerra ad oggi* (Roma: Donzelli, 1987), pp. 118–53.

Amatori, F., and A. Colli, *Impresa e industria in Italia dall'Unità a oggi* (Venezia: Marsilio 1999).

Amatori. F., and G. Jones (eds), *Business History Around the World* (Cambridge: Cambridge University Press, 2003).

[Anastasopoulos] Αναστασόπουλος, Γ., *Ιστορία της Ελληνικής Βιομηχανίας 1840–1940, Τόμος Α (1840–1884)* (Αθήνα: Ελληνική Εκδοτική Εταιρεία, 1946/7).

[Asdrachas] Ασδραχάς, Σ., *Βίωση και Καταγραφή του Οικονομικού* (Αθήνα: Εθνικό Ίδρυμα Ερευνών, 2007).

Audretsch, D. B. (ed.), *Entrepreneurship: Determinants and Policy in a European–US Comparison* (Boston, MA, Dordrecht and London: Kluwer Academic Publisher, 2003).

—, *The Entrepreneurial Society* (Oxford: Oxford University Press, 2007).

Audretsch, D. B., and A. R. Thurik, 'What's New about the New Economy? Sources of Growth in the Managerial and Entrepreneurial Economies', *Industrial and Corporate Change*, 1 (2001), pp. 267–315.

Bairati, P., *Vittorio Valletta* (Turin: UTET, 1983).

Balconi, M., *La siderurgia italiana (1945–1990): Tra controllo pubblico e incentivi di mercato* (Bologna: Il Mulino, 1991).

[Bakounakis] Μπακουνάκης, Ν., *Πάτρα 1828–1860, Μία Ελληνική Πρωτεύουσα στον 19ο αιώνα* (Αθήνα: Καστανιώτης, 1995).

Bancaja, *Actividad y ocupación por niveles de estudios*, Working Paper 33, Human Capital Series (Valencia: Fundación Bancaja, 2003).

Barbero, M. I., 'Business History in Latin America: Issues and Debates', in Amatori and Jones, *Business History around the World*, pp. 317–37.

—, 'Business History in Latin America: A Historiographical Perspective', *Business History Review*, 3 (2008), pp. 555–75.

Barbero, M. I., and C. Dávila, 'Introduction: A View from Latin America', *Entreprises et Histoire*, 54 (2009), pp. 6–15.

Barnia, N., R. W. Eberts and M. S. Fogarty, 'Universities and the Startup of New Companies: Can We Generalize from Route 128 and Silicon Valley?', *Review of Economics and Statistics*, 4 (1993), pp. 761–6.

Barro, R. J., and R. M. McCleary, 'Religion and Economic Growth across Countries', *American Sociological Review*, 5 (2003), pp. 760–81.

Bates, T., 'Entrepreneur Human Capital Inputs and Small Business Longevity', *Review of Economics and Statistics*, 4 (1990), pp. 333–58.

—, 'Financing Small Business Creation: The Case of Chinese and Korean Immigrant Entrepreneurs', US Census Bureau, Working Papers, 96–9 (Washington, DC: Center for Economic Studies, 1996).

Baumol, W. J., 'Entrepreneurship in Economic Theory', *American Economic Review*, 2 (1968), pp. 64–71.

—, 'Entrepreneurship: Productive, Unproductive and Destructive', *Journal of Political Economy*, 5:1 (1990), pp. 893–921.

Baumol, W. J., and R. Strom, 'Useful Knowledge of Entrepreneurship: Some Implications of the History', in Landes et al. (eds), *The Invention of Enterprise*, pp. 527–42.

Baumol, W. J., E. Litan, and C. J. Schramm, *Good Capitalism, Bad Capitalism and the Economics of Growth and Prosperity* (New Haven, CT: Yale University Press: 2007).

Becattini, G., *Dal distretto industriale allo sviluppo locale: Svolgimento e difesa di un'idea* (Turin: Bollati Boringhieri, 2000).

Benaul, J. M., 'Els empresaris de la industrialització: Una aproximació des de la indústria textil llanera catalana', 1815–1870', *Recerques*, 31 (1995), pp. 93–113.

Berghoff, H., 'Public Schools and the Decline of the British Economy, 1870–1914', *Past and Present*, 129 (1990), pp. 148–67.

Berle, A., and G. Means, *The Modern Corporation and Private Property* (New York: Macmillan, 1932).

Berta, G., *Le idee al potere: Adriano Olivetti tra la fabbrica e la comunità* (Milan: Edizioni di Comunità, 1980).

Bigazzi, D., 'Grandi imprese e concentrazione finanziaria: La Pirelli e la Fiat nel mercato mondiale', in *Storia della società italiana, vol. XX: L'Italia di Giolitti* (Milan: Teti Editore, 1981), pp. 87–143.

Bigazzi, D., *La storia d'impresa in Italia: Saggio bibliografico: 1980–1987* (Milano: Franco Angeli, 1990).

Blaug, M., 'Entrepreneurship Before and After Schumpeter', in R. Swedberg, *Entrepreneurship: The Social Science View* (Oxford: Oxford University Press, 2000), pp. 76–88.

Bodenheimer, S., 'The Ideology of Developmentalism: American Political Science's Paradigm – Surrogate for Latin American Studies', *Berkeley Journal of Sociology*, 15 (1970), pp. 95–173.

Boix, R., and V. Galletto, 'El mapa de los distritos industriales de España', *Economía Industrial*, 359 (2006), pp. 165–84.

—, 'The New Map of the Industrial Districts in Spain and the Comparison with Italy and the United Kingdom: Improving International Comparison of Industrial Districts with Common Methodologies' (Regions in Focus? Regional Studies Association International Conference, Lisbon, 2–5 April 2007).

Bolasco, S., *Analisi multidimensionale dei dati: Metodi, strategie e criteri d'interprestazione* (Roma: Carocci Editore, 1999).

Bonacich, E., and J. Modell, *The Economic Basis of Ethnic Solidarity: Small Business in the Japanese-American Community* (Berkeley, CA: University of California Press, 1980).

Bonelli, F., *Lo sviluppo di una grande impresa in Italia: La Terni dal 1884 al 1962* (Turin: Einaudi, 1975).

—, 'Il capitalismo italiano: Linee generali d'interpretazione', in *Storia d'Italia. Annali 1: Dal feudalesimo al capitalismo* (Turín: Einaudi, 1978), pp. 1195–255.

—, 'Alberto Beneduce, il credito industriale e le origini dell'IRI', in IRI, *Alberto Beneduce e i problemi dell'economia italiana del suo tempo* (Rome: Atti della giornata di studio per la celebrazione del 50° anniversario dell'istituzione dell'Iri, Edindustria, 1985).

Boswell, T., and J. R. Curtis, *The Cuban-American Experience: Culture, Images and Perspectives* (Totowa, NJ: Rowman & Allanheld, 1984).

Boulding, K. E., *The Meaning of the Twentieth Century: The Great Transition* (New York: Harper & Row, 1965).

Brand Council, The, *Top Brands: El libro de las grandes marcas en España*, I (Madrid: Top-Brands and The Brand Council, 2002).

Brew, R., *El desarollo económico de Antioquia desde la Independencia hasta 1920* (Bogota: Publicaciones del Banco de la República, 1977).

Bricco, P., *Olivetti, prima e dopo Adriano: Industria, cultura, estetica* (Naples: L'Ancora del Mediterraneo, 2005).

Bucheli, M., *Bananas and Business: The United Fruit Company in Colombia, 1899–2000* (New York: New York University Press, 2005).

Buitoni, B., and G. P. Gallo, *Pasta e cioccolato: Una storia imprenditoriale* (Perugia: Protagon, 1992).

Cabana, F., *Fabricants i empresaris* (Barcelona: Enciclopédia Catalana, 1992–4).

—, *SA Damm: Mestres cervesers des de 1876* (Barcelona: SA Damm, 2001).

— (ed.), *Cien empresarios catalanes* (Madrid: LID, 2006).

—, *La saga dels cotoners* (Barcelona: Proa, 2006).

Cafagna, L., *Dualismo e sviluppo nella storia d'Italia* (Venice: Marsilio, 1989).

Cantillon, R., *Essai sur la nature du commerce en général* (1755; Paris: Institut national d'etudes demographiques, 1952).

Cardoso, F. H., 'The Industrial Elite', in Lipset and Solari (eds), *Elites in Latin America*, pp. 94–114.

Cardoso, F. H., and E. Faletto, *Dependência y desarrollo em América Latina* (Mexico: Siglo XXI, 1969).

Carlsson, B., Z. J. Acs, D. B. Audretsch and P. Braunerhjelm, *The Knowledge Filter, Entrepreneurship and Economic Growth*, Paper 2007–057 (Jena: Jena Economic Research Papers, 2007).

Carreras, A., and X. Tafunell, 'La gran empresa en la España contemporánea: Entre el Mercado y el Estado', in F. Comín, and P. Martín Aceña (eds), *La empresa en la historia de España* (Madrid: Civitas, 1996), pp. 73–90.

—, 'Spain: Big Manufacturing Firms between State and Market, 1917–1990', in A. D. Chandler, F. Amatori and T. Hikino (eds), *Big business and the wealth of nations* (Cambridge, UK: Cambridge University Press, 1999), pp. 277–304.

Carreras, A., X. Tafunell and E. Torres Villanueva, 'La historia empresarial en España', in Erro (ed.), *Historia empresarial*, pp. 319–437.

Cassis, Y., *Big Business: The European Experience in the Twentieth Century* (Oxford: Oxford University Press, 1999).

Cassis, Y., and I. Pepelasis Minoglou (eds), *Entrepreneurship in Theory and History* (Basingstoke: Palgrave Macmillan, 2005).

— (eds), *Country Studies in Entrepreneurship: A Historical Perspective* (Basingstoke: Palgrave Macmillan, 2006).

Casson, M., *The Entrepreneur: An Economic Theory* (Oxford: Martin Robertson, 1982).

Casson, M., and A. Godley, 'Entrepreneurship and Historical Explanation', in Cassis and Pepelasis Minoglou (eds), *Entrepreneurship in Theory and History*, pp. 25–59.

Casson, M., et al. (eds), *The Oxford Handbook of Entrepreneurship* (Oxford: Oxford University Press, 2006).

Castellano, C., *L'industria degli elettrodomestici in Italia: Fattori e caratteri* (Turin: Giappichelli, 1965).

Castronovo, V., *Giovanni Agnelli* (Turin: UTET, 1971).

CECA, *Estadísticas básicas de España, 1900–1970* (Madrid: CECA, 1975).

Cerutti, M., 'Regional Studies and Business History in Mexico since 1975', in Dávila and Miller (eds), *Business History in Latin America*, pp. 116–27.

—, 'Estudio introductorio', in M. Cerutti, *Empresas y grupos empresariales en América Latina, España y Portugal* (Monterrey: Universidad Autónoma de Nuevo León, Universidad de Alicante, 2006), pp. 9–40.

Cetin, F., *My Grandmother: A Memoir* (London: Verso, 2008).

[Chadziioannou] Χατζηϊωάννου, Μ. Χ., *Οικογενειακή Στρατηγική και Εμπορικός Ανταγωνισμός Ο Οίκος Γερούση τον 19ο Αιώνα* (Αθήνα: ΜΙΕΤ, 2003).

Chilcote, R., 'Dependency: A Critical Synthesis of the Literature', *Latin American Perspectives*, 1 (1974), pp.4–29.

Ciccone, A., and E. Papaioannou, 'Red Tape and Delayed Entry', *Journal of the European Economic Association*, 2:3 (2007), pp. 444–58.

Cipolla, C., *Before the Industrial Revolution* (London: Metheun, 1976).

Clark, X., T. J. Hatton and J. G. Williamson, 'Explaining US Immigration 1971–1998', *Review of Economics and Statistics*, 2 (2007), pp. 359–73.

Clogg, R., *A Concise History of Modern Greece* (Cambridge: Cambridge University Press, 1992).

Coase, R., 'The Nature of the Firm', *Economica*, 4 (1932), pp. 386–405.

Cochran, T., *The Puerto Rican Businessman: A Study in Cultural Change* (Philadelphia, PA: University of Pennsylvania Press, 1959).

—, 'The Entrepreneur in Economic Change', *Explorations in Entrepreneurial History* (Summer 1965), pp. 25–37.

Coleman, D. C., 'Gentlemen and Players', *Economic History Review*, 1 (1973), pp. 252–75.

Coleman, J. S., 'Social Capital in the Creation of Human Capital', *American Journal of Sociology*, (Supplement) 94 (1988), pp. 95–120.

Colitti, M., *Energia e sviluppo in Italia: La vicenda di Enrico Mattei* (Bari: De Donato, 1979).

Colli, A., 'Fumagalli, Eden', in *Dizionario Biografico degli Italiani*, vol. 50, pp. 720–2.

—, *I volti di Proteo: Storia della piccola impresa in Italia nel Novecento* (Turín: Bollati Boringhieri, 2002).

—, *Il quarto capitalismo: Un profilo italiano* (Venice: Marsilio, 2002).

—, *The History of Family Business, 1850–2000* (Cambridge: Cambridge University Press, 2003).

Colli, A., P. Fernández-Pérez and M. B. Rose, 'National Determinants of Family Firm Development? Family Firms in Britain, Spain and Italy in the Nineteenth and Twentieth Centuries', *Enterprise and Society*, 4:1 (2003), pp. 28–64.

Collins, J., 'Cultural Diversity and Entrepreneurship: Policy Responses to Immigrant Entrepreneurs in Australia', *Entrepreneurship and Regional Development*, 15 (2003), pp. 137–49.

Congregado, E., L. Hernández, J. M. Millán, J. L. Raymond, J. L. Roig, V. Salas, J. L. Sánchez-Asín and L. Serrano, *El capital humano y los emprendedores en España* (Valencia: IVIE / Bancaja, 2008).

Consejo Económico y Social, *El proceso de creación de empresas y el dinamismo empresarial*, Report 5/2005 (Madrid: CES, 2005).

Constant, A., Y. Shachmurove and K. F. Zimmermann, 'What Makes an Entrepreneur and Does it Pay? Native Men, Turks and Other Migrants in Germany', CEPR Discussion Paper, 4207 (Washington, DC, 2004).

Conti, F., 'I Perrone fra impresa e politica', in Hertner, *Storia dell'Ansaldo Vol. 3*, pp. 225–56.

Corcoran, M. P., 'Emigrants, Eirepreneurs and Opportunities', in R. H. Bayof and T. J. Meagher (eds), *The New York Irish* (Baltimore, MD: Johns Hopkins University Press, 1996).

Corley, T. A. B., 'Historical Biographies of Entrepreneurs', in Casson et al. (eds), *The Oxford Handbook of Entrepreneurship*, pp. 138–57.

Cuervo, A. (ed.), *Entrepreneurship: Concepts, Theory and Perspective* (Berlin: Springer, 2007).

Cuff, R., 'Notes for a Panel on Entrepreneurship in Business History', *Business History Review*, 1 (2002), pp. 123–32.

Dávila, C. (ed.), *Empresa e historia en América Latina: Un balance historiográfico* (Bogota: Conciencias, Tercer Mundo Editores, 1996).

—, 'Business History in Colombia', in Dávila and Miller (eds), *Business History in Latin America*, pp. 83–115.

—, 'La historia empresarial en América Latina', in Erro (ed.), *Historia empresarial*, pp. 349–81.

—, 'Books that Made a Difference: *On the Theory of Social Change: How Economic Growth Begins*, by Everett Hagen', *Business History Review*, 1 (2006), pp. 131–4.

—, 'Introduction', *Business History Review*, 3 (2008), pp. 439–44.

—, 'Perfil biográfico de empresarios: Orientación conceptual y esquema de análisis', in C. Dávila, L. F. Molina, G. Pérez y J. M. Ospina, *Una mirada a la historia del mercadeo en Colombia: Testimonio de Enrique Luque Carulla, 1903–2006* (Bogota: Universidad de los Andes, Facultad de Administración, 2008), pp. 21–50.

Dávila, C., and B. Rodríguez, 'Naturaleza y perspectivas de la historia empresarial en Colombia', in M. I. Barbero and R. Jacob (eds), *La nueva historia de empresas en América Latina y España* (Buenos Aires: Temas Grupo Editorial, 2008), pp. 109–139.

Dávila, C., and R. Miller (eds), *Business History in Latin America: The Experience of Seven Countries* (Liverpool: Liverpool University Press, 1999).

De Diego-García, E., 'Historia de la Escuela de Organización Industrial' (unpublished manuscript, 2000).

De Miguel, A., and J. J. Linz, 'Nivel de estudios del empresariado español', *Arbor*, 219 (1964), pp. 33–63.

Decleva, E. 'Conti, Ettore', in *Dizionario Biografico degli Italiani*, vol. 28, pp. 389–99.

Denison, E. F., *The Sources of Economic Growth of the United States and the Alternative Before Us*, Supplementary Paper 13 (New York: Committee for Economic Development, 1962).

[Dertilis] Δερτιλής, Γ. Β., *Το 1909 και η διαδικασία κοινωνικών και θεσμικών μεταβολών στην Ελλάδα* (Αθήνα: Εξάντας, 1977).

—, *Ιστορία του Ελληνικού Κράτους 1830–1920*, 2 vols (Αθήνα: Εστία, 2005).

Deu, E., 'La construcción de telares mecánicos en Sabadell (1863–1960): Francesc Duran Cañameras y sus sucesores', *Revista de Historia Industrial*, 2 (1992), pp. 183–90.

Dizionario Biografico degli Italiani, 73 vols to date (Roma: Istituto Della Enciclopedia Italiana, 1960–).

Doria, M., *Ansaldo* (Milan: Franco Angeli, 1989).

—, *L'imprenditoria industriale in Italia dall'unità al 'miracolo economico': Capitani d'industria, padroni, innovatori* (Torino: Giappichelli, 1998).

—, 'Gli imprenditori tra vincoli strutturali e nuove opportunità', in F. Amatori et al., *Storia d'Italia. Annali 15: L'industria* (Torino: Einaudi, 1999), pp. 619–87.

Dritsas, M., 'Business History in Greece: The State of the Art and Future Prospects', in Amatori and Jones (eds), *Business History around the World*, pp. 255–70.

Drucker, P., 'From Capitalism to Knowledge Society', in D. Neef (ed.), *The Knowledge Economy* (Boston, MA: Butterworth-Heinemann, 1998), pp. 15–34.

[*Encyclopedia Lexicon 'Elios'*] Νεώτερον Εγκυκλοπαιδικόν Λεξικόν 'Ηλίου' (Αθήνα, 1948–54).

Erro, C. (ed.), *Historia empresarial: Pasado, presente y retos de futuro* (Barcelona: Ariel, 2003).

European Commission, *Green Paper on Entrepreneurship in Europe* (Brussels: European Commission, 2003).

Evans, D. S., and B. Jovanovic, 'An Estimated Model of Entrepreneurial Choice under Liquidity Constraints', *Journal of Political Economy*, 97 (1989), pp. 808–27.

Evans, D. S., and L. C. Leighton, 'Some Empirical Aspects of Entrepreneurship', *American Economic Review*, 3 (1989), pp. 519–35.

Everitt, B. S., *Cluster Analysis* (London: Edward Arnold, 1993).

Federico, G., and P. A. Toninelli, 'Business Strategies from Unification up to the 1970s', in Giannetti and Vasta (eds), *Evolution of Italian Enterprises*, pp. 191–238.

Feldmann, H., 'Protestantism, Labor Force Participation, and Employment across Countries', *American Journal of Economics and Sociology*, 4 (2007), pp. 795–816.

Fernández, R., and J. F. Ocampo, 'The Latin American Revolution: A Theory of Imperialism, Not Dependence', *Latin American Perspectives*, 1 (1974), pp. 30–61.

Fernández-Aguado, J., *Historia de la Escuela de Comercio de Madrid y su influencia en la formación gerencial española, 1850–1970* (Madrid: AECA & ICOTME, 1997).

Fernández-Pérez, P., 'Small Firms and Networks in Capital Intensive Industries: The Case of Spanish Steel Wire Manufacturing', *Business History*, 49:5 (2007), pp. 647–67.

Fernández-Pérez, P., and N. Puig, 'Knowledge and Training in Family Firms of the European Periphery: Spain in the Eighteenth to Twentieth Centuries', *Business History*, 1 (2004), pp. 79–100.

—, 'Bonsais in a Wild Forest? A Historical Interpretation of the Longevity of Large Spanish Family Firms', *Revista de Historia Económica: Journal of Iberian and Latin American Economic History*, 3 (2007), pp. 459–97.

—, 'Global Lobbies for a Global Economy: The Creation of the Spanish Institute of Family Firms in International Perspective', *Business History*, 5 (2009), pp. 712–33.

Fernández-Pérez, P., and M. B. Rose (eds), *Innovation and Entrepreneurial Networks in Europe* (Oxford: Routledge, 2010).

Fishlow, A., 'Alexander Gerschenkron: A Latecomer who Emerged Victorious. Review Essay of A. Gerschenkron, *Economic Backwardness in Historical Perspective: A Book of Essays* (1962)' (EH.net Project 2001, Significant Works in Economic History, posted in 2003).

Fleming, W. J., 'The Cultural Determinants of Entrepreneurship and Economic Development: A Case Study of Mendoza Province, Argentina, 1861–1914', *Journal of Economic History*, 1 (1979), pp. 211–24.

Fontana, G. L. (ed.), *Schio e Alessandro Rossi: Imprenditorialità, politica, cultura e paesaggi sociali del secondo Ottocento* (Rome: Edizioni di Storia e Letteratura, 1985).

Foreman-Peck, J., 'A Political Economy of International Migration 1815–1914', *Manchester School*, 4 (1992), pp. 359–76.

—, 'Measuring Historical Entrepreneurship', in Cassis and Pepelasis Minoglou (eds), *Entrepreneurship in Theory and History*, pp. 77–108.

Foreman-Peck, J., and I. Pepelasis Minoglou, 'Entrepreneurship and Convergence: Greek Businessmen in the Nineteenth Century', *Rivista di Storia Economica*, 3 (2000), pp. 279–303.

Foreman-Peck, J., and J. Smith, 'Business and Social Mobility into the British Elite, 1870–1914', *Journal of European Economic History*, 3 (2004), pp. 485–518.

[Franghiadis] Φραγκιάδης, Α., *Ελληνική Οικονομία 19ος 20ος Αιώνας* (Αθήνα: Νεφέλη, 2007).

Franzinelli, M., and M. Magnani, *Beneduce: Il finanziere di Mussolini* (Milan: Mondadori, 2009).

Fuà, G., and C. Zacchia (eds), *Industrializzazione senza fratture* (Bologna: Il Mulino, 1983).

Galambos, L., 'The Emerging Organizational Synthesis in Modern American History', *Business History Review*, 3 (1970), pp. 279–90.

Gallo, M. A., 'Family Businesses in Spain: Tracks Followed and Outcomes Reached by Those among the Largest Thousand', *Family Business Review*, 4 (1995), pp. 245–54.

Galve, C., and V. Salas, *La empresa familiar en España: Fundamentos económicos y resultados* (Bilbao: Fundación BBVA, 2003).

Gamboa, L., *Les barcelonettes a Puebla, 1845–1928* (Puebla: Instituto de Ciencias Sociales y Humanidades, Benemérita Universidad Autónoma de Puebla, 2004).

García, R., 'Business History in Argentina', in Dávila and Miller (eds), *Business History in Latin America*, pp. 17–42.

—, *Historia empresarial e historia económica en Argentina: Un balance a comienzos del siglo XXI*, Monografía 95 (Bogota: Facultad de Administración, Universidad de los Andes, 2007).

García-Ruiz, J. L., *Grandes creadores en la historia del management* (Barcelona: Ariel, 2003).

—, 'Cultural Resistance and the Gradual Emergence of Modern Marketing and Retailing Practices in Spain, 1950–1975', *Business History*, 3 (2007), pp. 367–84.

García-Sanz, A., 'Empresarios en la España del antiguo régimen: Ganaderos trashumantes, exportadores de lana y fabricantes de paños', in F. Comin and P. Martín Aceña (eds), *La empresa en la historia de España* (Madrid: Editorial Civitas, 1996), pp. 93–113.

García-Tabuenca, C., J. De Jorge-Moreno and F. Pablo-Martí, *Emprendedores y espíritu empresarial en España en los albores del siglo XXI* (Madrid: Fundación Rafael del Pino, 2004).

García-Tabuenca, C., J. L. Crespo-Espert, F. Pablo-Martí and F. J. Crecente-Romero, *La actividad emprendedora: Empresas y empresarios en España, 1997–2006* (Madrid: Fundación Rafael del Pino, 2008).

Garruccio, R., 'Genealogia di una riflessione su imprenditorialità, innovazione e potere' (Milano, 2008).

Gartner, W. B., K. G. Shaver, N. M. Carter and P. D. Reynolds (eds), *Handbook of Entrepreneurial Dynamics: The Process of Business Creation* (Thousand Oaks, CA: Sage, 2004).

Gekas, S., and M. C. (C)Hadziioannou, 'The Trade-Minded Greek Entrepreneurs, 1780s–1900s' (Haifa: Papers from the Workshop on Entrepreneurship and Culture: Near and Middle Eastern Perspectives, organized by the Onassis Foundation and Haifa University, 2008).

Gerschenkron, A., *Economic Backwardness in Historical Perspective: A Book of Essays* (Cambridge, MA: Belknap Press of Harvard University Press, 1962).

—, 'Reviewed Work: On the Theory of Social Change: How Economic Growth Begins by Everett E. Hagen', *Economica*, 32 (1965), pp. 90–4.

—, 'La modernización empresarial', in M. Weiner, *Modernización* (Mexico: Roble, 1969), pp. 311–24.

Gersick, K. E., J. A. Davis, M. McCollom and I. Lansberg, *Generation to Generation: Life Cycles of the Family Business* (Cambridge, MA: Harvard Business School Press, 1997).

Giannetti, R., 'L'istruzione e la formazione del capital umano', in P. Toninelli (ed.), *Lo sviluppo economico moderno dalla rivoluzione industriale alla crisi energetica (1750–1973)* (Venezia: Marsilio, 1997), pp. 511–31.

Giannetti, R., and M. Vasta (eds), *Evolution of Italian Enterprises in the Twentieth Century* (Heidelberg and New York: Phisica-Verlag, 2006).

Global Entrepreneurship Monitor, *National Entrepreneurship Assessment: Italy* (Babson Park, MA: GEM, 1999).

—, *Informe Ejecutivo GEM España 2005* (Madrid: Instituto de Empresa, 2006).

—, *GEM Colombia 2006: Reporte de resultados* (Bogota: Universidad de los Andes, Universidad Icesi, Universidad del Norte, Pontificia Universidad Javeriana, 2007).

Godley, A., *Jewish Immigrant Entrepreneurship in New York and London 1880–1914: Enterprise and Culture* (London: Palgrave, 2001).

—, 'Migration of Entrepreneurs', in Casson et al. (eds), *The Oxford Handbook of Entrepreneurship*, pp. 601–10.

Godley, A., and O. Westall (eds), *Business History and Business Culture* (Manchester: Manchester University Press, 1996).

Gramsci, A., *Note sul Machiavelli, sulla politica e sullo stato moderno* (Torino: Einaudi, 1966).

—, *Il Risorgimento* (Torino: Einaudi, 1966).

Granovetter, M., 'Business Groups and Social Organization', in N. Smelser and R. Swedberg (eds), *Handbook of Economic Sociology* (Princeton, NJ: Princeton University Press, 2005), pp. 429–50.

Grebler, L., J. W. Moore and R. C. Guzman, *The Mexican-American People: The Nation's Second Largest Minority* (New York: Free Press, 1970).

Guagnini, A., 'The Formation of Italian Electrical Engineers: The Teaching Laboratories of the Politecnici of Turin and Milan, 1887–1914', in F. Cardot (ed.), *Histoire de l'électricité dans le monde 1880–1980* (Paris: PUF, 1987), pp. 283–99.

Guillén, M. F., *Guía bibliográfica sobre organización de la empresa española hasta 1975*, Working Paper 9502 (Madrid: Fundación Empresa Pública, 1995).

—, *The Rise of Spanish Multinationals: European Business in the Global Economy* (New York: Cambridge University Press, 2005).

Guinjoan, M., C. Murillo and J. Pons, *L'empresa familiar a Catalunya: Quantificació i característiques* (Barcelona, CIDEM/Fundació Joaquim Molins, 2004).

Guiso, L., P. Sapienza and L. Zingales, 'Does Culture Affect Economic Outcomes?', *Journal of Economic Perspectives*, 2 (2006), pp. 23–48.

Gutiérrez, M., *Full a full: La indústria paperera de l'Anoia (1700–1998): Continuïtat I modernitat* (Igualada: Publicacions Abadia Montserrat, 1999).

[Hadziiosif] Χατζηιωσήφ, Χ., *Η Γηραιά Σελήνη Η Βιομηχανία στην Ελληνική Οικονομία 1830–1940* (Αθήνα: Θεμέλιο, 1993).

Hagen, E. E., *On the Theory of Social Change* (Homewood, IL: Dorsey Press, 1962).

—, *The Economics of Development* (Homewood, IL: Richard D. Irwin, 1980).

Halperin, T., '"Dependency Theory" and Latin American Historiography', *Latin American Research Review*, 1 (1982), pp. 115–30.

Harrison, L. E., *Underdevelopment is a State of Mind: The Latin American Case* (Cambridge, MA: Harvard University Center for International Affairs, 1985).

Harrison, L. E., and P. L. Berger (eds), *Developing Cultures: Case Studies* (New York: Routledge, 2006).

Harrison, L. E., and Huntington, S. (eds), *Culture Matters: How Values Shape Human Progress* (New York: Basic Books, 2000).

Harrison, L. E., and J. Kagan (eds), *Developing Cultures: Essays on Culture Change* (New York: Routledge, 2006).

Hartmann, H., *Education for Business Leadership: The Role of the German Hochschulen* (Paris: OEEC, 1955).

Hatton, T. J., 'How Much Did Immigrant "Quality" Decline in Late Nineteenth Century America?', *Journal of Population Economics*, 13 (2000), pp. 509–25.

Hatton, T. J., and A. Leigh, 'Immigrants Assimilate as Communities, Not Just as Individuals' (The Economics of Migration, Diversity and Culture Conference, Bologna, September 2006; paper revised in 2007).

Hertner, P. (ed.), *Storia dell'Ansaldo Vol. 3: Dai Bombrini ai Perrone 1903–1914* (Bari: Laterza, 1996).

Hicks, M., 'The Recruitment and Selection of Young Managers by British Business, 1930–2000' (PhD dissertation, Oxford University, 2004).

Huntington, S., 'Foreword: Cultures Count', in Harrison and Huntington (eds), *Culture Matters*, pp. xiii–xvi.

Ichihashi, Y., *Japanese in the United States: A Critical Study of the Problems of the Japanese Immigrants and Their Children* (1932; New York: Arno Press, 1969).

James, H., *Family Capitalism: Wendels, Haniels, Falcks, and the Continental European Model* (Cambridge, MA: Harvard University Press, 2006).

Jeremy, D. J. (ed.), *Dictionary of Business Biography: A Biographical Dictionary of Business Leaders Active in Britain in the Period 1860–1980*, 5 vols (London: Butterworths, 1984–6).

Jeremy, D. J., and G. Tweedale (eds), *Dictionary of Twentieth-Century Business Leaders* (London: Bowker, 1994).

Jones, C., *The Chinese in America* (Minneapolis, MN: Lerner Publication, 1972).

Jones, G., and M. B. Rose, *Family Capitalism*, special issue of *Business History*, 4 (1993).

Jones, G., and R. D. Wadhwani, *Entrepreneurship and Business History: Renewing the Research Agenda*, Working Paper 07–007 (Harvard Business School, 2006).

— (eds), *Entrepreneurship and Global Capitalism* (Cheltenham: Edward Elgar Publishing, 2007).

—, 'Entrepreneurship', in G. Jones and J. Zeitlin (eds), *The Oxford Handbook of Business History* (Oxford: Oxford University Press, 2008), pp. 501–28.

Kaldor, N., 'The Relation of Economic Growth and Cyclical Fluctuations', *Economic Journal*, 253 (1954), pp. 53–71.

Kantis, H., P. Angelelli and V. Moori Koenig, *Developing Entrepreneurship* (Washington, DC: Interamerican Development Bank, 2007).

Kay, C., *Latin American Theories of Development and Underdevelopment* (London: Routledge, 1989).

Kilby, P., 'Hunting the Heffalump', in P. Kilby (ed.), *Entrepreneurship and Economic Development* (New York: Free Press, 1971), pp. 1–40.

—, 'The Heffalump Revisited', *Journal of International Entrepreneurship*, 1 (2003), pp. 13–29.

Kirzner, I. M., 'Entrepreneurial Discovery and the Competitive Market Process: An Austrian Approach', *Journal of Economic Literature*, 1 (1997), pp. 60–85.

Klapper, L., L. Laeven and R. Rajan, 'Entry Regulation as a Barrier to Entrepreneurship', *Journal of Financial Economics*, 3 (2006), pp. 591–629.

Knight, F. H., *Risk, Uncertainty and Profit* (New York: Houghton Mifflin, 1921).

Knudsen, T., and R. Swedberg, 'Capitalist Entrepreneurship: Making Profit through the Unmaking of Economic Orders', *Capitalism and Society*, 4:2 (2009), pp. 1–26.

[Kostelenos et al.] Κωστελένος, Γ., et al., *Ακαθάριστο Εγχώριο Προϊόν: 1830–1939* (Αθήνα: ΚΕΠΕ, 2007).

Kostis, K., 'The Formation of the Greek State', in F. Birtek and T. Dragonas (eds), *Citizenship and the Nation-State in Greece and Turkey* (New York: Routledge, 2005), pp. 18–36.

[Kostis and Tsokopoulos] Κωστής, Κ., and Β. Τσοκόπουλος, *Οι Τράπεζες στην Ελλάδα 1898–1928* (Αθήνα: Παπαζήσης, 1988).

Kung, S. W., *Chinese in American Life: Some Aspects of Their History, Status, Problems and Contributions* (Seattle, WA: University of Washington Press, 1962).

Lacaita, C. G., 'Ingegneri e scuole politecniche nell'Italia liberale', in S. Soldani and G. Turi (eds), *Fare gli italiani: Scuola e cultura nell'Italia contemporanea*, 2 vols (Bologna: Il Mulino, 1993), vol. 1, pp. 213–53.

Laird, P. W., *Pull: Networking and Success since Benjamin Franklin* (Cambridge, MA: Harvard University Press, 2006).

Landes, D. S., *The Unbound Prometheus: Technological Change and Industrial Developement in Western Europe from 1750 to the Present* (Cambridge: Cambridge University Press, 1969).

—, *The Wealth and Poverty of Nations: Why Some are so Rich and Some are so Poor* (London: Abacus; New York: W. W. Norton, 1998).

—, *Dynasties: Fortunes and Misfortunes of the World's Great Family Businesses* (New York: Viking, 2006).

Landes, D. S., J. Mokyr and W. J. Baumol (eds), *The Invention of Enterprise* (Princeton, NJ: Princeton University Press, 2010).

Lebart, L., 'Complementary Use of Correspondence Analysis and Cluster Analysis', in M. Greenacre and J. Blasius (eds), *Correspondence Analysis in the Social Sciences* (London: Academic Press, 1994), pp. 162–78.

Lee, R. H., *The Chinese in the United States of America* (Hong Kong: Hong Kong University Press, 1960).

Leff, N. H., 'Entrepreneurship and Economic Development: The Problem Revisited', *Journal of Economic Literature*, 1 (1979), pp. 46–64.

Leibenstein, H., *General X-Efficiency Theory and Economic Development* (Oxford: Oxford University Press, 1978).

Lepore, G. F., and C. Claudio Sonzogno, *L'impero della chimica* (Rome: Newton Compton, 1990).

Levie, J., 'Immigration, In-Migration, Ethnicity and Entrepreneurship in the United Kingdom', *Small Business Economics*, 2:3 (2007), pp. 143–69.

Lipman, A., *El empresario bogotano* (Bogota: Tercer Mundo, 1966).

—, *The Colombian Entrepreneur in Bogota* (Coral Gables, FL: University of Miami Press, 1969).

Lipset, S., 'Values, Education and Entrepreneurship', in Lipset and Solari (eds), *Elites in Latin America*, pp. 3–60.

Lipset, S., and A. Solari (eds), *Elites in Latin America* (New York: Oxford University Press, 1967).

Locke, R. R., *The End of Practical Man: Entrepreneurship and Higher Education in Germany, France and Great Britain, 1880–1940* (Greenwich, CT: JAI Press, 1984).

Lofstrom, M., 'Labour Market Assimilation and the Self Employment Decision of Immigrant Entrepreneurs', *Journal of Population Economics*, 15 (2002), pp. 83–114.

Luján, N., *La lucha contra el frío y el calor, y en favor de la higiene: Contribución de una familia de industriales catalanes a lo largo de 75 años* (Barcelona: Compañía Roca Radiadores, 1992).

McClelland, D. C., *The Achieving Society* (Princeton, NJ: Van Nostrand, 1961).

McDonogh, G. W., *Good Families of Barcelona: A Social History of Power in the Industrial Era* (Princeton, NJ: Princeton University Press, 1986).

Marcuello, C. (ed.), *Capital social y organizaciones no lucrativas en España* (Bilbao: FBBVA, 2007).

Marshall, A., *Industry and Trade: A Study of Industrial Technique and Business Organization; and of their Influences on the Conditions of Various Classes and Nations* (1919), 3rd edn (London: Macmillan, 1927).

Marshall, A., *Principles of Economics*, 8th edn (London: Macmillan, 1977).

Mas, M., F. Pérez, E. Uriel and L. Serrano, *Capital humano: Series históricas (1964–1992)* (Valencia: Fundación Bancaja, 1995).

Mayor, A. *Etica, trabajo y productividad en Antioquia* (Bogota: Tercer Mundo, 1984).

Miguel, A. de, and J. J. Linz, 'Nivel de estudios del empresariado español', *Arbor*, 219 (1964), pp. 33–63.

Miller, R., *Britain and Latin America in the Nineteenth and Twentieth Centuries* (London: Longman, 1993).

—, 'Business History in Latin America: An Introduction', in Dávila and Miller (eds), *Business History in Latin America*, pp. 1–16.

Mokyr, J., 'Eurocentricity Triumphant', *American Historical Review*, 4 (1999), pp. 1241–6.

—, 'Entrepreneurship and the Industrial Revolution in Britain', in Landes et al. (eds), *The Invention of Enterprise*, pp. 183–210.

Monitor Group, *Paths to Prosperity: Promoting Entrepreneurship in the Twenty-First Century* (Cambridge, MA: Monitor, 2009).

Monreal, J. (ed.), *Formación y cultura empresarial en la empresa española* (Madrid: Civitas, 2004).

Moreno, J., 'Estrategias de expansión de una empresa familiar catalana: Agrolimen, 1937–2007', *Revista de Historia Industrial*, 3 (2009), pp. 49–89.

Mori, G. 'L'economia italiana dagli anni Ottanta fino alla Prima guerra mondiale', in G. Mori (ed.), *Storia dell'industria elettrica in Italia 1 Le origini: 1882–1914* (Rome-Bari: Laterza, 1992), pp. 3–106.

—, 'L'industria dell'acciaio in Italia', in Hertner (ed.), *Storia dell'Ansaldo Vol. 3*, pp. 31–66.

Morris, C., 'Review of David Landes, The Wealth and Poverty of Nations', *New York Times, Sunday Book Review* (29 October 2006).

Mortara, A. (ed.), *I protagonisti dell'intervento pubblico in Italia* (Milan: CIRIEC and Franco Angeli, 1984).

Moskos, C., *Greek Americans: Struggle and Success*, 2nd edn (New Brunswick, NJ: Transaction, 1989).

[Moulias] Μούλιας, Χ., *Το Λιμάνι της Σταφίδας, Πάτρα, 1828–1900* (Πάτρα: Περί Τεχνών, 2000).

Mouzelis, N., 'The Concept of Modernization: Its Relevance for Greece', *Journal of Modern Greek Studies*, 2 (1996), pp. 215–27.

Muñoz, P. A., *EOI, 1955–2005: 50 años en vanguardia* (Madrid: EOI, 2005).

Nadal, J., 'Los Bonaplata: Tres generaciones de industriales en la España del siglo XIX', *Revista de Historia Económica*, 1 (1983), pp. 79–95.

—, *Moler, tejer y fundir: Estudios de historia industrial* (Barcelona: Ariel, 1992).

—, 'Los Planas, constructores de turbinas y material eléctrico (1858–1949)', *Revista de Historia Industrial*, 1 (1992), pp. 63–94.

Nuccio, O., and F. Spinelli, 'The Historical Primacy of the Italian Entrepreneur', *Review of Economic Conditions of Italy*, 1 (2000), pp. 189–98.

Núñez, C. E., and G. Tortella (eds), *La maldición divina: Ignorancia y atraso económico en perspectiva histórica* (Madrid: Alianza Editorial, 1993).

Osti, G. L., and R. Ranieri, *L'industria di Stato dall'ascesa al potere: Trent'anni nel gruppo Finsider* (Bologna: Il Mulino, 1993).

Palafox, J., J. G. Mora and F. Pérez, *Capital humano, educación y empleo* (Valencia: Fundación Bancaja, 1995).

Pamuk, O., *Istanbul, Memories of a City* (London: Faber & Faber, 2005).

[Papageorgiou and Pepelasis Minoglou] Παπαγεωργίου, Στ., and Ι. Πεπελάση Μίνογλου, *Τιμές και Αγαθά στην Αθήνα (1834): Κοινωνική Συμπεριφορά και Οικονομικός Ορθολογισμός της Οικογένειας Βάσσου Μαυροβουνιώτη* (Αθήνα: ΜΙΕΤ, 1988).

[Papathanassopoulos] Παπαθανασόπουλος, Κ., *Εταιρεία Ελληνικής Ατμοπλοίας (1855–1872), Τα αδιέξοδα του προστατευτισμού* (Αθήνα: ΜΙΕΤ, 1988).

[Papayiannakis] Παπαγιαννάκης, Λ., *Οι Ελληνικοί Σιδηρόδρομοι (1882–1910) Γεωπολιτικές, οικονομικές και κοινωνικές διαστάσεις* (Αθήνα: ΜΙΕΤ, 1982).

Parker, S. C., *Economics of Self-Employment and Entrepreneurship* (Cambridge: Cambridge University Press, 2004).

Pascual, P., and J. Nadal, *El coure II La Farga Lacambra: Un estudi socioeconòmic* (Vic: Eumo/La Farga Group, 2008).

Penrose, E. T., *The Theory of the Growth of the Firm* (Oxford: Basil Blackwell, 1959).

Pepelasis Minoglou, I., 'Between Informal Networks and Formal Contracts, International Investment in Greece during the 1920s', *Business History*, 2 (2002), pp. 40–64.

—, 'Non-Bank Financial Corporates, 1832–1909: A Note in Greek Banking History' (Malta: Papers from the European Association for Banking and Financial History Conference, 2007).

—, 'Women and Greek Family Capitalism, 1780–1940', *Business History Review*, 3 (2007), pp. 517–38.

—, 'The Greek Joint-Stock Company and Institutional Change, 1830–1909' (unpublished draft, December 2009).

[Pepelasis Minoglou] Πεπελάση Μίνογλου, Ι., 'Επιχειρηματικότητα', in *Η Ανάπτυξη της Ελληνικής Οικονομίας τον 19ο Αιώνα (1830–1914) επιμ Κ. Κωστής και Σ. Πετμεζάς* (Αθήνα: ALPHA BANK, 2006), pp. 463–96.

Pérez-Brignoli, H., 'The Economic Cycle in Latin America Agricultural Export Economies, 1880–1930: A Hypothesis for Investigation', *Latin American Research Review*, 2 (1980), pp. 3–33.

Pirani, M., 'Tre appuntamenti mancati dell'industria italiana', *Il Mulino*, 6 (1991), pp. 1045–51.

Planas, J., 'El Instituto Agrícola Catalán de San Isidro y la organización de los intereses agrarios' (1880–1936)', *Revista Española de Estudios Agrosociales y Pesqueros*, 217 (2008), pp. 13–48.

Polese, F., *Alla ricerca di un'industria nuova: Il viaggio all'estero del giovane Pirelli e le origini di una grande impresa (1870–1877)* (Venice: Marsilio, 2004).

[Polemis] Πολέμης, Δ., *Τα Ιστιοφόρα της Ανδρου* (Ανδρος: Καϊρειος Βιβλιοθήκη, 1991).

Porter, M. E., *The Competitive Advantage of Nations* (New York: Free Press, 1990).

Poutziouris, P. Z., C. X. Smyrnios and S. B. Klein (eds), *Handbook of Research on Family Business* (Aldershot: Edward Elgar, 2006).

Pozzi, D., *Dai gatti selvatici al cane a sei zampe: Tecnologia, conoscenza e organizzazione nell'AGIP e nell'ENI di Enrico Mattei* (Venice: Marsilio, 2009).

Puig, N., 'Educating Spanish Managers: The United States, Modernizing Networks and Business Schools in Spain, 1950–1975', in R. P. Amdam, R. Kvalshaugen and E. Larsen (eds), *Inside the Business Schools: The Content of European Management Education* (Oslo: Abstrakt Press, 2003), pp. 58–86.

—, 'La empresa en Cataluña: Identidad, supervivencia y competitividad en la primera región industrial de España', in J. L. García-Ruiz and C. Manera (eds), *Historia empresarial de España: Un enfoque regional en profundidad* (Madrid: LID, 2006), pp. 27–56.

Puig, N., and P. Fernández-Pérez, 'The Education of Spanish Entrepreneurs and Managers: Madrid and Barcelona Business Schools, 1950–1975', *Paedagogica Historica*, 5 (2003), pp. 651–72.

—, 'La gran empresa familiar española en el siglo XX: Claves de su profesionalización', *Revista de Historia de la Economía y de la Empresa*, 2 (2008), pp. 93–122.

—, 'A Silent Revolution: The Internationalization of Large Spanish Family Firms', *Business History*, 3 (2009), pp. 462–83.

Putnam, R. 'Bowling Alone: America's Declining Social Capital', *Journal of Democracy*, 6:1 (1995), pp. 65–78.

Romano, R., 'Borghi, Giovanni', in *Dizionario Biografico degli Italiani*, vol. 34, pp. 498–500.

Romer, P., 'Economic Growth', in *The Concise Encyclopaedia of Economics* (2007), available at: http://www.econlib.org/library/Enc1/EconomicGrowth.html.

Rose, M. B. (ed.), *Family Business* (Aldershot: Edward Elgar, 1995).

Rubinstein, W. D., *Men of Property: The Very Wealthy in Britain since the Industrial Revolution* (London: Croom Helm, 1981).

—, *Capitalism, Culture, and Decline in Britain 1750–1990* (London and New York: Routledge, 1993).

Rugafiori, P., 'Agostino Rocca (1895–1978)', in Mortara (ed.), *I protagonisti*, pp. 383–403.

—, *Ferdinando Maria Perrone: Da Casa Savoia all'Ansaldo* (Turín: UTET, 1992).

Safford, F., 'Significación de los antioqueños en el desarrollo económico colombiano: Un examen crítico de la tesis de Everett Hagen', *Anuario Colombiano de Historia Social y de la Cultura*, 3 (1965), pp. 18–27.

Saiz, P., and P. Fernández-Pérez, 'Intangible Assets and Competitiveness in Spain: An Approach through Trademark Registration Data in Catalonia, 1850–1946' (EBHA-BHC Conference, Milan, 11–13 June 2009).

Saloutos, T., *The Greeks in the United States* (Cambridge, MA: Harvard University Press, 1964).

Sanderson, M., *The Universities and British Industry, 1850–1970* (London: Routledge & Kegan Paul, 1972).

Santos, M., *Los economistas y la empresa: Empresa y empresario en la historia del pensamiento económico* (Madrid: Alianza, 1997).

Sanuy, F., *Informe Sanuy: Defensa del petit comerç i crítica de La Caixa* (Barcelona: La Campana, 2005).

Schultz, T. W., 'The Value of the Ability to Deal with Disequilibria', *Journal of Economic Literature*, 3 (1975), pp. 827–46.

Schumpeter, J. A., *The Theory of Economic Development: An Enquiry into Profits, Capital, Credit and Interest in the Business Cycle* (Cambridge, MA: Harvard University Press, 1934).

—, *Business Cycles: A Theoretical, Historical, and Statistical Analysis of the Capitalist Process* (New York: McGraw-Hill, 1939).

—, *Capitalism, Socialism and Democracy* (New York: Harper & Row, 1942).

—, *L'imprenditore e la storia dell'impresa: Scritti 1927–1949*, ed. A. Salsano (Torino: Bollati Boringhieri, 1993).

Segreto, L. *Giacinto Motta: Un ingegnere alla testa del capitalismo industriale italiano* (Rome-Bari: Laterza, 2005).

Shane, S. A., 'Explaining Variation in Rates of Entrepreneurship in the United States: 1899–1988', *Journal of Management*, 5 (1996), pp. 747–81.

—, *A General Theory of Entrepreneurship: The Individual-Opportunity Nexus* (Aldershot: Edward Elgar, 2003).

Sheshinski, E., R. J. Strom and W. J. Baumol, *Entrepreneurship, Innovation and the Growth Mechanism of the Free-Enterprise Economies* (Princeton, NJ: Princeton University Press, 2007).

Sicilia, D., 'Cochran's Legacy: A Cultural Path Not Taken', *Business and Economic History*, 1 (1995), p. 34.

Siqueira, A. C. O., 'Entrepreneurship and Ethnicity: The Role of Human Capital and Family Social Capital', *Journal of Developmental Entrepreneurship*, 1 (2007), pp. 31–46.

Smelser, N. J., and S. M. Lipset (eds), *Social Structure and Mobility in Economic Development* (Chicago, IL: Aldine, 1966).

Smith, A., *An Inquiry into the Nature and Causes of the Wealth of Nations* (1776; New York: Modern Library, 1937).

Solà-Gussinyer, P., *Història de l'associacionisme català contemporani: Barcelona i comarques de la seva demarcación* (Barcelona: Generalitat de Catalunya, Departament de Justícia, 1993).

Solà-Parera, A. 'Actituds i comportaments de la gran burgesia barcelonina a mitjan s. XIX', *Quaderns de l'Institut Català d'Antropologia*, 3:4 (1981), pp. 101–27.

—, 'Una família burgesa de la Plana de Vic: Els Moret, de Roda', in A. Solà-Parera et al., *Osona i Catalunya al segle XIX: Estudis d'història* (Vic: Eumo Editorial, 1990), pp. 201–20.

—, *Aigua, indústria i fabricants a Manresa, 1759–1860* (Sant Vicenç de Castellet: Centre Estudis Bages, 2004).

Solé, A., 'Reshaping Entrepreneurship after a Civil War: The Case of the Industrial Districts in Catalonia during the 1930s' (EBHA Conference, Bergen, 21–3 August 2008).

Solow, R. M., 'A Contribution to the Theory of Economic Growth', *Quarterly Journal of Economics*, 70 (1956), pp. 65–94.

Sombart, W., *El apogeo del capitalismo*, 2 vols (1902; Mexico: Fondo de Cultura Económica, 1946).

Subbrero, G., 'La Ferrero di Alba: Appunti per un profilo storico', in F. Chiapparino and R. Romano (eds), *Il cioccolato: Industria, mercato e società in Italia e Svizzera (XVIII–XX sec.)* (Milan: Franco Angeli, 2007), pp. 151–68.

[Syrmaloglou] Συρμαλόγλου, Δ., *Φορολογία η Χρεοκοπία, Η φορολογική πολιτική στη Βουλή των Ελλήνων 1862–1910* (Αθήνα: Μεταμεσονύκτιες Εκδόσεις, 2007).

Tàpies, J., and J. L. Ward (eds), *Family Values and Value Creation: The Fostering of Enduring Values within Family-Owned Businesses* (London: Palgrave Macmillan, 2008).

Temin, P., 'The American Business Elite in Historical Perspective', in E. Brezis and P. Temin (eds), *Elites, Minorities and Economic Growth* (Amsterdam: Elsevier, 1999), pp. 19–39.

[Theodorou and Loukos] Θεοδώρου, Β., and Χ. Λούκος, *Το Αρχείον της Βιομηχανίας 'Κλωστήριον και Υφαντήριον Ε. Λαδόπουλου και Υιοι εν Σύρω* (Αθήνα: Εταιρεία Μελέτης Νεοελληνισμού-Μνήμων, 1996).

Thomadakis, S., 'Monetary Arrangements and Economic Power in Nineteenth-Century Greece: The National Bank in the Period of Convertibility (1841–77)', *Journal of the Hellenic Diaspora*, 4 (1985), pp. 55–90.

—, 'Coordinated Industrialization Institutional Agendas for Less Favoured Countries', in M. Storper, S. Thomadakis and L. Tsipouri (eds), *Latecomers in the Global Economy* (London: Routledge, 1998), pp. 107–28.

Thünen. J. H. von, *Isolated State: An English Edition of Der Isolierte Staat* (1826; Oxford: Pergamon Press, 1966).

Todeschini, G., *Un trattato di economia politica francescana* (Roma: Istituto Storico Italiano per il Medioevo, 1980).

Toninelli, P. A., *Industria, impresa e stato: Tre saggi sullo sviluppo economico italiano* (Trieste: Edizioni dell'Università di Trieste, 2003).

—, *Storia d'impresa* (Bologna: Il Mulino, 2006).

Toniolo, G., 'Oscar Sinigaglia (1877–1953)', in Mortara (ed.), *I protagonisti*, pp. 405–30.

Torres Villanueva, E. (ed.), *Los 100 empresarios españoles del siglo XX* (Madrid: LID, 2000).

Tortella, G. (ed.), *Education and Economic Development since the Industrial Revolution* (Valencia: Generalitat Valenciana, 1990).

—, *The Development of Modern Spain: An Economic History of the Nineteenth and Twentieth Centuries* (Cambridge, MA: Harvard University Press, 2000).

Tortella, G., J. L. García-Ruiz, J. M. Ortiz-Villajos, and G. Quiroga, *Educación, instituciones y empresa: Los determinantes del espíritu empresarial* (Madrid: Academia Europea de Ciencias y Artes, 2008).

Turani, G., *I sogni del grande Nord* (Bologna: Il Mulino, 1996).

Twinam, A., 'Miners, Merchants and Farmers: The Roots of Entrepreneurship in Antioquia, 1763–1810' (PhD dissertation, Yale University, 1976).

Valdaliso, J. M., *El espíritu emprendedor en España: un análisis histórico* (Madrid: Instituto Superior de Formación del Profesorado/Ministerio de Educación y Ciencia, 2005).

—, *La familia Aznar y sus negocios* (Madrid: Marcial Pons, 2006).

Valls, F. *La Catalunya atlántica: Aiguardents i texitis a l'arrencada industrial catalana* (Vic: Eumo, 2004).

Van der Sluis, J., C. M. Van Praag and W. Vijverg, *Education and Entrepreneurship in Industrialized Countries*, Discussion Paper TI 2003–046/3 (Amsterdam: Tinbergen Institute, 2003).

Van Praag, C. M., and J. S. Cramer, 'Roots of Entrepreneurship and Labour Demand: Individual Ability and Low Risk Aversion', *Economica*, 269 (2001), pp. 45–62.

Veblen, T., *The Theory of Business Enterprise* (New York: Scribner's, 1904).

[Vaxevanoglou] Βαξεβάνογλου, Α., *Οι Έλληνες Κεφαλαιούχοι 1900–1940: Κοινωνική και Οικονομική Προσέγγιση* (Αθήνα: Θεμέλιο, 1994).

Velasco-Barroetabeña, R., and M. Saiz-Santos, *Políticas de creación de empresas y su evaluación*, Working Paper 118 (Madrid: Fundación Alternativas, 2007).

Vidal Olivares, J. (ed.), *Cien empresarios valencianos* (Madrid: LID, 2005).

Villari, L., *Le avventure di un capitano d'industria* (Turín: Einaudi, 2008).

[Vovolinis, *Lexicon*] Βοβολίνης, Κ., *Μέγα Ελληνικόν Βιογραφικόν Λεξικόν* (Αθήνα, 1958).

Weber, M., *The Protestant Ethic and the Spirit of Capitalism* (1905; New York: Dover, 2003).

Wiener, M. J., *English Culture and the Decline of the Industrial Spirit 1850–1980* (Cambridge: Cambridge University Press, 1981).

Wilken, P., *Entrepreneurship: A Comparative and Historical Study* (Norwood, NJ: Ablex Publishing Corporation, 1979).

Wilson, J. F., and A. Thomson, *The Making of Modern Management: British Management in Historical Perspective* (Oxford: Oxford University Press, 2006).

Wong, Y., 'Entrepreneurship, Marriage and Earnings', *Review of Economics and Statistics*, 4 (1986), pp. 693–9.

Xu, B., 'A Re-Estimation of the Evans-Jovanovic Entrepreneurial Choice Model', *Economic Letters*, 58 (1998), pp. 91–5.

INDEX